How can we care about growin
moorings in the process? And
ing a theologically sound look at practical ministry that will help your
church grow and change the right way. I've known and seen the fruit
of Andrew's ministry, and I commend this book to pastors and leadership teams.

Ed Stetzer
Dean, Talbot School of Theology at Biola University, California

Don't read this book if you're comfortable and relaxed in ministry and
want to remain that way. I found *Growth and Change* compelling and
uncomfortable. It's compelling in that, with laser-like clarity, Andrew
brings us to the great truths of the Bible and shows how and why these
eternal realities must change our lives. And it's uncomfortable in that
Andrew then shows us the Bible's charge to Christian leaders to take
up our responsibility for fruitful gospel preaching. He demonstrates
that the Scriptures will not let us hide behind passive 'faithfulness'—
God gives the growth, but we carry a level of responsibility for results.
Andrew then spells out what a burning gospel desire will look like as
we lead: a willingness to bear the pain of change. This book is theologically deep and biblically thorough, and it burns with a passion for the
lost. This is the book to read with your church leadership team. I guar-
antee you won't be the same team once you've finished reading it.

Al Stewart
National Director, Fellowship of Independent Evangelical
Churches Australia

This is a *brilliant* book, full of the genius insights of a highly effective
church pastor and movement leader. But more than that, it's an incredibly *important* book, certainly for evangelical churches in the UK! It's
so important because it provides a carefully argued biblical base for
church leaders facing our responsibility under God for the ministry outcomes of our churches—wisely steering between the worldly ideas of
godless, corporate megachurches and the equally damaging passive,
pietistic minimalism that has gripped so many Bible-teaching churches

in the UK. At points it's painful to read how our failure to lead change is inhibiting the salvation of souls. But I honestly believe this could prove to be one of the most important books (after the Bible, of course) for church leaders in our time. While I've been trying to embrace and commend in outline the principles in this book for a decade, I'm so thankful to God that they're now finally available to leaders everywhere in more depth in this written form. May God be glorified in the salvation of many in countless churches as a result!

Richard Coekin
Senior Pastor, Dundonald Church, Raynes Park
Mission Director, Co-Mission church planting network, London

This is easily one of the most thoughtful books I've read on leadership or institutional change. Carefully and compellingly written, and helpfully supported throughout with Scripture, it articulates much wisdom on the greatest of challenges and opportunities we have: the need to change, and the dire consequences and compromises of not doing so. Every leader of a church or Christian organization should read this.

The Rev Dr Robert S Kinney
Director of Ministries, The Charles Simeon Trust, Chicago

Andrew Heard confronts the disturbing reality that most evangelical churches are not making "mature disciples of Christ in ever-increasing numbers". He challenges our simplistic theological presuppositions that stifle growth, wrestling deeply with "the complex interplay between two apparently contradictory ideas: God's sovereignty and genuine human agency".

Principles of implementing change are established without being prescriptive. The core message resonates throughout: "Leading for change is not primarily a matter of techniques and skill sets, but of deep conviction—of being fuelled by a heart that pulsates with the gospel, with God's love for the lost, and with God's love for his people".

Andrew's convictions have been forged in the real world of growing EV Church and equipping pastors. This makes for an engaging read, during which Andrew anticipates our objections and difficulties. Every pastor and church leader must read *Growth and Change*. Debate with your teams and repent for the sake of hell-bound souls and Christ's honour.

Colin Marshall
Author, *Growth Groups*
Co-author, *The Trellis and the Vine* and *The Vine Project*

I **loved** *Growth and Change*! I felt both convicted and encouraged.

Far too often our ministries emphasize our faithfulness over God's. In other words, we can stop expecting God to work through our work, and settle for kingdom-less results. With great wisdom and clarity, Andrew Heard rekindles (or reignites) our hope that God desires to advance his kingdom through our service, while challenging us to share the responsibility for making that happen.

Jeremy Conrad
Executive Director, The Calvary Family of Churches, USA

Some people think it's a matter of the 'trellis' *or* the 'vine'. From both experience and theological conviction, Andrew Heard powerfully argues otherwise in this heartfelt book. He urges church leaders to do the painful but necessary work not only of reforming traditions and structures and programs, but of examining our hearts as we approach faithful biblical leadership. The result is a stirring call to radically rethink our trellises for the sake of growing the vine.

Tony Payne
Author, *The Trellis and the Vine*

In *Growth and Change*, Andrew Heard is having a 'fierce conversation' with the reader—not a harsh conversation but one that is clear and gentle, yet very much needed. He speaks to the elephant in the room: as evangelicals, we proclaim that the gospel is powerful to save, yet in many of our churches we don't see the inevitable gospel growth that should follow.

Carefully unpacking the Scriptures, Andrew shows that the Bible gives leaders a real responsibility for the outcomes of our ministry—

something that is often denied. Faithfulness must include fruitfulness, not be set against it. Andrew is forcing us to ask hard questions about what we leaders do, or don't do, that is getting in the way of gospel growth. This is combined with an urgent call to willingly embrace the inevitable pain that always marks outcome-driven ministry. Andrew rightly wants our prime motivation to be the desire of our Lord Jesus Christ to make mature disciples. I also appreciate his pastoral eye on the potential collateral damage when leaders take a greater ownership of responsibility. I look forward to the many sequels that should flow from this book.

Ray Galea
Senior Pastor, Fellowship Dubai, UAE

Growth and Change is uncomfortably comforting! With steely determination, Andrew Heard issues a clarion call for painful change because of the purposes of our unchanging God. A passionate and gospel-fuelled challenge for the glory of Jesus.

Richard Chin
National Director, Australian Fellowship of Evangelical Students

Andrew Heard planted EV Church more than 25 years ago. He also leads an organization called Reach Australia that has helped plant scores of healthy, evangelistic and multiplying churches. For many years, he's been wrestling with difficult church-growth topics—including the relationship between inputs and outputs, balancing faithfulness and fruitfulness, the relationship between God's sovereignty and our activity, the importance of numbers, and principled pragmatism. *Growth and Change* will do for pastors and Christian leaders what JI Packer's classic *Evangelism and the Sovereignty of God* has done for outreach-focused Christians. It mines the riches of Scripture and carefully critiques the heart of the reader. I found it very challenging—and very enriching.

Ben Pfahlert
National Director, Ministry Training Strategy, Australia

The purpose of this book is clear and very unsettling: it calls church leaders to growth and change. This book cannot be dismissed as it is firmly rooted in the Bible, displays deep theology, and oozes wisdom. This is unsurprising, as Andrew Heard has a worldwide reputation for arousing a vision for the lost, penetratingly challenging structures for the glory of God, and being a wonderful practitioner of what he teaches. While calling for change, this book is also nuanced and recognizes the challenges and objections leaders face. I recommend this book to every pastor as both a rigorous theology and a wise, heart-warming call to best practice and obedience.

Archie Poulos
Head, Department of Ministry, Moore Theological College
Director, Centre for Ministry Development, Sydney

Andrew Heard's passion for Christ, his gospel and the growth of his church has long been a great encouragement to me. He has evangelistic fire in his belly, and my prayer is that reading this book will help rekindle that same fire in many readers. In this book, I love the way Andrew seeks to keep the focus on Christ and evangelism even when talking about the priorities and processes of church growth. We want churches to grow as more people are introduced to the Saviour and are drawn to gather with other believers. We want churches to grow as they resource disciples to go and make other disciples. We want churches to grow as a testimony to "the manifold wisdom of God" who rescues men and women from diverse backgrounds and experiences and joins them to one another. I am grateful that Andrew has written this book with the fruit of his many years of serving the Lord of the gospel, who is the Lord of the church. I know he would want each reader to test what he has written against the word of God, perhaps even to challenge some of his conclusions, or his reading of the Bible or of how we have arrived at where we are, but above all to be willing to be led into whatever change might be necessary if we are to reach our community and the world with the life-giving message of Jesus.

Dr Mark D Thompson
Principal, Moore Theological College, Sydney

Andrew Heard has helped me see with gospel freshness the power and wonder and urgency of the grace and love of God in Christ Jesus. The truths and principles Andrew brings to our attention from the word of God have profoundly energized my soul to give my all for the glory of the Lord Jesus. I'm glad this book has been written so that many others can benefit from Andrew's clarity, insight and passion. When it's for the cause and glory of Christ, who wouldn't embrace change?

Allan Blanch
Minister, Dubbo Presbyterian Church, New South Wales

Andrew Heard writes as a pastor to pastors. He has a passion to see the lost saved and believers growing deep in their discipleship. This book provides a theological framework and tools to help Christian leaders ask the hard questions about their gospel heart and the effectiveness of their ministry. Andrew highlights that having specific goals and assessing if they have been met is confronting, but also that this feedback loop is empowering. It helps us, under the sovereign hand of God, to take "some measure of responsibility" for achieving outcomes and to make changes, even painful ones, when they could increase fruitfulness. This is a must-read for all ministry workers and leadership teams. It has the potential to make a real change to Christian thinking and practice.

Sue Harrington
Trinity Network, South Australia

Very few people have challenged my ministry thinking and practices as much as Andrew Heard. He has a unique ability to see where we have gotten into 'ruts' and to boldly, yet graciously, push us to see if we need to make changes in our churches for the good of the gospel. I hope every pastor reads this book and is stretched and challenged like I have been to consider how we can all do better at taking responsibility for leading our churches to see disciples made and grown.

Phil Colgan
Senior Minister, St George North Anglican Church, Sydney

When it comes to the topic of leading and growing healthy, evangelistic churches, there are few people I'd sooner listen to than Andrew Heard. Andrew brings wisdom, experience, passion, and theological sure-footedness to the sometimes-fraught world of church growth. Reading *Growth and Change* will push you, inspire you, and perhaps occasionally discourage you. But ultimately it will spur you on in the work of the Lord. What it won't do is make you feel comfortable. Andrew wants to see more people come to know Jesus. To do that, we need change. Change is never comfortable. Andrew's argument is not that it's comfortable or easy, but that it's worth it.

Rory Shiner
Senior Pastor, Providence City, Perth

Andrew Heard, one of Australia's most significant and successful church planters and ministry leaders, has written a unique book for church planters and ministry leaders. Those who pioneer new churches are usually marked as entrepreneurial characters with a pragmatic approach to leadership—'find what works and do it'. In *Growth and Change*, Andrew has taken the time to outline his approach and ministry values based on biblical principles. This book contains much practical and helpful information, but it is not just pragmatism; it's an attempt at a biblical framework for church leadership. The church in Australia and across Western nations will be indebted to Andrew for taking the time to write *Growth and Change*.

Karl Faase
CEO, Olive Tree Media
Host, *Jesus the Game Changer* and *Faith Runs Deep* video series and the *Daily Nudge* radio spot

GROWTH *and* CHANGE

The danger and necessity of
a passion for church growth

ANDREW HEARD

with Geoff Robson

Matthias Media
(St Matthias Press Ltd ACN 067 558 365)
Email: info@matthiasmedia.com.au
Internet: matthiasmedia.com.au
Please visit our website for current postal and telephone contact information.

Matthias Media (USA)
Email: sales@matthiasmedia.com
Internet: matthiasmedia.com
Please visit our website for current postal and telephone contact information.

ISBN 978 1 922980 13 7

Cover design by Carol Lam.
Typesetting by Lankshear Design.

All websites cited in this book were accessed on 9 June 2023.

CONTENTS

FOREWORD

At a time when, in the Western world, not a few commentators are discussing the shrinking of our churches, we have come to expect to see books and articles that try to point the way forward. We reflect on the rising number of people who, when asked what religion they espouse, proudly tick 'None', and when we reflect on the remarkable turnover rate of pastors who pour themselves into their church ministries for a few years before abandoning them in deep discouragement, we conclude that it is not surprising to find a plethora of books promising to lead us out of the wilderness and into the promised land of growth and evangelistic fruitfulness. Some writers take us by the hand and lead us into the uplands of cultural apologetics; others take pains to distinguish merely anecdotal accounts from rigorous statistical analysis; still others offer 'how to' strategies of one sort or another. Nevertheless, the worrying trends continue, and, as useful as some of these books may be, quite frankly most of them seem a trifle anaemic—simply not up to the strenuous challenges of our age.

Enter *Growth and Change*, the new book by Andrew Heard. I am usually loath to proclaim that such-and-such a book is the 'best' in its field. Best for what? Best for whom? But if there is one book that happily serves as the exception to the rule, Heard's book is it. The range of its coverage is remarkable: careful analysis of what 'dechurching' means in different subcultures, wise wrestling with several theological conundra, and more than a quarter of a century of 'hands on' church experience, not only in the congregation that Heard has served but also in many congregations where Heard has been influential in re-shaping the priorities of ministers and congregants alike, very often with stunning results.

In the name of faithfulness, some churches put a premium on tradition. It is easy to see why the clarion call for unchanging sameness has its own beauty in a culture of rapid change: the very repetitions are reassuring. One sympathizes with the old saw advanced by CS Lewis: he could put up with almost any kind of liturgy, he averred, as long as it does not change too much or too often. But on the other hand, in a very traditional congregation the commitment to traditional forms may be little more than a kind of ecclesiastical virtue-signalling. Meanwhile, if at least part of the purpose of our public meetings is to communicate the gospel faithfully and tellingly, and we perceive that our traditional forms serve obfuscation rather more than communication, something *ought* to change. Conversely, endless innovation may have more to do with titillating the saints than with declaring the whole counsel of God. Large numbers may be a mark of God's singular blessing on a particular ministry, but they may signal little other than professional-quality entertainment, bought at the cost of sustained biblical and theological ignorance.

As Heard points out, sometimes the polarities in our approaches to church planting are tied to certain theological commitments. Those of us who spring from a rather Arminian background may feel under some pressure to produce 'results', and in consequence drift into what 'works' or at least seems to work, even if the gospel is quietly slipping out of our hands. Those of us who spring from a rather more Reformed background may become so quick to remind each other that it is God alone who saves, and he knows those who are his, that we may drift toward a sort of soteriological fatalism, a long way removed from the portrait of a God who cries, "Turn!

Turn ...! Why will you die ...?" (Ezek 33:11). How shall we simultaneously cleave without hesitation or embarrassment to the sweeping sovereignty of God depicted in Scripture, while espousing without a tremor of reluctance the moving portrayals of a God who is not willing that any should perish? Getting these portrayals right will go a long way toward strengthening our evangelistic and church-planting commitments.

These are only a few of the tensions with which the Scriptures are replete. Andrew Heard is a reliable guide to the biblical, theological, evangelistic and pastoral issues that will confront all Christian leaders who aim for growth, recognize the need for change, and hunger to work out of a rich and faithful biblical theology. Andrew is well known and well trusted in Australia, his homeland. Now we pray that his influence may multiply exponentially around the world.

—DA Carson

1

CHANGE AND THE UNCHANGING GOD

Serving the God who is committed to change

This book is designed to help you think about a very important and very emotional topic: *change*. And not just change in some generalized sense, but a kind of change that could have great significance in your life: change to our churches, our gospel ministries, and our Christian leadership.

What's your initial reaction to the whole idea of change? How does it make you feel? Does the thought of change fill you with excitement and hope, or with nervousness and dread?

The experts confirm what we know through intuition and experience: even positive changes—getting married, having a child, starting a new job—are among the most stressful events we will face in life. Yet there are people who welcome change, or even go looking for it. Maybe you're one of them. Maybe you live by the mantra 'a change is as good as a holiday', or you share the sentiment expressed by legendary basketball coach John Wooden: "failure is not fatal, but failure to change might be".

Or maybe you're at the other end of the spectrum: what you crave more than anything is stability. Maybe you've worked hard to carve out a life or a ministry with maximum predictability and minimal uncertainty. Or perhaps your world has been chaotic for too long, and the very last thing you're looking for is more change. It's even possible that you feel stuck in the mud and you know some changes would be beneficial, but you don't know where to start, so you choose the safety of routine over an uncertain future: 'better the devil you know'.

No matter how you feel about change, we can all agree that change is rarely, if ever, easy. The very idea of change requires a lot of hard work and a lot of careful thought—not to mention that it involves a great deal of emotion.

As with any topic, it's right to begin our thinking about change with theology. And straight away we are confronted with a potentially unsettling truth: those of us who know and love the God of the Bible cannot be opposed to change as a matter of principle. For we follow a God who is committed to bringing about change.

The irony here is that God, in his deepest being, does *not* change (Mal 3:6). In fact, God's unchanging nature is precisely *why* he is all about change.

The God at the heart of the universe is forever perfect, holy, good, loving and glorious. And this perfect, unchanging God made us in his image to live in a right relationship with him. But because we fell into sin, we don't properly occupy the position for which God designed us. We—his image bearers, the very pinnacle of his creation—have all fallen short of his glory in all kinds of ways (Rom 3:23). Left to our own devices, we cannot and will not live in a right relationship with him or with each other.

But the perfect, holy, unchanging God is not content to leave this situation as it is. He is determined to redeem us, to bring us back to himself. As he works to restore us, his unchanging nature empowers this work, assuring us that he will never cease in his pursuit of restoration. He works relentlessly to bring us back to our original glory—in fact, to a glory that surpasses our original standing. God is at work to move his people from death to life, from one degree of glory to another, from corruptible to incorruptible, from mortal to immortal. God is completely committed to changing things *because* he is unchanging.

And think about what this commitment to change cost him.

The most famous verse in the Bible puts it this way: "For God so loved the world, that he gave his only Son, that whoever believes in him should not perish but have eternal life" (John 3:16). To bring about the change that he wanted in us, God sent his beloved Son to dwell among us. When he came to earth, Jesus Christ suffered abuse and rejection from the very people that he had made in his image (John 1:10–11). He humbled himself to the point of suffering death on a cross (Phil 2:9).

"In this is love, not that we have loved God but that he loved us and sent his Son to be the propitiation for our sins" (1 John 4:10). This verse wonderfully expresses the heart of God, who would pay such a price for sinners like us. God the Father gave up his only Son to death, and he did it for us. This is the extent of God's commitment to changing us, to defeating sin and restoring his creation, and ultimately to bringing about a glorious new creation with no more death, mourning, crying or pain—the glorious city of God, where the redeemed "from every tribe and language and people and nation" will be gathered together to praise their Saviour (Rev 5:9).

The change that God brings happens on at least three levels. First, he seeks to change *our status*: by his grace, he rescues fallen sinners, justifying us—declaring us not guilty—and taking us from condemned to forgiven. But this is only the first level of change. He also brings about a change in *our very being*: we are taken from being dead in sin to now being alive in Christ, reborn by the Spirit of God through the word of God. And thirdly, he works within Spirit-indwelt believers to bring us *from immaturity to maturity*, that we

might more and more reflect the glory of Christ. And all this anticipates the final great change with the redemption of believers' bodies
at Christ's final return (e.g. Rom 12:2; 2 Cor 3:18; Gal 4:19; Col 1:22;
2 Corinthians 4).

God is absolutely committed to change. This is not 'change for
change's sake'. He is deeply purposeful about the change that he pur-
sues. It is all fuelled by his unchanging nature, and it all happens for
the sake of his glory and for the good of those he saves. And our Lord
was willing to pay the ultimate price to bring about this change.

Proactively pursuing change

My purpose in writing this book is to promote change. The changes
I'm writing about are less significant than the changes God is bringing, as described above, yet they directly relate to what I've described.
For the change at the centre of this book is centred on our churches,
our ministries, and our Christian leadership. These are not just
random changes. I write to encourage purposeful changes that might
genuinely serve God's greater purpose of restoring a fallen people to
himself and to the glory he intends for us.

In particular, I write to encourage Christian leaders to initiate
change.

As much as we might like to be in the driver's seat, sometimes
change is forced upon us by circumstances well outside our control.
These circumstances often take the form of challenges and hardships, but we are sometimes compelled to change by more positive
situations. For example, revival—the rapid growth of the church in
one place—has sometimes forced churches, leaders and ministries
to adapt.

Perhaps the most obvious example of this is found in the New
Testament. In the opening chapters of Acts, we read of the early
church growing quickly through an outpouring of the Spirit of God.

Thousands were brought to faith in Christ. But this created a problem, as tensions arose among the growing group of disciples. In response, the apostles instituted a new structure for ministry: what is sometimes called the 'diaconate'. Seven men, known to be filled with the Spirit, were chosen to take over the ministry of distributing food among widows who were in need (Acts 6:1–3). This change enabled the apostles to continue in their core responsibilities: "we will devote ourselves to prayer and to the ministry of the word" (6:4). In a sense, the apostles simply embraced change because the pressure of growth forced it on them. This certainly isn't bad. They were wise enough to see what mattered most—their crucial role in leading the fledgling church—and readily brought about changes to meet the new need while guarding their priorities.

But change shouldn't only be forced upon us. Outside of times of revival or unexpected difficulty, it is possible for God's people—especially leaders among God's people—to make changes that facilitate numerical and spiritual growth. Put positively, I want to suggest that proactively initiating change in ourselves, our leadership and our churches can bring about the growth of our churches or ministries. Put negatively, our failure to change ourselves, our leadership and our churches can often be a significant hindrance to the numerical and spiritual growth of our churches or ministries.

For some, this will sound obvious. But I'm conscious that for others this will be a radically different way of thinking. I'm aware that to some it might even seem, at least on first reading, blasphemous. It could seem like I'm suggesting that *we* are the key to the conversion or the spiritual growth of people around us—but isn't this God's work? Doesn't Paul say as much? We might 'plant' and 'water' like Paul and Apollos, but God's work is decisive: "So neither he who plants nor he who waters is anything, but only God who gives the growth" (1 Cor 3:6–7). Perhaps you bristle at the impression that I might want to make organizational principles and management techniques a central piece in the spiritual growth of a church or a person. Can this be so?

Hence the need for this book.

As will become very clear, I'm not endorsing every inference that a person might draw from my statements about growth and change. Not for one second would I suggest that God is somehow subordinate to us and our activities—by no means!

And yet I am convinced that many of the ways we are running our churches and ministries, and many of the ways that we are exercising our leadership within our churches and ministries, has become a significant hindrance to the fundamental growth of the church, both numerically and spiritually. Or, again to put it positively, I'm convinced that with some significant changes to church life and to our leadership patterns and practices, we will see a greater penetration of the gospel into the lost community around us and so see many more people saved. I'm convinced that we can see more men, women and children come to faith in Christ and grown to maturity in Christ.

In short, I am convinced that we need to make some changes.

Embracing the pain of change

Of course, it's one thing to state that change is needed. It's another thing entirely to bring about meaningful change. And we won't make the necessary changes to facilitate growth until we are motivated to make those changes. Most fundamentally, this means we need to be convinced that changes will truly make a difference. But something more is needed: *we need to be willing to embrace the pain of change.*

This last statement leads us to a critical principle operating throughout this book—and throughout our lives and ministries: *we won't change the things that need to be changed until the pain of not changing is greater than the pain of changing.*

All meaningful change is costly and painful. A person concerned about their weight might know that some changes in diet and exercise will help them to be healthier, but those changes will cost them. The dream of change is easy, but in practice it is hard work. It's hard work to choose water over soft drink or salad over fried chicken, to go for a walk or get to the gym instead of sitting on the couch. They may feel bad about their poor health; they may grieve their situation. But until the pain of not changing is greater than the pain of changing, they won't follow through on their good intentions, change their habits, and make real changes.

The same principle applies to gospel ministry. We might quickly and easily agree with the idea that some changes would be useful, but actually changing things in church can be very difficult. Unless we share God's heart for the lost in such a way that it pains us greatly to see people perish without Christ, and unless that pain exceeds the pain that we know will accompany our efforts to make changes, we will almost always opt for the status quo. Of course, this is not the only factor that will determine whether we work to bring about change. But it's a significant and inescapable part of the equation.

Anyone who's tried to bring change in the church will surely agree that it's painful. For one thing, it's tremendously hard work—maintaining the status quo requires much less effort. On top of that, just try moving one piece of furniture, or changing the songs you sing together, or playing around with the order of the service, and see what reaction you get. With EV Church, we had only existed as a church for a decade before we clearly needed to make some significant changes. But, astonishingly, the suggestion that we needed to change was met with horror. Some people even appealed to the history of the church—all ten years of it!

Professor Robert Quinn is a secular expert in organizational culture and leadership. In his book *Deep Change*, he writes these powerfully disturbing words:

Virtually every dominant coalition, in every organization, has a sacred and self-sealing model. It represents the most sacred of common belief patterns because it justifies the present behaviour of the most powerful coalition. It justifies the current equilibrium and limits change to incremental rather than transformational efforts.[1]

Quinn's point is that every group of people forms a pattern of behaviour that becomes critical to their own sense of belonging and participation. This pattern of behaviour "seals" and defines the group; the life of each member becomes bound to the group staying the way it is. Any change threatens each member's sense of belonging, and so the group resists change, or at least limits change to minor areas. There is too much at stake for anything more to be allowed.

All organizations or groups of people are like this, but churches face a unique additional factor that makes change difficult: as we shape our life together, we tend to add an almost-spiritual sense of 'ought': 'This is the way God intends it, and perhaps God has blessed us while we were doing it this way'. Therefore, so the logic goes, changing things can mean defying God! This ratchets up the challenge of change by a few notches.

Change and the Christian leader

In the face of these challenges, the key (humanly speaking) to bringing change to a church or ministry is the leadership. Leaders are the church's most important human resource—not, of course, in the sense that God loves them more or they possess some special spiritual privileges, but in the sense that God charges them to "shepherd the flock of God that is among you, exercising oversight" (1 Pet 5:2). This divine charge entails having a special responsibility and authority to bring about the changes that are needed. A leader's actions affect the whole church in a special way: Paul tells Timothy, "Keep a close watch on yourself and on the teaching. Persist in this, for by so doing you will save both yourself and your hearers" (1 Tim 4:16). Church leadership is critical, and change in a church flows (mostly) from its leaders.

But here is yet another issue: getting leaders to change can be a challenge of its own. Even the most dynamic leaders can settle into patterns of behaviour. It's like driving on the beach: once a few cars have driven the same path on the sand, a deep rut forms. And if you drive too close to the rut, you just slide right in. Ruts have their own kind of gravity. And once you're in, getting out requires considerable, intentional effort—maybe even a push or a pull from a friend.

Throughout this book, I will argue that change in our churches and ministries is necessary. We will think about the kinds of changes that are necessary, and why. These changes will range from the small to the large: we need to be willing to change our roster structures, the shape of our yearly programs, and the pattern of our gatherings. But we also need to be willing to change our leadership styles, our personnel, our eldership structure, or perhaps even the very message we preach (though read the next chapter very carefully for more on this point!). In some cases, it will be obvious that change is needed; in other cases, a painful process of analysis and self-examination might be necessary before we can see the changes that should take place. But in the end, the key is a healthy appreciation that change is crucial, and that we cannot live if we don't change.

And so, fundamental to the change process is good and proper motivation. This book is about much more than some simple suggestions on ministry management or revamping your church structure. It is primarily about a deeper work within us. It is about being stirred to feel the pain of *not* changing, in order that we might truly own the need to make changes and therefore have the drive and motivation to continue with the change process over the long haul.

This deeper work is clearly the task of the Holy Spirit, for only God can truly bring about the change of heart that we need. Yet God works through his people. It is my prayer that he might use something of what I offer as fuel for his work in our hearts. For without this deeper work of God, we won't make the changes that are needed if we are to see the gospel bring about the conversion and spiritual transformation that is necessary in people's lives.

The glories and challenges of our work

The next chapter of this book will set the whole enterprise in its proper context. Any pursuit of growth and change needs to be conducted with a careful eye to the dangers inherent in a desire to grow. In fact, these dangers are so significant that I see the next chapter as the most important chapter in the whole book.

The following section will focus on the need to change and the pain of not changing. These chapters are a call to be passionate about seeing the church grow—both spiritually and numerically. They are important because of the principle articulated above: change won't happen until the pain of not changing is greater than the pain of changing.

From there, we will deal with the boundaries and freedoms of change. What are we free to change? What can't be changed? The last part of the book (including the appendix) offers some preliminary suggestions on practicalities—learning to lead, fundamental decisions related to ministry structure, resourcing your ministry, and the like.

Some readers will find parts of the book confronting and challenging. This is deliberate. It is my desire to stir us to see the need for change, and even to create sufficient pain that we will be moved to bring real change. But though my approach may be confronting or perhaps even painful, I do it all with the greatest affection and admiration for those who embrace appropriate leadership within God's people. And I do it with a deep desire to encourage those who minister within God's church.

The work we do as leaders and servants of the church of Christ is the greatest work to which any person can give themselves: "The saying is trustworthy: If anyone aspires to the office of overseer, he desires a noble task" (1 Tim 3:1). It is an extraordinary thing to exercise some level of responsibility among the people of God—a people bought with the precious blood of Christ himself.

The great 19th-century pastor and preacher Charles Spurgeon is said to have captured these sentiments with a characteristic turn of phrase: "If God calls you to be a preacher, do not stoop to become a king". Perhaps Spurgeon was just echoing Martin Luther, who is said to have remarked: "If I could today become king or emperor, I would not give up my office as preacher". Leadership and service of any kind within and among the people of God is a truly great thing.

But it is not uncommon for leaders to lose this perspective.

Some time ago, I was speaking with a young pastor who was leading a small church in a struggling context. He had experienced some months of grief and pain in his ministry. The work was slow, and there was little understanding or support for all he was trying to do. He found himself drifting into depression. But around this time, he read some words from Martyn Lloyd-Jones's book *Preaching and Preachers*. Lloyd-Jones wrote of the importance of bringing the word of God to human hearts:

> The work of preaching is the highest and the greatest and the most glorious calling to which anyone can ever be called. ... I would say without any hesitation that the most urgent need in the Christian Church today is true preaching; and as it is the greatest and the most urgent need in the Church, it is obviously the most urgent need of the world also.[2]

As he reflected on these powerful observations, the young pastor found his soul deeply nourished. Despite the struggles, despite the pressures and the pain, the work mattered. It mattered more than any other work he could be doing. He was enabled and encouraged to press on.

The work we do as leaders, pastors and servants within the community of faith is the greatest work imaginable. This is not to denigrate the many kinds of good and important work that God's people can do in this world; it is simply to recognize that the work of serving and leading the people of God, of proclaiming the word of God, aligns with what God is doing in the world as he gathers a people who belong to the Lord Jesus Christ—a people who will live for his glory and will make his name known in the world through their witness and their godly lives. The importance of this work is surely why Paul exhorts the Corinthians to honour men such as Timothy and Stephanas: they were "doing the work of the Lord" (1 Cor 16:10, 15). Indeed, he encouraged the whole church as they played their part in this work: "be steadfast, immovable, always abounding in the work of the Lord, knowing that in the Lord your labour is not in vain" (15:58).

The greatness of our work isn't always obvious when you look at our external entailments. We don't get paid like someone doing an important task; we don't receive the respect and regard to match other valued workers in our community. In fact, in Australia, surveys have shown that a minister of religion's reputation sits around the same level as a used-car salesman—which isn't meant to offend used-car salesmen, though it might.

But when the eyes of faith look at Christian leadership, they see something altogether different. They see beauty: "How beautiful are the feet of those who preach the good news!" (Rom 10:15). As I call for change, it is my intention to reconnect us with the beauty and the eternal value of our task and to encourage us in this great work.

And for those readers who are not leaders, my prayer for you is that you'll be moved to encourage your leaders in their work and support them as they bring about the changes that are needed. I hope your passion for the gospel will be renewed. And I hope you'll begin to see how you can be a positive agent for change within your church or ministry.

But while I will seek to encourage pastors, I will also speak some hard truths. And the truth is that, in many cases, we can do much better! For that reason, I intend to foster some pain—but only so that it might help us to generate the kind of change that our churches need. But even change is not the end, but a means to an end. The end, the thing that really matters, is to see many more men and women come to receive the saving knowledge of Jesus Christ and be deepened in their lives with him, to the glory of God.

This is a book about big things. I write to encourage big things to happen, not for our satisfaction or our glory, but because there are big things at stake—the glory of God, and the salvation of men and women from hell.

Passages for further reflection

- John 3:16
- 1 Corinthians 3:5–9
- 1 Timothy 2:1–4
- 1 Timothy 3:1

Questions for personal or team reflection

- Do you share God's heart for the lost?
- Are you ready and willing to embrace the pain of change so that more people might be saved?

Quote for personal or team reflection

"The work of preaching is the highest and the greatest and the most glorious calling to which anyone can ever be called." (Martyn Lloyd-Jones)

THE DANGER OF A PASSION
FOR GROWTH

Clear and present danger

My aim in this book is no secret: I am writing to promote change—the kind of change that leads to growth in our churches and ministries. The whole project is unashamedly about fostering a passion for growth and a willingness to make the necessary changes to bring about that growth.

But we can't go any further before identifying a major issue. It is critical that this passion for growth exists alongside an awareness of the profound *dangers* of a passion for growth. The desire to see our churches and ministries grow is very, very dangerous.

This may seem like an odd observation to make, but it is critical. If we develop a passion for church growth without being aware that this is one of the most dangerous passions a person can have, then the passion will destroy us and our work. What's more, it's one thing for the leaders of a church to be passionate about growth, but when that passion extends to the members of the church, the situation becomes even more dangerous.

Please don't assume that I'm exaggerating when I talk about this danger or that I'm about to flip this around and explain how this is really a positive kind of 'danger' (it's 'dangerous' to the establishment or to people's comfortable lives). I'm not. I'm being deadly serious. Passion for growth is a clear and present danger to the health of our churches.

What do I mean?

Sinner-driven churches

The most dangerous people in our Christian community are the leaders who long to see growth in their ministries and the evangelists who are most concerned to see people in our communities added to our churches. In fact, let me provide some nuance to that statement: the most dangerous people are the leaders and evangelists who not only long to see growth, but who also sympathize deeply with the needs and concerns of the people we are seeking to reach. I'm talking about leaders who feel most keenly the needs of the unconverted sinner and the pain and difficulties that unconverted sinners experience because of the way we do things in our churches.

This is the most dangerous type of leader, for this is the leader who does everything with the wrong audience as his or her primary concern. Their dominant question is, 'How will the world react to this thought, this teaching, or this action?'

It ought to be obvious why this is so dangerous: it leads to a ministry that 'self-censors'. The leader who is most concerned about how an unconverted person receives what is said or done will see almost every issue through the lens of what will make it hard or easy for that person to connect with church. And because they long to see these people won to Christ and connected with his people, they will be hypersensitive to anything that might potentially make it hard for them to connect. In our context, this means it will be very unlikely that a growth-oriented church will speak clearly about issues such as the exclusive claims of Christ, the Bible's teaching on homosexuality, the differences between men and women, judgement, hell, or the true nature of sin as proud rebellion against God.

The more passionate a person is to see their church or ministry grow, and the more their sympathies rest with the sinner, the more susceptible they become to the danger of silence or compromise. It is possibly an overstatement to suggest that all heresies find their genesis in a desire to make the Christian faith more appealing to an unbelieving world, but there is a strong element of truth to this notion. Consider, for example, the stated motivation of the 19th-century liberals who were convinced that talk of miracles would make the gospel foolish to a generation who now had the light bulb. Consider the ministry of John Shelby Spong (1931–2021), whose express desire was to make the gospel more accessible to his own daughters, leading him to rid his 'gospel' of all talk of blood or propitiation or wrath. And we could list countless other examples.

Leaders and churches can become 'sinner-driven' in a desire to reach the sinner. And being 'sinner-driven' is deadly.

We are very aware of how secular businesses can become consumer-driven: they exist to entice people to buy their product, and will bend and shift almost anything to increase sales. This is to be expected in the secular marketplace. But a sinner-driven church can adopt an almost identical set of values. We will shift and change whatever is necessary to make church more attractive to the community of people we are trying to attract. Barriers to acceptance of church life are identified and then removed, driven very largely by the principle that if our 'customers' encounter barriers then we must have done something wrong. Before you know it, the barriers being removed are core gospel thoughts, ideas and practices. 'Make church more celebratory', we are told. 'Pursue inspiration instead of education.' 'Public Bible reading is clunky and hard to follow; drop it in favour of something that will engage a modern audience.'

Consider Paul's charge to his protégé Timothy. Notice the contrast between Timothy's duty to "preach the word" and the disaster that awaits when unconverted sinners are allowed to set the agenda:

> I charge you in the presence of God and of Christ Jesus, who is to judge the living and the dead, and by his appearing and his kingdom: preach the word; be ready in season and out of season; reprove, rebuke, and exhort, with complete patience and teaching. For the time is coming when people will not endure sound teaching, but having itching ears they will accumulate for themselves teachers to suit their own passions, and will turn away from listening to the truth and wander off into myths. (2 Tim 4:1–4)

The danger of worldly respect

Closely related to the danger of the 'sinner-driven church' is the subtle but dangerous pattern of passionate, mission-minded leaders and churches being tempted by the prospect of gaining the community's respect. The logic, it seems, is that if the community thinks highly of our church or denomination, if we can just gain some cultural heft, we will win a hearing for the gospel. People will listen to us. We long for the church and its leadership to be well regarded so that the community might listen to the life-saving message. Fuelled by this goal, we begin to shift our focus. We embrace practices which are designed to establish our credibility in the eyes of the world. But at this point we are only a short step away from losing that which makes us the church: the truth of the gospel and the distinctives of gospel priorities.

It ought to be obvious, but it must be constantly said: it isn't our ministry practices or the message we preach that is to win the respect of outsiders; it is our daily lives. Jesus said, "let your light shine before others, so that they may *see your good works* and give glory to your Father who is in heaven" (Matt 5:16). The apostle Peter said,

"*Keep your conduct among the Gentiles honourable,* so that when they speak against you as evildoers, they may *see your good deeds* and glorify God on the day of visitation" (1 Pet 2:12). But the message we preach always was and always will be "foolishness to those who are perishing", "an aroma that brings death" (1 Cor 1:18; 2 Cor 2:16, NIV).

Our gospel will be viewed this way because it is, at least from one perspective, a prophetic call to the world to lay down its arms: to stop its futile and wicked rebellion against the Creator. One of the shortest descriptions of the gospel in the New Testament is found in 2 Corinthians 4: "For what we proclaim is not ourselves, but Jesus Christ as Lord, with ourselves as your servants for Jesus' sake" (v 5). Here is the message in just four words: *Jesus Christ is Lord.* What are those words if not fighting words? To the unforgiven sinner, these words declare: "Jesus Christ is Lord. You are not Lord. So, turn back! Repent. Bow the knee. Find forgiveness by the only means possible—the gift of grace found in the Lord Jesus Christ himself. If you don't turn back, you will face his just judgement."

For those of us who have found this forgiveness, the gospel message is, of course, "an aroma that brings life" (2 Cor 2:16, NIV). But that aroma is only sweet once you have acknowledged the fatal dent it makes in your pride. For pride is the essence of sin, and it is this pride that sees most people remain outside of Christ and unforgiven. We simply cannot make the message of Christ sweet to those who refuse to bow. It will continue to be the stench of death—until the Spirit of God uses that very same message to give birth to a whole new heart. When a church is preaching the biblical gospel, some will respond with repentance and faith, while others will respond with hostility.

Pastor and theologian Iain Murray writes, "From apostolic times onwards, whenever the gospel has entered with discriminating power, it has been with disturbance, opposition and personal reproach for its preachers".[1] Murray goes on to quote Martin Luther:

> Those who are in the teaching office should teach with the greatest faithfulness and expect no other remuneration than to be killed by the world, trampled under foot, and despised by their own. ... Teach purely and faithfully, and in all you do expect not glory but dishonour and contempt, not wealth but poverty, violence, prison, death, and every danger.[2]

Here is the significant danger facing the person who is most passionate about growth. It is very hard to witness outrage against our message; it is painful to feel that we have lost a hearing, to watch our friends becoming alienated against the gospel, and to see the opportunity to win people to Christ slipping through our fingers. And so, the 'sinner-sympathetic evangelist' says, "We must be doing something wrong".

And, of course, perhaps we *are* doing something wrong. Perhaps our daily lives lack the integrity and character that is needed to commend the gospel; we may need to repent. Or perhaps we are falling too heavily on the truth side of the "speaking the truth in love" equation (Eph 4:15). We may be speaking the truth, and therefore comfort ourselves that we are being faithful to Christ, when really we are just being obnoxious and harsh. We are failing the 'love test' and ending up as mere noisy gongs or clanging cymbals (1 Cor 13:1).

Yet these possibilities must not be used to dismiss the very real danger. Leaders need to decide: whose friendship matters most? The world's, or our heavenly Father's? These words of the apostle John are sobering: "Do not love the world or the things in the world. If anyone loves the world, the love of the Father is not in him" (1 John 2:15). Jesus warned that the servant isn't greater than the master:

> "If they persecuted me, they will also persecute you. If they kept my word, they will also keep yours. But all these things they will do to you on account of my name, because they do not know him who sent me. (John 15:20–21)

GROWTH AND CHANGE

What kind of leadership do we need in our churches? What kind of leaders do we aspire to be? The kind the world will respect? Or the kind that speak as a prophetic voice to a lost world, knowing it will bring much disturbance, opposition and personal reproach—even knowing that our voice may appear to hinder the growth of our churches?

These are fundamental questions. And this is why this chapter sits so early in the book. In fact, it's the most important chapter in the whole book. Without resolving this issue, and without keeping it clearly resolved in our hearts and minds, any passion for growth and determination to change will always be ill-fated.

Leading through the dangers

There are fundamental values necessary to minister as Christ's ambassador in this age. One such value is a deeply embedded determination and passion to be, above all else, a faithful representative of Christ in an age that is instinctively and innately opposed to him.

The simple fact is that we cannot be friends with the city. We can love it—or, to express it more helpfully, we can love its people (not to mention the people of the rural area and the village and the isolated station). But our love for the city is not a kind of love that can be reciprocated. Beware the leader who needs or wants to be liked and wants to position the church as the loved and respected member of the broader community.[3]

Indeed, it is possible to minister in one generation, even for the purpose of winning people to the kingdom, in such a way that we destroy the next generation's grasp of the gospel and so hinder the long-term work of gospel ministry. Francis Schaeffer made this point in a slightly different context—different in its specific setting, but identical in its underlying concern. At the 1966 Berlin Conference on Evangelism, he warned:

If we do not make clear by word and practice our position for truth as truth and against false doctrine, we are building a wall between the next generation and the gospel. And twenty years from now, men will point their finger back at us and say of us, this is the result of the flow of history.[4]

This is a warning of such importance that it needs to shape a person long before they are anywhere near taking responsibility for a community of faith. And this mindset will be tested again and again in many ways over the course of a leader's ministry. Our great need is leaders who not only understand the truths and the priorities of the gospel, but who are also emotionally bound up with these truths and priorities in such a way that a shift away from biblical faithfulness becomes unthinkable. The very idea of abandoning the truth of the gospel should hurt deeply.

Where such a shift does occur, it is often in reaction to apparent failings of previous generations of leadership.

For example, we see the outsider criticizing the previous leader, or the church in general, for a perceived arrogance and harshness. Therefore, to win the respect of these critics or to gain a hearing with them—and out of a desire to see them saved (a wonderful motivation)—we seek to establish ourselves as distinct from those who are disliked; we present our message in such a way that the sinner is struck by its warmth and inclusiveness. This will very often lead to growth. We will gain positive feedback, and perhaps even great affirmation, as the representatives of a kind of Christianity that is so much more appealing.

But here is the critical thing to note: this path will only ever buy short-term growth—and this short-term gain will bring long-term pain.

The long-term pain comes because, in short order, one of two things will happen. The first possibility is that we will have to display a very different side of the gospel as we shift into proclaiming that this message of love and inclusivity does, in fact, have some hard edges: there is an eternal judgement for those outside of Christ; Jesus is the only way to escape God's wrath; salvation isn't only from the penalty of sin, but also from its power, which necessitates change in those who are converted. When we take this path, we have moved into a kind of 'bait-and-switch' ministry. This will create disillusionment and even disdain within the broader community. We will lose the world's friendship—and we will be confronted with the reality that the world never wanted us, and it never will.

Seeking to avoid this trap, we may fall into the second danger: changing our presentation of the gospel so that we never disappoint our newly won audience. This may start with leaders comforting themselves with the thought that they will keep their preaching more 'positive', and will simply deal with harder issues in smaller, more private areas of ministry. But the reality here is that a leader who doesn't model an ownership of difficult truths—and who won't do so *publicly*—will slowly build a church filled with people who likewise won't own those hard truths. This then creates an even-more-powerful movement that encourages the pragmatic leader towards being silent on anything that might offend the outsider. Thus, a church or ministry slides into compromise. By this stage, systems and structures are likely to be dependent on the cash flow of a church that was built through 'community-compatible preaching'. It will be a very courageous leader who is prepared to jeopardize their livelihood to stand for truths that many oppose—especially when many of those who oppose these truths are now within the church.

When we fall into these kinds of errors, it is often because we have failed to appreciate the great strengths of the generations that came before us—generations that are now routinely condemned as having been harsh, unloving and sectarian. In reality, these generations did much to "guard the good deposit entrusted to [them]" (2 Tim 1:14) and to faithfully preserve the message that we are to proclaim. While some may claim that our forebears gave the church a negative reputation—a reputation that was perceived as inhibiting growth—the fact is that, over the long haul, faithful leaders have kept the seeds of the all-powerful gospel alive and well; they have modelled that a God-centred life and a Christ-centred ministry is not beholden to the shifting sands of popular culture.

One example from my part of the world will illustrate the point. It's an incident that took place in 1970. I was too young to understand it or even notice it at the time, but I later came to see its significance. In that year, Pope Paul VI visited Australia for the first time. During his visit, he called the leaders of various religious organizations to gather with him to pray. Sir Marcus Loane, who was then Anglican Archbishop of Sydney, famously refused to attend the event. For Archbishop Loane, attending would have been an act of significant compromise, for it would have overlooked the serious doctrinal differences between Roman Catholics and Protestants (such as his own Anglican denomination).

Archbishop Loane's refusal was, by its very nature, highly public. It caused outrage around Australia. Local newspapers received countless letters to the editor, there was widespread community debate and discussion, and the incident made headlines as far away as *The New York Times*.[5] To many 'church growth' observers, it was a public relations disaster. How can Christianity appeal to the world if its leadership acts in such seemingly divisive ways? Many were so outraged that they resolved never to set foot in an Anglican church in Sydney again. Other churches readily capitalized on the uproar by presenting a far softer image to the community—one of inclusiveness and broad incorporation. These churches won the acclaim of many, even as another church was being condemned.

But more than half a century later, the very churches that were condemned in this moment are, broadly speaking, alone in experiencing growth in the last two or three decades. This growth has not been spectacular by many standards. But the churches Sir Marcus Loane led have, for the most part, remained determinedly faithful to the apostolic gospel and its exclusive claims in a world that is increasingly pluralistic. As a result, they have experienced slow but steady growth while most other churches and denominations have declined.

It is not hard to see why such an act would contribute to faithful leadership and to long-term growth. The many men and women who understood what Archbishop Loane was doing were nurtured in a similar determination to live for God's approval, not other people's approval. They saw themselves functioning as prophetic voices in a world that would always have reason to despise the message of Christ. They fostered the same set of values in the leaders who came after them, which in turn strengthened the hands of innumerable young men and women to trust the God of the gospel and to stand firm, even when short-term or more narrowly defined strategic considerations would insist it was time to soften.

The pursuit of cultural relevance

All this bears on the issue of our churches and our ministries pursuing *relevance*.

At EV Church, we are very keen to be culturally savvy. We want to notice those things that make us disconnected culturally from the groups we are trying to reach. It is a guaranteed principle of growth that the fewer cultural hurdles a person needs to jump over, the easier it is to connect into the community of faith. These are important values for our church, and they have a significant influence on how we conduct our ministry. We are very conscious of the call to imitate the apostle Paul, who became "all things to all people, that by all means [he] might save some" (1 Cor 9:22, 11:1).

But—and this is a major *but*—the gospel calls us to "bear the reproach [Jesus] endured" (Heb 13:13). It calls us to expect that we will be "publicly exposed to reproach and affliction" (Heb 10:33). Jesus destroyed any chance of being culturally respected by the Jewish leadership when he gave himself over to death, even death on a cross. As a strategy to connect to the Jewish elites of his day, the cross was a total failure. In this Jesus was like Moses, who had to make a choice between being culturally acceptable to the Egyptian cultural elites or being with God's people. His choice "to be mistreated with the people of God [rather] than to enjoy the fleeting pleasures of sin" was the right one, but it was a choice to accept "reproach" for the sake of God (Heb 11:25–26). In other words, he chose to endure disgrace among those he may have had a desire to win. This should be no surprise. After all, we follow a master who was hated and persecuted by the world, and who promised that his followers would experience the same things (John 15:18–21).

Ultimately, our choice for Christ is a choice to stand against or outside the cultures of our times, along with all the shame that this choice brings. This choice is always hard for those who are most intent on growth.

The church is to be "a pillar and buttress of the truth" in a world of darkness and active opposition to the truth (1 Tim 3:15). The very nature of this image is that it requires strength and determination (God-given strength and determination, no doubt) to stand when every influence around—including our passion for growth—is pulling us towards compromise and softness.

Faithful to Christ, come what may

In essence, our ministries are to be about communicating the truth. The truth matters more than popularity, more than worldly success, and more than crowds. Jesus Christ and his pleasure must matter to us much more than the favour of the world—because Jesus Christ alone is the way, and the truth, and the life. For those with eyes to see it, this truth is far more appealing than the shifting sands of approval from our relativistic world. We must cultivate a hunger—among ourselves and others—to build our lives on the true rock, Jesus, and on all the truth found in him.

We know that for many, however, this will hold no appeal at all. As Jesus himself taught, "the gate is narrow and the way is hard that leads to life, and those who find it are few" (Matt 7:14). Our world is the way it is because it has deliberately thrown off the loving rule of a holy God and has preferred self-rule, along with all that entails.

And so, we embrace an oft-repeated appeal: we make it our aim to be faithful to Christ and to his word, come what may. We make it our ambition to preach the word of God in season and out of season, to rebuke, to correct and to encourage—for we know that the time is coming, and in fact has now arrived, when people will not endure sound teaching.

A passion for growth and a willingness to change are essential. But this passion for growth is dangerous—very dangerous.

Passages for further reflection

- John 15:18–21
- 1 Corinthians 1:18–31
- 2 Corinthians 4:1–6
- 2 Timothy 4:1–5

Questions for personal or team reflection

- Has your care for the unconverted sinner ever led you to compromise? Is it leading you to compromise right now?
- Whose friendship and approval are most important to you: the world's, or your heavenly Father's?

Quote for personal or team reflection

"Those who are in the teaching office should teach with the greatest faithfulness and expect no other remuneration than to be killed by the world, trampled under foot, and despised by their own. ... Teach purely and faithfully, and in all you do expect not glory but dishonour and contempt, not wealth but poverty, violence, prison, death, and every danger." (Martin Luther, quoted by Iain Murray)

3

THE NECESSITY OF A PASSION FOR GROWTH

The limits of 'just be faithful'

For many, the content of the previous chapter is deeply understood and keenly felt. It dominates any and every discussion on the topic of church or ministry growth. Every contemplation of change brings with it a note of trepidation and warning: 'Be careful! Don't push it!' I have great sympathy with this position. I've seen the dangers of a passion for growth turn into reality far too often.

It is therefore very tempting to leave the discussion there. Many do this, and then retreat to a popular but easily misapplied phrase: 'Just be faithful'.

The Scriptures, of course, call on us to be faithful: "it is required of stewards that they be found faithful" (1 Cor 4:2). This is absolutely true in many ways. Yet this is often applied in a simplistic way to suggest that the *only* thing that matters is a bold, heroic and *faithful* stand on the truth. Any attention to the impact of our ministry is dismissed as being outside of our purview. Take preaching as an example: we preach without regard to anyone's reactions or to whether we see growth or decline. If our passage talks about sin, smash it—and anyone who happens to be present—out of the park. Will this mean people leave the church? Sure. But this kind of pastorate operates on the motto "We're not here to make friends". This kind of approach is thought to protect us from any danger of compromise. It's all so simple.

But it's also thoroughly inadequate.

For there is just one problem with this way of thinking and this approach to ministry: the Bible.

So much of what the Bible teaches leaves us unable to live with simplistic mantras like 'just be faithful'. The Bible compels the careful reader to be absolutely passionate about growth, even with all the dangers of potential compromise this brings.[1]

In this chapter, I will unpack the biblical data which makes clear that growth is to be our passion. This chapter isn't just 'filler', and it's not just here so the book can tick a box of 'theological correctness' by referring to the Bible. Critical to the life and growth of a community of faith is a proper grasp of the deep truths that ought to drive us. What matters in this life? Can we, or should we, prioritize some things over others? Amid the many good things that could fill our lives and our ministries, what might emerge as the highest priority? And is it really necessary to make changes to my ministry? Is it worth the pain?

It is only possible to answer these questions properly with a clear sense of the biblical perspective on life and what matters in it. We can only have the courage and the longstanding determination needed to lead a ministry into the kind of change that might facilitate real gospel growth if we know with razor-sharp clarity what we should be doing and why we should be doing it. When we are foggy about what really matters, it is impossible to lead with any real power. Clarity is king for leaders. Clarity brings confidence, courage, stamina and drive.

The larger point here is that although it is immensely dangerous to be passionate about growing the church, it is impossible to be long in the Bible and be left without this passion. It is impossible to be long in the Bible and to be close to the heart of God without holding a passionate desire to see the church grow—not only spiritually, but also numerically. It is impossible to not be filled with a great sense of urgency. This passion and this urgency ought to well up in fervent prayer and in a heartfelt drive to make a difference.

Why should we have this passion?

In this chapter, I'm going to offer five reasons—five truths that leap off the pages of the Bible, address our hearts and foster this passion. I'll then conclude by adding one final truth. This might sound like the slow-witted man's way of saying that I'm offering six truths. But I want to treat the sixth point separately because it stands in a unique relationship to the others and demonstrates another profoundly important point.

From there, having unpacked the great biblical truths that should make us passionate for growth, the next chapter will consider a perennial question among all Christians: how should this passion for growth properly express itself specifically in a concern for *numerical* growth?

Let's begin by turning to our five foundational truths.

Deep truths that clarify our purpose and fuel our passion

1. The biblical vision for Christ and his church

One of the spiritual blessings God has given us in Christ is to know his eternal plan and purpose, which is to "unite all things in [Christ], things in heaven and things on earth" (Eph 1:10). In all things, God is working to a plan—a grand, eternal scheme to make his Son the head over all things, with all things being united together in him and all things brought into subjection to the one Lord of all. This is God's good purpose to make all things right. We praise God for this plan, and we rejoice in it—including giving thanks and rejoicing for our part in it.

The Greek words translated "unite all things" may well carry a larger idea than the sum of their compound parts. The key word behind this phrase was used in some contexts in the ancient world to indicate a 'summing up'. If this is Paul's intention here, then God's grand purpose is full, expansive and rich: he intends to unite all things in Christ and to 'sum up' everything in him. Whatever the precise details, it is clear that Jesus is central to life and existence; all God's purposes focus on him. As Paul tells us in Colossians 1, all things—including us—were made not only *through* the Son and *by* the Son, but also *for* the Son (Col 1:16). You and I exist for him, and everything we do should be done for his glory.

As Ephesians unfolds, Paul shows that the firstfruits of this grand, eternal plan are seen in the earthly reality of the thing he calls "the church". This can seem completely at odds with how most people perceive the church today, but it is an inescapable conclusion from Paul's writing. The church is the body of Christ, established through his own blood (Eph 2:13). It is the assembly of those who were once hostile but are now reconciled not only to God, but also to one another, having been saved to live their lives for the honour and glory of Christ. The evidence of this great reconciling work is that Jew and Gentile, once deeply divided, are now made to be "one new man" (2:15), "a dwelling place for God by the Spirit" (2:22).

Before the watching universe, God is revealing the glory of his great plan to unite all things in Christ. And the church is the vanguard of this cosmic work. The gathering of this body—united around Jesus Christ, comprised of those who were once divided but are now united, brought together to know their God and to live lives that please and honour him—declares "the manifold wisdom of God" to the universe (3:10).

The second half of Ephesians applies these great truths to the church as a community of believers. Paul urges this new people of God to be "eager to maintain the unity of the Spirit in the bond of peace" (4:3; see 4:1–6) and to use their diversity to enable the "building up" of this united body (4:12; see 4:7–16). There is the sense that this new community of believers, once hostile to God and to one another but now reconciled, ought to do two things: expand and grow numerically; and deepen in what it means to be brought back under the lordship of the risen Christ. To enable us to pursue these twin tasks, Jesus gave four foundational gifts: "the apostles, the prophets, the evangelists, the shepherds and teachers" (Eph 4:11). And why did he give these gifts?

> To equip the saints for the work of ministry, for building up the body of Christ, until we all attain to the unity of the faith and of the knowledge of the Son of God, to mature manhood, to the measure of the stature of the fullness of Christ, so that we may no longer be children, tossed to and fro by the waves and carried about by every wind of doctrine, by human cunning, by craftiness in deceitful schemes. Rather, speaking the truth in love, we are to grow up in every way into him who is the head, into Christ, from whom the whole body, joined and held together by every joint with which it is equipped, when each part is working properly, makes the body grow so that it builds itself up in love. (4:12–16)

In sum, the foundational gifts are given so that the body of Christ might be *built*. God's grand plan in Christ is directly bound up with adding people to his church and transforming those who have been added.[2] Within this fallen and broken world, a new community emerges that is made alive to the true God, united in him, and set free to serve him in holiness and righteousness—for our good and his glory.

In other words, central to our very purpose as humans is participation in God's eternal plan—a plan, now revealed to those of us he has chosen, to sum up everything in Christ and to "unite all things in him". All that we do should be done for the glory of Christ. But

Paul makes clear that the church *and its growth* are central to God's Christ-centred plans for all things. Life is not a matter of people 'making it up as we go', and neither is church life. We are not left in the dark. We now know why we were created, why we live, what our future holds, and what is God's great purpose for our lives and our eternity. All things—including the building of the church—are about Jesus: his glory, and his acclaim.

And God's purpose in this building of the church is both *extensive* and *intensive.*

It is *extensive* in that it includes both "you who were *far off*" and "those who were *near*"—Gentile and Jew alike (Eph 2:17), telling us that all nations and all peoples are included in God's plans. Or to use the vision of Revelation 5, God's glorious vision is seen in Jesus, the Lamb, being praised because "by your blood you ransomed people for God from every tribe and language and people and nation" (Rev 5:9). God's purpose isn't local or regional. It is the vision of the mustard seed which, though small when it is planted, grows to be the largest of all plants (Mark 4:30–32). God's purpose for his church is extensive. His heart is for multitudes of people from every nation to be saved.

At the same time, it is *intensive.* In an important passage in Colossians, Paul speaks to the driving concern to present people mature in Christ. Three times in one sentence, he references the fact that God's concern is for "everyone" to be grown to maturity in Christ: "Him [Jesus] we proclaim, warning *everyone* and teaching *everyone* with all wisdom, that we may present *everyone* mature in Christ" (Col 1:28). Again, we see that God's vision to glorify himself in Christ is bound up with the growth of his church—*extensive* growth in numbers, and *intensive* growth in the depth of each person's Christian maturity.

What, therefore, matters? What concern should we have as those who know the deep mystery of God that is now revealed (see Eph 1:9, 3:3–5)? We can't be content to 'just be faithful' *if* we mean a 'faithfulness' that has no regard for the growth of God's church. What matters is that we concern ourselves with growth and change —as individuals, and as a community of faith—because this growth and change are directly connected to God's great purpose to save more people and to deepen them in what it means to live their new life in Christ. The growth of the church is integral to the glorious, Christ-centred biblical vision.

2. The reality of heaven and hell

Is it possible to find a more sobering, mind-clearing, perspective-giving truth than the fact that there is a heaven and a hell, and that every person is destined for one or the other?

Both are real. Both are forever. One is a future to long for; the other is a future to avoid at all costs. And if both are real, they necessarily overshadow every moment of this age and every perceived value and attainment of this age. There are many things that distinguish one person from another in our cultural contexts: age, gender, profession, ethnicity, and the like. But these distinctions count for very little in light of the fact that heaven or hell awaits each one of us.

You cannot read the life of Jesus and miss the fact that these eternal realities were not only part of his world of thought, but in fact dominated his thought. His first expression of public teaching concerned the coming kingdom (Matt 4:17). The controlling thought throughout the 'Sermon on the Mount' (Matthew 5–7) was the same kingdom. The opening section of the sermon, the 'beatitudes' (Matt 5:1–12), relies entirely on the reality of the future kingdom, where present circumstances will be reversed. Later in the sermon, Jesus warns:

> "If your right eye causes you to sin, tear it out and throw it away. For it is better that you lose one of your members than that your whole body be thrown into hell. And if your right hand causes you to sin, cut it off and throw it away. For it is better that you lose one of your members than that your whole body go into hell." (5:29–30)

This idea was so important to Jesus that he repeated it later in his ministry.

> "And if your hand or your foot causes you to sin, cut it off and throw it away. It is better for you to enter life crippled or lame than with two hands or two feet to be thrown into the eternal fire. And if your eye causes you to sin, tear it out and throw it away. It is better for you to enter life with one eye than with two eyes to be thrown into the hell of fire." (18:8–9)

Notice here that Jesus speaks simply of entering "life". In his thought, *life*—starkly stated, with no qualifier—is set in contrast to entering (literally) "the Gehenna of fire".[3]

Back in the Sermon on the Mount, heaven and hell are recurring themes:

> "Unless your righteousness exceeds that of the scribes and Pharisees, you will never enter the kingdom of heaven." (5:20)

> "You have heard that it was said to those of old, 'You shall not murder; and whoever murders will be liable to judgement.' But I say to you that everyone who is angry with his brother will be liable to judgement; whoever insults his brother will be liable to the council; and whoever says, 'You fool!' will be liable to the hell of fire." (5:21–22)

> "Do not lay up for yourselves treasures on earth, where moth and rust destroy and where thieves break in and steal, but lay up for yourselves treasures in heaven, where neither moth nor rust destroys and where thieves do not break in and steal. For where your treasure is, there your heart will be also." (6:19–21)

> "Enter by the narrow gate. For the gate is wide and the way is easy that leads to destruction, and those who enter by it are

many. For the gate is narrow and the way is hard that leads to life, and those who find it are few." (7:13–14)

"Not everyone who says to me, 'Lord, Lord,' will enter the kingdom of heaven, but the one who does the will of my Father who is in heaven. On that day many will say to me, 'Lord, Lord, did we not prophesy in your name, and cast out demons in your name, and do many mighty works in your name?' And then will I declare to them, 'I never knew you; depart from me, you workers of lawlessness.'" (7:21–23)

Each statement expresses Jesus' depth of concern for eternal realities—and this was only his first sermon! Outside of the sermon, the parables of chapter 13 trade heavily on eternal realities, and Jesus regularly returns to the idea of future judgement:

"I tell you, many will come from east and west and recline at table with Abraham, Isaac, and Jacob in the kingdom of heaven, while the sons of the kingdom will be thrown into the outer darkness. In that place there will be weeping and gnashing of teeth." (8:11–12)

"Do not fear those who kill the body but cannot kill the soul. Rather fear him who can destroy both soul and body in hell." (10:28)

"What will it profit a man if he gains the whole world and forfeits his soul? Or what shall a man give in return for his soul?" (16:26)

Jesus' death is itself a testimony to the dominance of eternal realities. It was "for the joy that was set before him" that he "endured the cross, despising the shame" (Heb 12:2). He came to bring a kingdom that is "not of this world" (John 18:36).

Surely it is impossible to read the life of Jesus without being struck by how much of his life is lived under these great and terrible future realities. In fact, you can't make sense of his life or of the choices he made without seeing how the reality of heaven and hell shaped his priorities. The horror of hell loomed large for Jesus, as did the blessing of restoration to God's rule through forgiveness and mercy that will come in a future, eternal kingdom.

These eternal realities bring crystal clarity to life and its many decisions now. Why didn't Jesus allow himself to be consumed by social-justice issues and by the abundant good that could have been done by healing the sick? Because Jesus saw a larger canvas, and he lived under the greater realities of a future heaven or hell that awaits every person.

This shift in perspective, this clarity of thought and purpose, happens to everyone who grasps these eternal realities. Take, for example, the rich man in Luke 16. Finding himself in hell and discovering that his own anguish could never be relieved (v 24), his only thought was for his brothers to hear and heed the truth (v 28). Peter and the other apostles are very quickly consumed with pleading with anyone and everyone they meet to "save yourselves from this crooked generation" (Acts 2:40); anything the human authorities threaten does very little to silence them. Peter knows that this present world will be "burned up and dissolved" and looks forward to "new heavens and a new earth in which righteousness dwells" (2 Pet 3:10–13). Everything that Paul does is done to save some, and in this he understands himself to be following in the footsteps of the Lord Jesus:

> To the Jews I became as a Jew, in order to win Jews. To those under the law I became as one under the law (though not being myself under the law) that I might win those under the law. To those outside the law I became as one outside the law (not being outside the law of God but under the law of Christ)

that I might win those outside the law. To the weak I became weak, that I might win the weak. I have become all things to all people, that by all means I might save some. I do it all for the sake of the gospel, that I may share with them in its blessings. … I try to please everyone in everything I do, not seeking my own advantage, but that of many, that they may be saved. Be imitators of me, as I am of Christ. (1 Cor 9:20–23, 10:33–11:1)

It is very significant that there is such a push by some to rid Christianity of this eternal framework. But to do so requires a massive culling of the teaching of Jesus and his apostles. So much of what Jesus said and did was dominated by these powerful future realities that loomed large over his life, and which should now loom large over our lives.

Grasping this eternal framework brings clarity today. In light of the twin future realities of heaven and hell, what truly matters now? Can we be content to 'just be faithful' when there is so much at stake?

3. The fact of the cross

Jesus died on the cross while still a relatively young man. He died before his life really took off. He never travelled. He never had a career. He never married. And he never maximized his healing gifts. He could've healed every sickness or fed every starving mouth. He could've resolved every dispute. But none of these things were his primary focus. In fact, he sometimes moved on before fulfilling his potential as a healer (Mark 1:37–38). He did this because of a higher priority. In the first instance, it was the desire to preach (Mark 1:38). But ultimately what really impinged on his concern for immediate needs was the priority of going to the cross to deal with humanity's greatest need.

At a crucial moment in his ministry, Jesus "set his face to go to Jerusalem" (Luke 9:51), though he knew the suffering that awaited him there: three times he warns his disciples that he is going up to Jerusalem to be rejected and killed (Luke 9:22, 9:44, 18:31–33). His giving himself over to death on a cross was intentional and deliberate, despite its impact on his ability to engage in other service activities. The fact that he makes the cross his priority, in light of other options, says something powerfully important. It tells us that the cross was far more important—or at least far more foundational—than any other good Jesus could have achieved.

What did the cross achieve? At heart, it was a ransom for many (Mark 10:45) and achieved reconciliation between God and humanity. In it, "God was reconciling the world to himself, not counting their trespasses against them" (2 Cor 5:19). This is only possible, and only true, because at the cross Jesus was dying in our place: "For our sake he made him to be sin who knew no sin, so that in him we might become the righteousness of God" (2 Cor 5:21).

It is true that the cross achieved many things. It paved the way for a new creation, it provides the perfect example of selfless love, and it informs the way we think about and deal with all of life's challenges. But foregrounded and emphasized throughout the New Testament is the power of the cross to achieve pardon for sinners—the forgiveness of sins, the removal of guilt, and a restored relationship with God.

What matters is not the brute fact of the cross, but what the cross means and what it achieves. For the apostle Paul, it is of "first importance" not just that Christ died, but that "Christ died *for our sins in accordance with the Scriptures*" (1 Cor 15:3). The apostle Peter takes the same view: "Christ also suffered once *for sins*, the righteous for the unrighteous, *that he might bring us to God* ..." (1 Pet 3:18). The Old Testament sacrificial system established that a sacrifice needed to be offered to deal with sin; the New Testament makes clear that Jesus is that sacrifice: "when Christ had offered for all time a single sacrifice *for sins*, he sat down at the right hand of God ..." (Heb 10:12).

Let the following verses wash over you—they are just a selection of what could be said, but notice the picture they paint of why Christ came and what his death achieved.

> But he was pierced for our transgressions;
>> he was crushed for our iniquities;
> upon him was the chastisement that brought us peace,
>> and with his wounds we are healed. (Isa 53:5, prophesying Jesus' death around 700 BC)

"The Son of Man came not to be served but to serve, and to give his life as a ransom for many." (Mark 10:45)

[John the Baptist] saw Jesus coming toward him, and said, "Behold, the Lamb of God, who takes away the sin of the world!" (John 1:29)

"This is my commandment, that you love one another as I have loved you. Greater love has no one than this, that someone lay down his life for his friends. You are my friends ..." (John 15:12–14)

All have sinned and fall short of the glory of God, and are justified by his grace as a gift, through the redemption that is in Christ Jesus, whom God put forward as a propitiation by his blood, to be received by faith. (Rom 3:23–25)

God shows his love for us in that while we were still sinners, Christ died for us. (Rom 5:8)

He who did not spare his own Son but gave him up for us all, how will he not also with him graciously give us all things? (Rom 8:32)

For the word of the cross is folly to those who are perishing, but to us who are being saved it is the power of God. ... We preach

Christ crucified, a stumbling block to Jews and folly to Gentiles, but to those who are called, both Jews and Greeks, Christ the power of God and the wisdom of God. (1 Cor 1:18, 23–25)

I delivered to you as of first importance what I also received: that Christ died for our sins in accordance with the Scriptures, that he was buried, that he was raised on the third day in accordance with the Scriptures, and that he appeared to Cephas, then to the twelve. (1 Cor 15:3–5)

The love of Christ controls us, because we have concluded this: that one has died for all, therefore all have died ... in Christ God was reconciling the world to himself, not counting their trespasses against them, and entrusting to us the message of reconciliation. ... For our sake he made him to be sin who knew no sin, so that in him we might become the righteousness of God. (2 Cor 5:14, 19, 21)

You know the grace of our Lord Jesus Christ, that though he was rich, yet for your sake he became poor, so that you by his poverty might become rich. (2 Cor 8:9)

Christ redeemed us from the curse of the law by becoming a curse for us—for it is written, "Cursed is everyone who is hanged on a tree" ... (Gal 3:13)

And you, who were dead in your trespasses and the uncircumcision of your flesh, God made alive together with him, having forgiven us all our trespasses, by cancelling the record of debt that stood against us with its legal demands. This he set aside, nailing it to the cross. (Col 2:13–14)

The saying is trustworthy and deserving of full acceptance, that Christ Jesus came into the world to save sinners, of whom I am the foremost. (1 Tim 1:15)

But when Christ appeared as a high priest of the good things that have come, then through the greater and more perfect tent (not made with hands, that is, not of this creation) he entered once for all into the holy places, not by means of the blood of goats and calves but by means of his own blood, thus securing an eternal redemption. (Heb 9:11–13)

When Christ had offered for all time a single sacrifice for sins, he sat down at the right hand of God ... (Heb 10:12)

We have confidence to enter the holy places by the blood of Jesus, by the new and living way that he opened for us through the curtain, that is, through his flesh ... (Heb 10:19)

He himself bore our sins in his body on the tree, that we might die to sin and live to righteousness. By his wounds you have been healed. (1 Pet 2:24)

Christ also suffered once for sins, the righteous for the unrighteous, that he might bring us to God ... (1 Pet 3:18)

In this is love, not that we have loved God but that he loved us and sent his Son to be the propitiation for our sins. (1 John 4:10)

There is no end to our many felt needs—sickness, inequality, oppression, greed, hurt and death. But the cross proclaims that our deepest need is the forgiveness of our sins, reconciliation between God and humanity.

The personal break that sin creates between God and humanity is the root from which all other evils flow and from which they take their power. Dealing with sin and with God's righteous judgement against it is at the heart of all other needs. To steal an expression that is more commonly applied to politics, Jesus' death was the true 'drain-the-swamp' moment.

But it was more than this. Yes, his death will right all other wrongs. The new creation will be a place where God wipes every tear from our eyes, where "death shall be no more, neither shall there be mourning, nor crying, nor pain anymore" (Rev 21:4). But even these are the fruit of a much larger concern: *that God and humanity are reconciled.* The greatest glory of Eden (Genesis 2) isn't the wonderful and abundant provision of food, nor is it the absence of sickness and war; it is that God and humanity walk together in the garden. God is with his people. The other blessings are wonderful, but they are only the beautiful context for the relational peace that existed. Now, because we have been justified through faith in Jesus' blood shed for us (Rom 3:24–25), "we have *peace with God* through our Lord Jesus Christ" (Rom 5:1). The final chapters of Revelation are glorious in their depiction of a restored creation, but central to it all and over it all is the fact that God will be with his people. There will be no temple, for God dwells with his people; there will be no sun or moon, for the glory of God will give light to the city of God (Rev 21:22–25). Reconciliation and peace will be fully and perfectly enjoyed.

Jesus came for this work. He came to seek and to save the lost (Luke 19:10). He came not to be served but to serve, and to give his life as a ransom for many (Mark 10:45). He came so that God and sinner might be reconciled, and so that all things may be made right.

And he was prepared to pay the highest price to achieve what he came for. He gave up his life. This wasn't a side issue for Jesus. It wasn't an afterthought. Nor was it an afterthought for his heavenly Father, who paid dearly as well: "God so loved the world, that he gave his only Son, that whoever believes in him should not perish but have eternal life" (John 3:16). Both Father and Son paid such a price because the salvation of men and women is so important. This was and is their glory.

The fact of the cross—of Jesus Christ emptying and humbling himself to the point of a humiliating death—demonstrates the urgency and the primacy of that which the cross achieves: God reconciling the world to himself, no longer counting our sins against us. This urgency is captured in Paul's words to the Corinthians:

> Therefore, we are ambassadors for Christ, God making his appeal through us. We implore you on behalf of Christ, be reconciled to God. (2 Cor 5:20)

4. The brevity of life

These first three truths should be enough to clarify and to compel. But when you add the fact that our lives are so brief, there is a growing pressure to be clear on what really matters. We only have a few short years, relatively speaking, before health and life disappear. The Bible reminds us that we are "a mist that appears for a little time and then vanishes" (Jas 4:14). We should pray with Moses, "teach us to number our days that we may get a heart of wisdom" (Ps 90:12). What is worth doing in these few short years?

Jesus lived with great clarity, aware that time was short. It is telling that the prayer he taught his disciples was dominated by eternal concerns. In a prayer that contains six requests, only one— "Give us this day our daily bread"—concerns itself with physical needs.[4] At every point, Jesus returns to the priority and importance of establishing the kingdom, which happens by his death and resurrection and by the proclamation of his death and resurrection. Jesus taught his disciples not to store up treasures on earth, but to store up treasures in heaven—to invest themselves in eternal things, not temporary things (Matt 6:19–21). He taught them not to be anxious about their food, their drink or their clothing, but instead to "seek first the kingdom of God and his righteousness" (Matt 6:25–34).

This presses upon us some wise and profoundly important questions: What am I going to do with the few short years that God gives me? What matters most? What should dominate my life, my concerns, my priorities, and my prayers? What will it profit me to gain the whole world and forfeit my soul? What will be gained by investing my energies and efforts in things that won't last?

As Jesus said, "Do not work for the food that perishes, but for the food that endures to eternal life" (John 6:27).

Some time ago, I was profoundly impacted by the words of a friend who was dying of cancer. As he lay on his death bed, he had a great deal of time to think, and he expressed very powerfully a proper biblical sense of how we ought to view life. Here's something he wrote near the end:

> I am seeing with greater clarity that all the beautiful and beguiling things of this world and of this life are merely shadows of the reality that is to come. This seems to be God's way. The Passover is swallowed up in the Cross. One greater than Moses comes to lead his children into their true inheritance. David, the Messiah King, submits to the Son of David whose suffering and death provide the full and perfect atonement. The temple gives way to the body of Christ. So many examples could be given. ... My poor illustration is this. It is as if, each day, a bus leaves from the Town Hall steps for the city of God. Each day I go to the point of departure and scan the passenger list to see if my name is there. It may not be there today, so I seek, so far as I am able, to press on in service, but each day is one day closer.[5]

5. Love

Here is our final deep truth—but not final in the sense of being least in importance. It is final in that it binds the others together and brings them into proper focus. Without love, we can end up with a very cool, detached appreciation of the first four truths. We can know that each of those points is true and right, yet we can remain largely unmoved by them because we are also sure that God will be glorified in salvation *and* in judgement. And so, we tell ourselves, whether a person comes to faith is not that important, because God will be glorified either way.

But love changes all this—the love of God, and our love for others that is meant to reflect his love.

God is love (1 John 4:8, 16). Yes, he is also light; he is also holy. But love is the essence of his being and character; it is his love that compels him to pursue a rebellious and sinful world instead of simply condemning it righteously.

The Old Testament prophecy of Hosea vividly captures Israel's awful rebellion against God, most memorably through God asking his prophet to marry "a wife of whoredom" (Hos 1:2)—a woman whose adulterous behaviour provided a living illustration of Israel's unfaithfulness to God. But after many chapters of pronouncing judgement against his rebellious and unrepentant people, God's heart for his people is revealed in these famous words:

How can I give you up, O Ephraim?
How can I hand you over, O Israel?
How can I make you like Admah?
How can I treat you like Zeboiim?
My heart recoils within me;
my compassion grows warm and tender.
I will not execute my burning anger;
I will not again destroy Ephraim;
for I am God and not a man,
the Holy One in your midst,
and I will not come in wrath. (11:8–9)

Yes, God can and will be glorified by judgement. Yes, he is the potter and we are the clay, and he has the right to do with us as he pleases. But judgement is his "strange" and "alien" work (Isa 28:21). He will not rest in judgement. He loves too much. He takes no pleasure in the death of the wicked (Ezek 18:23) and does not wish that any should perish (2 Pet 3:9); he "desires all people to be saved and to come to the knowledge of the truth" (1 Tim 2:4). And so, his love compels him to send his Son into the world, that whoever believes in him should not perish but have eternal life (John 3:16).

In Romans 10:21, Paul quotes the prophet Isaiah to describe God's attitude towards those who are not among "God's elect": "But of Israel he says, 'All day long I have held out my hands to a disobedient and contrary people'". Remember, these were people who were *not* among God's elect. They died in their sin. But here is an insight into the deepest heart of God even for the lost. He loves his world—a world, according to the theology of John's Gospel, that is in hostility and rebellion towards its Creator.

God's heart is a heart of love. He longs to save.

If we love like God loves, we will be urgent about the work of salvation—to save from hell, and to bring those that are being saved into the fellowship of his people, and into the life of love he calls us to.

The apostles didn't just present Jesus to the world in a detached and dispassionate way. In the first ever Christian sermon, Peter exhorted people—he pleaded with people—to accept the salvation on offer (Acts 2:40). Paul implored people—he begged them—to be reconciled to God (2 Cor 5:20). When Jesus approached Jerusalem and knew the judgement that awaited the city—even though that judgement was thoroughly deserved after centuries of rebellion—he wept (Luke 19:41). His love moved him to shed a flood of tears.

Jesus and his apostles grasped the loving heart of their sovereign heavenly Father. God is not cool towards his world. He *is* love, and in his love he will see people saved before he will see them condemned.

Richard Baxter expressed it so well in his classic work *The Reformed Pastor*. The language is old-fashioned (the book was originally published in 1656), but the sentiment is entirely relevant to our own day:

O sirs, surely if you had all conversed with neighbour death as oft as I have done, and as often received the sentence in yourselves, you would have an unquiet conscience, if not a reformed life, as to your ministerial diligence and fidelity; and you would have something within you that would frequently ask you such questions as these: 'Is this all thy compassion for lost sinners? Wilt thou do no more to seek and to save them? ... Shall they die and be in hell before thou wilt speak to them one serious word to prevent it? Shall they there curse thee for ever that didst no more in time to save them?' Such cries of conscience are daily ringing in mine ears, though, the Lord know, I have too little obeyed them. ... How can you choose, when you are laying a corpse in the grave, but think with yourselves, 'Here lieth the body; but where is the soul? and what have I done for it, before it departed? It was part of my charge; what account can I give of it?'

O sirs, is it a small matter to you to answer such questions as these? It may seem so now, but the hour is coming when it will not seem so.[6]

Given all these considerations—the biblical vision for God to be glorified in Christ (especially in the church), the reality of heaven and hell, the fact of the cross, the brevity of life, and God's love for his world—it is truly problematic to settle for the 'just be faithful' line. How can we 'just be faithful' without regard for whether people walk away? How can we 'just be faithful' without being moved to care deeply, and to sacrifice, and to make changes, so that the people around us may be saved and presented mature in Christ? Such an attitude is not just deficient; it is ungodly—that is, it is *not like God*. Our God does not desire the death of anyone, and he paid the ultimate price so that people could be saved. He wept over the crowds that walked away, and he held out his hands all day long to a disobedient and contrary people, beseeching them to turn back.

As I said earlier, clarity is king for leaders. Clarity is power in leadership. These five truths provide the clarity we need. What matters in life? What things should dominate our thinking and our concerns? Amid the many good and proper things we could do, what ought to take priority? In light of eternity, it is unavoidable that the thing that matters most is the priority of saving men and women from condemnation and judgement in hell, that they might "obtain the freedom of the glory of the children of God" (Rom 8:21) and be presented "mature in Christ" (Col 1:28).

'Plus one': The biblical imperative

These five biblical truths are immensely powerful. Taken together as a whole, they provide a logical framework to tell us that gospel ministry is primary, and they push us to review and rethink all our priorities. But the New Testament goes a step further by adding another element—what I sometimes call a 'plus one'. That is, the New Testament does not leave us to draw our own conclusions about priorities in life and ministry; it tells us very directly that the conclusions drawn from the above theological principles are well and truly on the mark.

In other words, a gospel-fuelled passion for growth and change is not just a logical inference; it is *a biblical imperative*.

Perhaps the most obvious place to find such an imperative is in the 'Great Commission' in Matthew 28. The last of Jesus' words recorded for us by Matthew stand as a thoroughly appropriate climax to the life of Jesus—a life that was consumed by eternal realities, shaped by his Father's will, lived with a heart of love, and ended in his sacrificial death on the cross. Having lived such a life and died such a death, and having been raised to life and given "all authority in heaven and on earth" (Matt 28:18), Jesus tells his disciples exactly what it must mean for them: "Go therefore and make disciples of all nations" (Matt 28:19).

There has been considerable debate around the proper audience for these words and their application to us today. Some have noted that the original audience was only the eleven disciples,[7] and have therefore concluded that these words don't function as a general command for all Christians. But when the Great Commission is set in the context of not only the flow of the whole biblical narrative but also the movement of Matthew's Gospel—together with the five foundational biblical truths expounded above—it is impossible to *not* see the Commission as shaping the priority and agenda of all believers.

One key to understanding Jesus' intended audience is in the repeated use of the word 'all':

- *All* authority in heaven and on earth has been given to the risen Jesus (by his heavenly Father) (v 18).
- The disciples are told to make disciples of *all* nations (v 19).
- The disciples are to teach new disciples to observe *all* that he has commanded them (v 20).
- He will be with them *always*—literally *"all* the days"—as they fulfill this Commission (v 20).

This is compelling evidence that the Commission is for all disciples everywhere, not just the original eleven. If the foundation of the Commission is Jesus' universal authority, the Commission applies far beyond the lifetime of the first disciples. If the Commission involves calling on all nations to respond, it will require all disciples in all times and places. And if Jesus follows the Commission with a promise to be with his disciples "all the days, to the end of the age", we should conclude that he means to address all his disciples, not just the eleven.

In their comprehensive book on a biblical theology of mission, theologians Andreas Köstenberger and Peter O'Brien conclude that the Great Commission shows "mission is the church's primary task between Christ's first coming and his return".[8] What's more, they note that "mission entails the nurturing of converts into the full obedience of faith, not merely the proclamation of the gospel".[9]

This draws our attention to the fact that the Great Commission has two dimensions—what I call the 'get' and the 'grow' of Christian ministry: *get* people saved, and *grow* them in the faith. But it also confirms that the command to make disciples extends to all disciples everywhere. And because the Commission is not fulfilled by evangelism alone but by the all-encompassing, ongoing work of evangelism and discipleship, it requires us to re-examine every aspect of life and ministry. It requires us to ask constantly: what changes are needed so that I might play my part in fulfilling Christ's all-encompassing mission in all the world? What changes are needed in my church or ministry?

Our five foundational biblical truths function like the unseen bulk of an iceberg that sits below the water. They are the reason that the handful of biblical commands are visible above the water line, pushed to the surface by those deeper realities. For example, the mission imperative of Matthew 28 makes perfect and powerful sense when seen as the natural outworking of Matthew's overall presentation of Jesus, not to mention that Matthew's presentation of Jesus relies on the deeper structures of the Bible's thought—such as the universal human need for salvation, God's faithfulness to his covenant promises, and his commitment to saving a people for himself.

To take another such example, Paul exhorts us to "be steadfast, immovable, always abounding in the work of the Lord, knowing that in the Lord your labour is not in vain" (1 Cor 15:58). This "work of the Lord" is not any and all work to which we might give ourselves, but the narrower kind of work associated with ministering for the growth and health of the church.[10] But this exhortation is the culmination of Paul's long argument about the truth and the importance of Jesus' resurrection: Christ has been raised from the dead as "the firstfruits of those who have fallen asleep", and in Christ all shall be "made alive" (1 Cor 15:20–22). And those great truths about the resurrection flow out of Paul's reminder of the saving gospel of Christ:

> For I delivered to you as of first importance what I also received: that Christ died for our sins in accordance with the Scriptures, that he was buried, that he was raised on the third day in accordance with the Scriptures, and that he appeared to Cephas, then to the twelve. (1 Cor 15:3–5)

Understanding the relationship between the foundational truths and the biblical imperatives that follow will help to guard us against being distracted by other more imaginative theologizing that can sound enticing, but that lacks the same kind of biblical warrant and can therefore confuse our priorities. Every few years or so, it seems, some new structure of thought is put forward, drawing certain possible inferences from theological themes. For instance, in recent times much has been made of the possible connection between this creation and the new creation. We are told that we have been misreading the Bible, and that there will be a high level of continuity between this age and the age to come. On this basis, we are then told that we must recognize the lasting benefits of work other than gospel work—that things such as art and culture will last, so Christians ought to invest more of their time and energies into these things.

I don't wish to diminish the importance or the wonder of art and culture. These are good, God-given gifts. What is noteworthy, however, is that the theological inference about investing time in such things doesn't find expression in any imperatives in the New Testament. When you do find that the inferences being drawn from larger theological truths also find expression in clear New Testament commands—as is the case with gospel work, with the work of making disciples—you know you are on solid ground.

Disciple making builds on our five foundational truths; it gives perfect and natural expression to them. *And* it is confirmed by the clear exhortations of Scripture: we are to pursue the conversion and the Christian growth of the people around us until the end of the age; we are to always abound in the work of the Lord; we are to imitate Paul as he imitates Christ by laying down his life for the salvation of others.

The central concern of all God's people ought to be the salvation of those around us. Or, in the language of the Great Commission, our driving passion should be to make disciples. We must be deeply committed to seeing the growth of God's church and the growth of God's people.

But should this passion for growth be equated specifically with a passion for *numerical* growth? That is the subject of our next chapter.

Passages for further reflection

- Hosea 11:8–9
- Matthew 6:19–34
- Matthew 28:18–20
- 1 Corinthians 10:31–11:1

Questions for personal or team reflection

- What truly matters to you? In view of eternity—in view of heaven and hell—what *should* truly matter to you?
- What changes are needed in your life so that you might play your part in fulfilling Christ's all-encompassing mission in all the world? What changes are needed in your church or ministry?

Quote for personal or team reflection

"O sirs, surely if you had all conversed with neighbour death as oft as I have done, and as often received the sentence in yourselves, you would have an unquiet conscience, if not a reformed life, as to your ministerial diligence and fidelity; and you would have something within you that would frequently ask you such questions as these: 'Is this all thy compassion for lost sinners? Wilt thou do no more to seek and to save them? ... Shall they die and be in hell before thou wilt speak to them one serious word to prevent it? Shall they there curse thee for ever that didst no more in time to save them?'" (Richard Baxter)

THE IMPORTANCE OF NUMBERS

Moving beyond "it isn't about numbers"

Christians are often reluctant to speak about numbers and attendance—whether numerical growth or numerical decline. And there are many good reasons for this reluctance. Thinking of numbers in the wrong way can reduce God's church to an ungodly theatre of personal ambition; it can reduce people to statistics on a spreadsheet that simply allow us to hit our KPIs. We've all seen numbers used and discussed in crass and unhealthy ways.

But we have gone too far and thrown the baby out with the bathwater when our rhetoric around church life explicitly states that "it isn't about numbers".

I most recently heard this at a church-planting conference where we were being exhorted to focus on evangelism. In this context, we were told that "it isn't about numbers". The speaker's point—as is usually the case with people who make this point—was delivered with a good heart and a reasonable concern. For we were being urged to continue in gospel proclamation no matter the outcome, and we were being warned that we ought never think of people as objects to collect. The intention behind "it isn't about numbers" is honourable.

But in seeking to help us avoid one error, it creates another. For our passion for growth, created and fuelled by the theological realities outlined in the last chapter, *must* express itself in a humble, sober and appropriate concern for numbers.

Let me unpack this claim with a brief comment on the logic of the issue, before turning more explicitly to the Scriptures. This may sound back to front, but approaching the issue this way will allow us to keep the bulk of our focus on what God's word says about numbers.

Thinking logically about numbers

The gospel is "the power of God for salvation to everyone who believes" (Rom 1:16). Upon believing the powerful word of Christ, a person is united to Christ by the work of the Spirit and becomes part of "the body of Christ" (see 1 Cor 12:27; Eph 4:12). But this "body" isn't only a spiritual reality; the body of Christ is visible in the world whenever and wherever local churches meet. Every local church is more than a part of the body of Christ; it *is* the body of Christ (see Col 1:24).[1]

So, this conclusion almost always follows: where people are becoming Christians, the visible body of Christ should grow numerically as new converts become part of local churches.

There are, of course, some exceptions to this. Some churches are in highly transient communities (such as mining towns in remote parts of Australia). Some churches are in areas where almost every convert moves out of the region because of upward mobility. Some churches face such hostile opposition that many converts are killed. Some churches are in retirement villages and see attendance fluctuate wildly for health reasons. There are numerous qualifications we could add. But these qualifications should not be used to squash an obvious truth: conversion growth is normally reflected in church growth.

Where there is no numerical growth, apart from the kinds of

exception mentioned, it would properly be a point of great concern. A lack of numerical growth in a church—by which I really mean a lack of *conversion* growth—would signal a grave problem.

Logically, then, numbers matter because they signify conversion.

But this isn't only established as a matter of logical deduction. Much more importantly, the Scriptures directly testify to the truth that numbers matter.

Thinking biblically about numbers

The gospel isn't merely a word about God's honour and glory—a word to be delivered with no regard to the response. It is, at its heart, a summons from God our ruler that *demands* a response. It is God's loving movement towards his hostile world, but a move made with purpose and intent: to reconcile the world to himself (2 Cor 5:19), to save the world (John 3:17), to win it back.

We could turn to so many parts of Scripture to establish this point, but let's begin by looking at Paul's words in 2 Corinthians 4:

> Since we have the same spirit of faith according to what has been written, "I believed, and so I spoke," we also believe, and so we also speak, knowing that he who raised the Lord Jesus will raise us also with Jesus and bring us with you into his presence. For it is all for your sake, so that as grace extends to more and more people it may increase thanksgiving, to the glory of God. (2 Cor 4:13–15)

Paul's expectation is that as he speaks the gospel that he believes, the grace of God will extend "to more and more people". He expects numerical growth. And he sees this numerical growth—and the increase in thanksgiving that it brings—as bringing honour and glory to God.

Or consider the opening of Luke's Gospel. When Jesus is born, the angels announce that they bring "good news of great joy that will be for all the people. For unto you is born this day in the city of David a Saviour, who is Christ the Lord" (Luke 2:10–11). Note the use of the word "Saviour". The gospel is good news because it is news of the Lord *who is a Saviour*. He doesn't just come to testify to the truth (although of course he does that). He comes to save; he comes to bring the forgiveness of sins. In other words, built into the gospel itself is the expectation of an appropriate response to the gospel. And that response sees people saved and converted. It brings numerical growth.

We could add to this the tone and tenor of the whole book of Acts (Luke's companion volume to his Gospel). Throughout the book, Luke speaks of numerical growth as people respond to the gospel being preached, even reporting the number of people responding. After Peter's first sermon, as he urges his hearers to repent and be baptized for the forgiveness of their sins, and as he pleads with them to save themselves "from this crooked generation" (Acts 2:40), Luke records the response: "So those who received his word were baptized, and there were added that day about three thousand souls" (2:41). And after then describing the fellowship of these early believers, Luke adds: "And the Lord added to their number day by day those who were being saved" (2:47). This kind of description could seem somewhat crass and alarming to many modern evangelicals— imagine the feedback if a missionary wrote this way in a newsletter! But it is part of God's inspired word.

But Luke doesn't stop there:

More than ever believers were added to the Lord, multitudes of both men and women. (Acts 5:14)

The word of God continued to increase, and the number of the disciples multiplied greatly in Jerusalem, and a great many of the priests became obedient to the faith. (6:7)

The hand of the Lord was with [the disciples who preached Jesus to the Hellenists], and a great number who believed turned to the Lord. The report of this came to the ears of the church in Jerusalem, and they sent Barnabas to Antioch. When he came and saw the grace of God, he was glad, and he exhorted them all to remain faithful to the Lord with steadfast purpose, for he was a good man, full of the Holy Spirit and of faith. And a great many people were added to the Lord. (11:21–24)

Now at Iconium [Paul and Barnabas] entered together into the Jewish synagogue and spoke in such a way that a great number of both Jews and Greeks believed. (14:1)

The churches were strengthened in the faith, and they increased in numbers daily. (16:5)

Luke's focus on numerical growth is not arbitrary. It carries forward an important theological idea introduced at the end of his Gospel, which itself is carrying forward ideas developed much earlier. In his post-resurrection appearances at the end of Luke's account, Jesus speaks about the divine necessity of not only his death and resurrection, but also the mission to the world:

"Thus it is written, that the Christ should suffer and on the third day rise from the dead, and that repentance for the forgiveness of sins should be proclaimed in his name to all nations, beginning from Jerusalem." (Luke 24:46–47)

Note the use of the word "should": the Son of man *should* suffer and rise from the dead. The death of Jesus was a necessary part of the divine plan, and it happened just as God promised in the Old Testament Scriptures. But the same thing applies to what comes next: repentance and forgiveness of sins *should* be preached to all nations. The mission of the gospel is as much a part of God's plan as the death and resurrection of Jesus. And the divine plan isn't simply that a message will be preached, but that a message *which brings repentance for the forgiveness of sins* will be preached *to all nations*. This takes us back to the notion from early in Luke: the gospel is "good news of great joy ... for *all the people*" because it is news about a "Saviour" (2:10–11)—one who will save people from their sins through his death and resurrection as this "good news of great joy" is proclaimed and as people respond in repentance.

This is the foundation upon which Acts builds. One of its major themes is the fulfilment of the mission: the preaching of the gospel, the response of repentance, and the forgiveness of sins that spreads to all the nations—first in Jerusalem, then in Judea and Samaria, then "to the end of the earth" (see Acts 1:8). In this context, Luke's focus on numbers serves an important purpose. It tells us that God's intention in sending his Son "to seek and to save the lost" (Luke 19:10) is being fulfilled; it tells us that "more and more people" (2 Cor 4:15)—i.e. more numbers!—are coming to know the grace of God, so that thanksgiving is overflowing to the glory of God.

Jesus came into the world to fulfill God's ancient promise to bless "all the families of the earth" (Gen 12:3). He suffered so that many might be saved. Paul imitated his Saviour by laying down his rights and preaching the gospel to all people so that many would come to salvation: "I have become all things to all people, that by all means I might save some" (1 Cor 9:22). True, he doesn't expect that all will be saved—but he certainly expects that some will be saved. And he has now told us to follow him as he follows Christ:

> So, whether you eat or drink, or whatever you do, do all to the glory of God. Give no offence to Jews or to Greeks or to the church of God, just as I try to please everyone in everything I do, not seeking my own advantage, but that of many, that they may be saved. Be imitators of me, as I am of Christ. (1 Cor 10:31–11:1)

In our day and age, there is an immediate reaction when numbers are mentioned in the context of setting our aims for Christian leadership. This reaction often includes the (absolutely true) observation that it is God who gives the growth. As Paul wrote: "I planted, Apollos watered, but God gave the growth. So neither he who plants nor he who waters is anything, but only God who gives the growth" (1 Cor 3:6–7).[2]

We will consider this truth more in a later chapter. But it is striking that the accounts in Acts never make the connection that "God gives the growth, therefore it isn't about numbers". On the contrary, Luke records numbers again and again. He rejoices in the number of people being converted, and he celebrates the salvation of the lost. In fact, we would be closer to the heart of the New Testament if we said, "God gives the growth, therefore it *is* about numbers". Numbers proclaim the victory of the gospel—the fulfilment of Paul's desire "that the word of the Lord may speed ahead and be honoured" (2 Thess 3:1). The Bible is clear that numbers matter.

Faithfulness, fruitfulness and success (revisited)

In recent times, it has been suggested that the language of 'fruitfulness' might be an appropriate way to resolve the tension that exists between those who pursue 'success' in ministry and those who focus on 'faithfulness'. This is the argument mounted by Tim Keller in his highly influential book *Center Church*. Keller's work in this area has been so significant that it is worth quoting at length:

> It is an oversimplification to say that faithfulness is all that matters. No—something more than faithfulness is needed to assess whether we are being the ministers we should be.
>
> As I read, reflected, and taught, I came to the conclusion that a more biblical theme for ministerial evaluation than either success or faithfulness is *fruitfulness*. Jesus, of course, told his

disciples that they were to "bear much fruit" (John 15:8). Paul spoke even more specifically. He spoke of conversions as "fruit" when he desired to preach in Rome: "that I might have some fruit among you also, even as among other Gentiles" (Rom 1:13 KJV). Paul also spoke of the "fruit" of godly character that a minister can see growing in Christians under his care. This included the "fruit of the Spirit" (Gal 5:22). Good deeds, such as mercy to the poor, are called "fruit" as well (Rom 15:28). ...

The gardening metaphor shows that both success and faithfulness by themselves are insufficient criteria for evaluating ministry. Gardeners must be faithful in their work, but they must also be skillful, or the garden will fail. Yet in the end, the degree of the success of the garden (or the ministry) is determined by factors beyond the control of the gardener. ...

The church growth movement has made many lasting contributions to our practice of ministry. But its overemphasis on technique and results can put too much pressure on ministers because it underemphasizes the importance of godly character and the sovereignty of God. Those who claim that "what is required is faithfulness" are largely right, but this mind-set can take too much pressure off church leaders. It does not lead them to ask hard questions when faithful ministries bear little fruit. When fruitfulness is our criterion for evaluation, we are held accountable but not crushed by the expectation that a certain number of lives will be changed dramatically under our ministry.[3]

It is certainly true that fruitfulness is a biblical theme which includes godly character and the deeds such a character produces—most famously, but not only, with the fruit of the Spirit in Galatians 5. Yet it also includes a sense of an increase in the number of converts. As Keller rightly noted, Romans 1:13 speaks of the "fruit" (or "harvest" in the ESV) of Gentile conversion. To this we could add Colossians

1:5–6, which speaks of "the word of truth, the gospel … bearing fruit and increasing" in the whole world. In John's Gospel, Jesus speaks of the urgency of accomplishing his Father's work, the work of "gathering fruit for eternal life" (John 4:34–38)—a clear allusion to conversion growth. Later, in John 12, he predicts that his death will bear "much fruit" (John 12:24), before moving immediately to talk again about "eternal life" (12:25). These references to "fruit" set one piece of the context for his use of the same word in John 15, where he speaks of the expectation for his disciples to "bear much fruit and so prove to be my disciples", which will glorify his Father (John 15:8). No doubt, other dimensions of fruit are intended—things such as love, obedience and prayerfulness. But as others have also noted, Jesus certainly includes the idea of the fruit of evangelistic witness and conversion growth.[4]

All this is to say that I'm not sure the language of fruitfulness does much to relieve me of expectations. In fact, I feel a great deal of pressure because of the expectation that we will "bear much fruit"!

So then, because the language of 'fruitfulness' is so closely linked to a desire for the numerical and spiritual growth of God's people, it lands very much on the 'success' side of the equation (as opposed to the 'faithfulness' side). And there's nothing wrong with that. 'Success' is a neutral term; its meaning in each context depends on the outcomes being sought and the methods being used to achieve these outcomes.[5]

However, with Keller, I believe the language of 'fruitfulness' is more appropriate than the language of 'success'—not because it avoids placing any kind of pressure on a ministry, but because it better expresses a kind of 'success' that is dependent on God. The language of 'fruitfulness' carries within it a strong sense of being dependent on the nourishing sap of the vine. We will achieve no 'success' without being united to Christ and dependent on him. As he says, "apart from me you can do nothing" (John 15:5).

But whatever label we choose, we must return to the larger point: the Scriptures are clear that numbers matter.

Numbers matter because people matter

The fact that numbers matter makes sense when we consider that the Great Commission is, in a very real sense, a rescue mission. We are hoping, praying and working to see people saved from their sins and from the righteous wrath of God.

Imagine yourself turning up to a ferry-boat disaster as a member of a rescue crew, tasked with gathering survivors. As you are about to set off in your rescue vessel, the captain calls the crew together for a final pep talk: "Just remember, team: it's not about numbers". Every member of the rescue crew would be looking at each other in total, mystified confusion: "What on earth is he talking about?!"

We need to take great care with our language. Perhaps our language about numbers is simply intended to safeguard the proud heart that easily finds its worth in things apart from our life in Christ. It is ugly when leaders compare themselves to one another based on the number of people attending their church. Perhaps we are rightly mindful of the warning Jesus gave to the 72 in Luke's Gospel, when they returned from their 'successful' mission. Without denying the success of their ministry, he added: "Nevertheless, do not rejoice in this, that the spirits are subject to you, but rejoice that your names are written in heaven" (Luke 10:20). In other words, rejoice not in what you can do for God, but in what God has done for you.

The dangers are real. But again, we can end up combating one problem by creating another.

If our concern is to guard against pride and against finding our joy and identity in the wrong things, then perhaps the best solution is to identify this danger explicitly and speak about it regularly. Keep saying to each other: the growth of our ministry must never be a means of measuring our worth before God; it is not the measure of our godliness; there are all kinds of reasons why one church may be larger than another, and not all these reasons are related to conversion growth.[6] Numbers should never become a matter of personal pride. It is truly God who gives the growth. Even the most 'fruitful' or 'successful' among us should always be ready to say to the Lord: "We are unworthy servants; we have only done what was our duty" (Luke 17:10). And whatever we've done has been done through his strength that so powerfully works in us (Col 1:29).

Talking openly about the real issues is a better solution than slipping into unhelpful clichés or half-truths like "it's not about numbers". For this can give the dangerous and unbiblical impression that it's not about *people*. The gospel is all about people! Numbers matter a great deal when those numbers are souls won to Christ and kept in Christ for eternity. Saying that numbers matter is just another way of saying that people matter.

In some circles today, leaders and churches that embrace the importance of numbers are a little out of fashion. There seems to be a shift away from the centrality of making disciples to anything else. One version of this danger is for churches to focus on 'transforming the city'.[7] No doubt, a significant number of converts in any city or town will bring some level of change to that community, which might be a wonderful outcome from a large-scale movement of God to make disciples in a particular region. But where is this imperative ever spelled out for us in the New Testament? We are in dangerous territory when we displace the top priority of making disciples with the possible fruit of that activity.

Our five foundational truths 'plus one' make it impossible to avoid a clear priority. Once we understand and embrace this, it will affect everything we do in our ministries. For example, it will profoundly affect our preaching: we preach as those who speak the very words of God—words that have the power of eternal life. When we preach these words, we aren't simply engaged in the activity of explaining syntax and grammar. We aren't running a discussion group for those who are interested. We are heralds of eternal life and death! The preacher speaks "as one who speaks oracles of God" (1 Pet 4:11). We minister on the edge of a great chasm. To use the language of Jonathan Edwards, we preach to people who "hang by a slender thread, with the flames of divine wrath flashing about it"— people who risk being cast forever into eternal condemnation.[8]

My sense is that many in our churches lack this heart for the lost. Evangelism is not the burning drive of the heart. I fear that, for many of us, winning the world for Christ becomes an afterthought. Many lack a true appreciation of what is at stake, of what drives God's heart, and of the price he paid to save people from hell. In the end, many lack a true love for the world and for the lost.

A lack of interest in numbers can be a symptom of these deeper problems, which are in fact spiritual problems in our churches and our leadership. No amount of restructuring, or adding programs, or thinking about systems, or reworking our processes, will fix a spiritual problem. The key, and the solution, is inward transformation and renewal as the Spirit of God applies the word of God to our hearts. If God can use this book to stir the heart of just one reader to truly burn with a desire to see the world saved, and to be willing to embrace the pain of change so that gospel growth can happen, then I will not have written in vain.

We are involved in something eternally significant. People need Christ more than they need anything else. All God's people have a role to play in bringing Christ to the people around us, but the role of leaders is critically important. To persist in this work, and to lead others to join us in this work, we need to believe and embrace the foundational truths which undergird the centrality of Christ and which will sustain us in the midst of stress and pain. We need to embrace the truth that numbers matter because people matter. We need deep inner conviction about God's purposes—conviction that will give us focus and joy in our work.

Perhaps now is a good time to pause and pray. How is your heart before God? Do you share God's heart for people? Do you share God's heart for the lost?

Passages for further reflection

- John 4:34–38
- John 15:1–8
- Acts 11:21–24
- 2 Corinthians 4:13–15

Questions for personal or team reflection

- What is your gut reaction to the topic of 'numbers'? Why?
- Have you inappropriately pursued 'success' in ministry? Or have you perhaps been too quick to think in terms of 'just being faithful'? Which of the two is the bigger danger for you, and why?

Quote for personal or team reflection

"Those who claim that 'what is required is faithfulness' are largely right, but this mind-set can take too much pressure off church leaders. It does not lead them to ask hard questions when faithful ministries bear little fruit. When fruitfulness is our criterion for evaluation, we are held accountable but not crushed by the expectation that a certain number of lives will be changed dramatically under our ministry." (Tim Keller)

RETHINKING OUR PRIORITIES

Gospel priorities and the 'sacred-secular' divide

In 1943, American psychologist Abraham Maslow published a now-famous paper called 'A theory of human motivation'.[1] In it, Maslow outlined a five-tiered theory for describing and analyzing human behaviour, proposing that the most basic needs—typically depicted at the bottom of a pyramid—must be met before people can and will properly turn their attention to other needs. This theory, now commonly known as 'Maslow's Hierarchy of Needs', can be represented by the diagram below.

As a piece of worldly wisdom, the theory has much to commend it. In fact, it comes to seem like common sense, a description of something that we all intuitively understand and practice. Yet while the theory may seem obvious, it is still useful in helping us to step back and examine why we behave the way we do and set priorities for ourselves as we do.

But the question should be asked: have Maslow and those who follow him properly understood our most basic needs? Or, to put it another way, what does the Bible reveal to us about our true

SELF-ACTUALIZATION
morality, creativity, spontaneity, acceptance, experience, purpose, meaning, inner potential

SELF-ESTEEM
confidence, achievement, respect of others, the need to be a unique individual

LOVE AND BELONGING
friendship, family, intimacy, sense of connection

SAFETY AND SECURITY
health, employment, property, family, social abillity

PHYSIOLOGICAL NEEDS
breath, food, water, shelter, clothing, sleep

'hierarchy of needs'? What would starting with the word of God, rather than with human-centred psychology, reveal to us about our needs and about the priorities that should follow?

Before answering those questions, we need to pause and think about the very notion of priorities in the Christian life. We have touched on this issue in chapter 3, but it is so important to the topic of this whole book that it is worth taking the time to consider it in more detail here.

For many years now, a lot of Christian thought has rejected the suggestion that some things are more important than others (as I've effectively been saying). This has been particularly voiced in the realm of work, where it is seen as wrong to suggest that any form of work—including gospel work—has more value (or less value) than any other form of work. But it has run more broadly into areas such as marriage and singleness, parenting, and what we might call 'acts of charity'.[2] It is argued that any suggestion that one activity should be prioritized over another creates second-class Christians, injures mission, breeds frustration, and runs the risk of inappropriately minimizing the importance of works of love and charity.

To argue for this position, a few different strategies are typically used. For example, there has been significant pushback against any apparent division between 'secular' and 'sacred'. There really is no such divide, we are told; such a division should never have been introduced, and Christian thinking should dispense with the notion. Another approach has been to reject a hard discontinuity between this age and the age to come. We are assured that there is, in fact, a firm continuity such that all work done in this age will impact the age to come. Therefore, it is simply wrong to privilege one activity over another. In other cases, the language of 'the kingdom of God' is broadened to include any activity of love and goodness, such that building a well in an impoverished desert region to bring water to thirsty people (for example) is an expression of bringing in the kingdom of God.

In each case, there is a very valid concern that needs addressing. It is certainly wrong that some Christians might be driven to imagine themselves second-class Christians, and any theology that requires this conclusion would be wrong.

Moreover, the Bible makes clear that God has a special heart for the poor, the oppressed and the downtrodden, and that he expects his people to share this heart. Consider the first chapter of Isaiah, where the wayward and sinful people of Judah are told: "learn to do good; seek justice, correct oppression; bring justice to the fatherless, plead the widow's cause" (Isa 1:17). Or the famous words of Micah 6:8: "what does the LORD require of you but to do justice, and to love kindness, and to walk humbly with your God?" The same sentiment carries into the New Testament—for example, in the words of James 1: "Religion that is pure and undefiled before God the Father is this: to visit orphans and widows in their affliction, and to keep oneself unstained from the world" (Jas 1:27). As already mentioned in chapter 2 of this book, there is a vital link between our good deeds and a positive response to the gospel we preach (Matt 5:16; 1 Pet 2:12).

It is surely concerning, then, if a particular theological view injures mission, breeds frustration among the people of God, or undermines the importance of works of love and charity.

Yet it is possible that in a desire to cure a particular symptom, the wrong medicine has been applied. It is even possible that the outcome is worse than the original problem.

The Bible very clearly pushes us to embrace and uphold the notion of priorities. Put simply, some things are more important than other things. Some ways of investing time and resources are more important, more worthwhile, than other ways of investing time and resources. This might not require us to divide the world into 'sacred' and 'secular', but it certainly divides the world along some very fundamental lines: the temporal and the eternal; the flesh and the spirit; this world and the world to come; what is most important and what is secondary.

So, for example, Jesus teaches:

> "If your right eye causes you to sin, tear it out and throw it away. For it is better that you lose one of your members than that your whole body be thrown into hell. And if your right hand causes you to sin, cut it off and throw it away. For it is better that you lose one of your members than that your whole body go into hell." (Matt 5:29–30)

He values spiritual life over health and wholeness in the physical world. Similarly:

"Do not lay up for yourselves treasures on earth, where moth and rust destroy and where thieves break in and steal, but lay up for yourselves treasures in heaven, where neither moth nor rust destroys and where thieves do not break in and steal. For where your treasure is, there your heart will be also." (Matt 6:19–21)

"Do not fear those who kill the body but cannot kill the soul. Rather fear him who can destroy both soul and body in hell." (Matt 10:28)

"What does it profit a man to gain the whole world and forfeit his soul? For what can a man give in return for his soul?" (Mark 8:36–37)

"Do not work for the food that perishes, but for the food that endures to eternal life, which the Son of Man will give to you." (John 6:27)

Jesus looked at the law and saw some matters as "weightier" than others (Matt 23:23). That is, he saw them as having a higher priority. He told a parable in which a rich man showed that he was a "fool" for laying up treasure for himself but not being "rich towards God" (Luke 12:13–21). Looking at the entire law, Jesus identified loving the Lord as "the great and first commandment" and loving your neighbour as yourself as "a second [that] is like it" (Matt 22:38–39).

The apostles of Jesus followed a very similar pattern. From among everything Paul taught, he identified some things as being "of first importance" (1 Cor 15:3–8). Because "the present form of this world is passing away" (1 Cor 7:31), we must not be engrossed in the things of this world. He drew a sharp contrast between "the desires of the flesh" and "the desires of the Spirit" (e.g. Gal 5:16–24).

Peter urged Christians to live "lives of holiness and godliness" because "the day of God" is coming and because one day "the heavens will pass away with a roar, and the heavenly bodies will be burned up and dissolved, and the earth and the works that are done on it will be exposed" (2 Pet 3:10–12). We are to "count the patience of our Lord as salvation" (3:15), seeing our wait for "the day of God" not as a meaningless delay or as a chance to indulge in the things of this world, but as an opportunity for more people to come to a saving faith in Christ (more on this important passage below). John warned:

> Do not love the world or the things in the world. If anyone loves the world, the love of the Father is not in him. For all that is in the world—the desires of the flesh and the desires of the eyes and pride of life—is not from the Father but is from the world. And the world is passing away along with its desires, but whoever does the will of God abides forever. (1 John 2:15–17)

Jude was "very eager" to write to God's people about "our common salvation", and was only dissuaded from writing in celebration of the gospel because the situation required him to urge his readers "to contend for the faith that was once for all delivered to the saints" (Jude 3).

Time and time again, the Bible prioritizes some things over others.

A biblical hierarchy of needs

Some years ago, I was visiting South Africa and was taken through one of the townships by a local pastor. As an Australian, very unaccustomed to an absolute division between the haves and the have-nots, I was shocked by the back-breaking poverty that some were facing. I asked my guide, 'How do you cope?' In response, he talked about "disaster fatigue": when you see the tragedy so often, sooner or later you stop seeing it. He wasn't happy or pleased about this situation, but it was their reality.

But then we began to discuss a bigger issue: our failure to see an even deeper problem—a problem that is invisible to the human eye.

It's the problem of the human heart and the human soul—in a word, the problem of *sin*.

If we could see this issue with our eyes, we would find it even more horrifying than the sight of abject poverty, because we wouldn't just see physical hunger and economic deprivation. We'd see the sin-stained hearts of prideful rebellion that exist in utter opposition to a loving God. As far as the Bible is concerned, the problem of sin—the problem of the human heart—is a far more serious problem than even the most horrifying physical hunger a society might face. Our problem is that, because of our sin, the wrath of God—the just judgement of God—is being revealed and will be revealed in all its fullness (Rom 1:18; Eph 5:6; Col 3:6; Rev 19:15). To his great credit, my South African friend understood and believed this truth, even though the awfulness of physical poverty confronted him every day.

As soon as we confess this 'invisible' reality, we have prioritized one issue over another. Salvation from sin and from the righteous wrath of God is the greatest human need. This is why the New Testament constantly emphasizes the spiritual nature of Jesus' mission:

> "Those who are well have no need of a physician, but those who are sick. I came not to call the righteous, but sinners." (Mark 2:17)

> "The Son of Man came not to be served but to serve, and to give his life as a ransom for many." (Mark 10:45)

> "I must preach the good news of the kingdom of God to the other towns as well; for I was sent for this purpose." (Luke 4:43)

> "For God so loved the world, that he gave his only Son, that whoever believes in him should not perish but have eternal life." (John 3:16)

"Everyone who drinks of this water will be thirsty again, but whoever drinks of the water that I will give him will never be thirsty again. The water that I will give him will become in him a spring of water welling up to eternal life." (John 4:13–14)

"My kingdom is not of this world. ... For this purpose I was born and for this purpose I have come into the world—to bear witness to the truth." (John 18:36–37)

When the fullness of time had come, God sent forth his Son, born of woman, born under the law, to redeem those who were under the law, so that we might receive adoption as sons. (Gal 4:4–5)

The saying is trustworthy and deserving of full acceptance, that Christ Jesus came into the world to save sinners ... (1 Tim 1:15)

Our great God and Saviour Jesus Christ ... gave himself for us to redeem us from all lawlessness and to purify for himself a people for his own possession who are zealous for good works. (Titus 2:13–14)

Since therefore the children share in flesh and blood, he himself likewise partook of the same things, that through death he might destroy the one who has the power of death, that is, the devil, and deliver all those who through fear of death were subject to lifelong slavery. (Heb 2:14–15)

He has appeared once for all at the end of the ages to put away sin by the sacrifice of himself. (Heb 9:26)

The reason the Son of God appeared was to destroy the works of the devil. (1 John 3:8)

The *spiritual* state of the human soul is of far greater concern than any other concern, and the *eternal* fate of those who die apart from Christ is far more important than any difficulty faced in this world.

As Jesus said, "do not fear those who kill the body but cannot kill the soul. Rather fear him who can destroy both soul and body in hell" (Matt 10:28). It is through Christ alone that we can be saved from "the wrath to come" (1 Thess 1:10; see also Rom 5:9).

The greatest human needs are not, in fact, our physiological needs, important as they are. The greatest human need is the forgiveness of sins, which happens as we come to the Lord Jesus in repentance and faith and so experience peace with God now (Rom 5:1) and salvation from the wrath to come. This will never be a person's *only* need, but it is *every* person's greatest need. This is the biblical hierarchy of needs that should change our thinking and reorder our priorities.

None of what I have said fits with the "wisdom of this age" (1 Cor 2:6); it requires a spiritual mind to understand and comprehend the seriousness of the spiritual need (see 1 Cor 2:14–16). And we don't arrive at a spiritual mind easily. We need the eyes of faith informed by the word of God; we need the Spirit of God to be at work to transform our thinking and bring us to an understanding of "the depths of God" (1 Cor 2:10).

The centrality of love and the importance of context

At this point, we find ourselves confronted by the need to embrace complexity. We can rightly affirm that salvation from sin is every person's greatest need—and that gospel proclamation is therefore our highest ministry priority—while also affirming that there are many other vital expressions of Christian love.

In other words, it is wrong to read the priority of the spiritual as exclusive of other needs such that we as individuals or our churches and ministries focus *only* on the spiritual and never pay any attention to the immediate, visible, physical needs of those around us. Those needs are still real, and they are still very important.

The summary used by American pastor John Piper is helpful here:

"Christians care about all suffering, especially eternal suffering".[3] The word "especially" draws us back to setting priorities that focus on the gospel as "the power of God for salvation to everyone who believes" (Rom 1:16) while also safeguarding us against becoming indifferent to other kinds of suffering. It is good and godly to be generous and to meet the physical, temporal needs of those around us, especially those who are brothers and sisters in Christ (e.g. Matt 25:36; 2 Cor 8:13–15; Gal 6:10; Jas 1:27, 2:15–16). We are close to the heart of our heavenly Father when we live this way, while also giving priority to preaching the gospel that can save people from eternal suffering.

In practice, this means that our competing priorities will exist in a complex and ever-evolving relationship.

To return to Maslow's diagram as an illustration, we would observe that the narrower priorities (self-esteem and self-actualization) should not be pursued at the expense of the core priorities (food, shelter, and the like). You don't stop caring about foundational needs as you pursue others; we all need to secure food, water, shelter and a place to sleep every day. These things may require very little thought or effort for wealthy Westerners, but they remain our basic needs.

At the same time, those who struggle to meet their basic needs will still care about other priorities. The homeless man begging for food will see his aching hunger as "of first importance", while still feeling deeply hurt and alienated by the people who walk past him, pretending he doesn't exist. The elderly woman lying on her death bed and struggling to draw breath will long to be surrounded by her family, and will remember with joy the love she has shown to others as part of a life well lived.

Applied to biblical thought, something has gone wrong if gospel proclamation is not our core priority, expressed in our own lives and in the life of our church in various ways. But equally, something has gone wrong if this priority is not mingled together with seeking to care for others and alleviate suffering in all kinds of other ways.

Perhaps it is best to speak of the priority of *love of God* and *love of neighbour* as the fundamental shape of life, out of which grows these more focused acts of love and service. In fact, the pursuit of disciple making ought never occur in a context where a person or church has given up on the broader concern to simply love their neighbour, whatever their presenting needs. Love is the heartbeat of the Christian life.

It's rare that life forces us to make a stark, either/or choice between gospel proclamation and other acts of service. Moreover, we make these decisions as part of a community. An individual's priority might be the saving of souls, yet they might spend the majority of their own time serving the immediate physical and emotional needs of their community and of the people around them. But they do so as part of a Christian community that, as a whole, prioritizes eternal salvation and growth in Christian maturity. And the individual will rightly sense a significant failure if he or she is playing no part in meeting those eternal, spiritual needs.

There is one final observation to draw from our use of Maslow's model: the importance of *context*.

Our context shapes our priorities. Think, for example, of wartime, where individuals or even an entire nation might face an immediate threat to life and safety. In this situation, all other priorities will take a back seat until these basic needs are secured. Once the immediate threat has passed and life returns to a more normal context, priorities will change.

What is the context in which we live our lives? If we answer this question biblically—as we must—we will find that *we are living in the last days*. And this fact introduces a unique set of circumstances that shifts how we think and how we live.

Two thousand years ago, Jesus came. He died for sins, was raised to life, and ascended to God's right hand. In these events, the kingdom of God was established. But instead of these events bringing an end to this creation as we know it—as the Old Testament seemed to anticipate, and as we might have logically expected—the present age has continued. The final judgement, the final destruction of Satan, and the new creation have all been delayed. The kingdom of God has been established, but it has not yet been consummated.[4]

Why the delay? Why has God done such a thing? Why has he stretched apart two things—the established kingdom and the consummated kingdom—that should properly be joined together?

The answer is found in 2 Peter 3: so there would be time for people to come to salvation.

> Scoffers will come in the last days with scoffing, following their own sinful desires. They will say, "Where is the promise of his coming? For ever since the fathers fell asleep, all things are continuing as they were from the beginning of creation." ... But do not overlook this one fact, beloved, that with the Lord one day is as a thousand years, and a thousand years as one day. The Lord is not slow to fulfill his promise as some count slowness, but is patient toward you, not wishing that any should perish, but that all should reach repentance. (2 Pet 3:3–4, 8–9)

The only reason given in Scripture for the gap between the kingdom of God being established and the kingdom being consummated is the salvation of the lost. We are given another day, another week, another year of life not to have more time to enjoy this fallen world—though it is certainly not wrong to enjoy it, and God in his kindness gives us all kinds of things to enjoy as we wait for the kingdom to be consummated. The fundamental reason we are given more time is so that more people may be saved. God has declared this as a 'time of amnesty'—a time when sinners can come forward, without fear of prosecution for their wrongdoing, and receive forgiveness from God through Christ. But it won't last forever. One day soon, Christ will return, bringing these 'last days' to an end and consummating the kingdom. The period of amnesty will end.

This is our context. It's the framework through which we must evaluate all possible priorities.

Given that this time is granted to us for the salvation of sinners, how should this change our priorities?

We should certainly stand ready to meet all the needs that people face in this "present evil age" (Gal 1:4). Love demands such a way of life. The heartbeat of any person saved by the God of love should be to prioritize love of God and love of neighbour.

But while we maintain our general concern, our context drives us to prioritize one particular act of love as we live in these last days: the act of seeking and saving the lost, of making disciples of all nations. "Now is the favourable time, now is the day of salvation" (2 Cor 6:2), and certain gospel priorities should follow. The limitless love of God should shape the way we respond to everything that happens in these last days. And the context of why these last days are happening should bring sharp focus to the priorities we set.

The danger of 'this-worldliness'

It is possible that, in our desire to avoid seeming to privilege one role over another, or one person over another, we've undermined what is most important. In doing so, we may be succumbing to a problem that the Bible intends to free us from: the problem of 'this-worldliness'.

'This-worldliness' is rife in our community and in our churches. Love of this world is constant and insidious. Our values, and the proposed solutions to our problems, are so readily absorbed through a 'this-worldly' lens. This has become even more problematic in the age of social media: people today—especially young people, for whom it is so easy to live life in a social-media bubble—are swamped with more this-worldly thinking than ever before. In our sinful nature, we are determined to make more of the here-and-now than of the life to come. We so easily slip into working for food that perishes, not for food that endures to eternal life. But this is exactly what Jesus critiqued.

Would we ever think to write, "Do not love the world or the things in the world" (1 John 2:15)? For John, "the world" is certainly not a reference to every single thing in the world; it is more of a reference to creation (especially people) rebelling against its Creator.[5] As Paul writes, "everything created by God is good, and nothing is to be rejected if it is received with thanksgiving, for it is made holy by the word of God and prayer" (1 Tim 4:4). But it is significant that John can even use such language. He begins in a place that is often very different from the place where we begin. We begin with an obsession with the world, and we would never want to give the impression that our engagement with the world requires great caution; John begins with an obsession with the age to come, and so can much more readily give the warning, "Do not love the world".

Remember that Paul tells us, "the present form of this world is passing away" (1 Cor 7:31). On one occasion I was speaking about this reality, and illustrated it by talking about a building that had been condemned and was scheduled to be destroyed. I suggested that this therefore doesn't seem like a great time to renovate the building. After I spoke, a Christian teacher came to speak to me and, with great pain, complained: "You're saying that my teaching career is of no value!" I'm pleased to have these types of conversations, because it means hard questions are being asked and a nerve has been struck—and that nerve *may* be that my Christian brother or sister is currently placing too high a value on their career. It might be possible—and was in this case—that teaching *in and of itself* is perceived to be intrinsically valuable, that educating people is always honouring to God and an outcome worthy of achieving.

But a moment's thought tells us this cannot be the case. Deeper, more searching questions are needed. What content and what ideas are being taught and learned? How can education always be good in and of itself when Jesus tells us that it is no good to gain the whole world and yet lose your soul, and when Jesus tells us not to work for food that perishes? It is possible for education to leave us with highly educated people going to hell, or even for the ideas taught to be contrary to God's word and to lead people to harden their hearts against God even more. Teaching can ultimately be worthless for the person who hasn't properly grasped the imperatives of the gospel.

Yet even this is far from the whole story. Once these realities have been acknowledged and owned, what place should we give to such activities? Do they have any value? Yes, of course! Education can be of enormous value. Christians were at the forefront of introducing and developing modern education in the West.[6] But the value of our activities—whatever the 'career' or field of work, and whatever the undertaking—needs careful expression and can only be properly understood with much more nuance.

It isn't sufficient, for example, to simply assert that art and culture have value because of a continuity between this age and the age to come. For such an assertion is so easily used by people who are 'this worldly' as a validation for their investment in the things of an age that will be "burned up and dissolved" (2 Pet 3:10). It certainly fails to radicalize people in the way that Jesus did.

But how do we keep a proper concern for the poor and the oppressed? How do we keep a heart that longs for justice in this world and aches over suffering in this world, without losing perspective on what matters most? How do we give proper place and proper value to teaching, and to the development of art and culture, and to the countless other activities in which we may invest our time?

There is simply no easy answer. There is no silver bullet that will cover every scenario. The key is that, once again, we must embrace complexity. We must learn to operate with a deeper structure of thought. And that is what the Bible offers us.

The New Testament might prioritize one thing over another, but it doesn't therefore despise the lower priority. See, for example, the way Jesus prioritizes one thing without disparaging the other:

> Woe to you, scribes and Pharisees, hypocrites! For you tithe mint and dill and cumin, and have neglected the weightier matters of the law: justice and mercy and faithfulness. These you ought to have done, without neglecting the others. You blind guides, straining out a gnat and swallowing a camel! (Matt 23:23–24)

Paul prioritizes singleness without disparaging marriage (1 Corinthians 7). The apostles prioritized devotion to prayer and the ministry of the word while ensuring that needy people were not being neglected in the daily distribution of food (Acts 6:1–6). "The work of the Lord" (1 Cor 15:58), gospel preaching, is certainly prioritized—which is unsurprising, given that the gospel is "of first importance" (1 Cor 15:3)—but without disparaging every other kind of work. In fact, Paul insists that believers engage in hard work and earn their living as an expression of love towards others:

> If anyone is not willing to work, let him not eat. For we hear that some among you walk in idleness, not busy at work, but busybodies. Now such persons we command and encourage in the Lord Jesus Christ to do their work quietly and to earn their own living. (2 Thess 3:10–12)

Yet gospel work remained at the centre of his concern, just as it is at the centre of God's concern for the world. It is as though God has a 'bullseye' to his work and 'outer rings' to his work: gospel work is the bullseye; his providential care for the world are the outer rings. Both are necessary, which means that neither can be neglected—but only one is primary. Only one can truly be said to be "not in vain" (1 Cor 15:58).

This means that prioritizing gospel work does not (or at least *must* not!) diminish the importance of works of charity. It is simply to note the vitally important truth that one is the root and the other is the fruit. We do not properly protect works of charity from being forgotten or disparaged by Christians by denying the primacy of gospel preaching. In fact, doing so strips the Bible of much of its language and ends up separating the fruit from the root, so that in the end the fruit will wither and die. The proper way to protect the importance of Christian charity is by recognizing that it is the necessary fruit of love that flows from a regenerate life. It is to the Father's glory that we produce much fruit. And gospel fruit is a much larger category than mission, as noted in chapter 4 when considering Jesus' meaning of 'fruit' in John 15.[7]

A warning to leaders

Let me conclude with a word of warning to pastors and ministry leaders: we need to be careful in the way we speak about these important truths among the people of God. We have the privilege of giving ourselves full-time (or in some cases part-time) to gospel work, of earning our living from the gospel and being freed up from normal work so that we can devote our time to prayer and preaching the word. It's possible for preachers to teach the truth about gospel priorities in an arrogant way, as though we are more favoured by God, or more important to God, or above reproach and untouchable because we are so valuable to God. We must take care not to speak in such a way that we elevate ourselves above those in our churches or ministries. The purpose of considering the Bible's teaching on priorities isn't so we can make ourselves as Christian leaders feel superior or others feel inferior, nor is it so we can denigrate the many good things in which God's people might invest themselves. It is so that we might be called back to the essence of our task, ask ourselves hard questions, and remind our people of what is "of first importance".

But neither should we fall into the opposite trap—the trap of saying that sharing the good news of Jesus is no more valuable than building a nice chair or cleaning the bathroom or balancing a spreadsheet. The gospel is "the power of God for salvation to everyone who believes" (Rom 1:16); a nice chair is for keeping you comfortable while you sit down to do your work or eat your dinner. Both things matter. But when we ask what is *more* important, what *most* aligns with what God is doing in the world, the two things can't compare. Preaching the gospel is more important than building a chair. Teaching the Bible is more important than cleaning the bathroom. Is the *person* who preaches the gospel more important than the person who builds the chair? No! Is the person who teaches the Bible more important than the person who cleans the bathroom? No! But is one activity of greater and more lasting value than the other? Yes! Should one activity be prioritized (without the other being totally neglected)? Yes!

And should the carpenter, the busy parent and the accountant be urged to give some of their time to preaching the word of God to others, since it is this word that has changed their lives and now has the power to change the lives of others? Absolutely! And should they still build, clean, and balance the books to the glory of God? Of course!

Passages for further reflection

- Mark 8:36–37
- John 6:27
- 1 Corinthians 2:6–16
- 1 John 2:15–17

GROWTH AND CHANGE

Questions for personal or team reflection

- Do you believe that the forgiveness of sins is every person's greatest need? How well do your priorities, or those of your church/ministry, align with your stated belief?
- "God so loved the world ..."; "Do not love the world ...". Have you properly understood both statements? Have you embraced this tension? Do both ideas have their proper place in your life and ministry?

Quote for personal or team reflection

"Christians care about all suffering, especially eternal suffering." (John Piper)

6

TYING TOGETHER THE THREADS (SO FAR)

The danger of compromise

I've argued that there are two dimensions that need to be held together at the same time: an awareness of the significant dangers of a passion for growth, and yet the absolute importance—indeed, the biblical necessity—of having that passion.

At the most basic level, this means there is no simple solution that will guard us against the dangers of compromise.

Some have attempted to avoid the danger of theological compromise by retreating into a ministry model dominated by standing for the truth, whatever the outcome. Perhaps they have witnessed the shipwreck that happens when leaders are so consumed by a passion for growth that those leaders and their churches wandered onto the path of compromise. In response, they conclude that the only safe position is to focus entirely on ensuring that the church is the pillar of truth. They and their churches will be concerned only with helping Christians mature and grow and with keeping true to "the faith that was once for all delivered to the saints" (Jude 3). If a few people are saved along the way, that's good—but we exist for Christians, and we will never compromise on anything.

This will certainly avoid any compromise fuelled by a desire to grow the church numerically. But it is far from the 'safe' position. For it is a betrayal of the heart of God—a heart that is so desirous of the salvation of men and women that he gave his only Son to win them. In avoiding one danger, many have fled down another path that ensures a church and its ministries are shut off from sharing the heart of God for the lost. Indeed, this position is its own form of theological compromise, so far has it moved from the heart of God revealed in the gospel. If such churches and leaders return again to this driving theme in the Scriptures, they will be pushed back towards the path that requires changing the way we do things—and even changing the things we do—to enable more people to hear and respond to the gospel.

And so, we are pushed down the path that has led many to compromise ...

My point is that there is nowhere safe; there is the danger of compromise in both directions. On the one hand, we flee from 'insider' Christianity, driven by the heart of God to focus outwardly. But as we do so, we run the risk of compromising the gospel. On the other hand, we flee from the compromise of the 'outsider' church to the apparent safety of 'just being faithful'. But as we do so, we run the risk of losing the heart of God for the lost.

One proposed solution is in some version of the slogan 'our methods might change, but our message never changes'. But there is no real safety to be found here. For there is no simple divide between our message and our methods. They are deeply intertwined.

This is one of the main points that the apostle Paul makes in 2 Corinthians. The ways that we minister, the methods we use, say a great deal about the way we understand and conceive of the gospel message itself. In other words, the cross isn't simply the message that saves; it also shapes the *way* we share that message. The cross is the what *and* the how of ministry. Following Paul's pattern, we renounce "disgraceful, underhanded ways" and "refuse to practice cunning or to tamper with God's word" (2 Cor 4:1–2). With Paul, we proclaim not ourselves "but Jesus Christ as Lord, with ourselves as your servants for Jesus' sake" (4:5). "We are not waging war according to the flesh"—yet our weapons have "divine power to destroy strongholds", and we are actively working to "destroy arguments and every lofty opinion raised against the knowledge of God, and take every thought captive to obey Christ" (10:3–5). We boast gladly of the things that show our weakness, for it is in our weakness that Christ's power rests on us and God's power is made perfect (11:30, 12:8–9).

It is almost as philosopher and media theorist Marshall McLuhan said (in a different context) in the 20th century: "the medium is the message". As one example, we live in a time where many churches have shifted away from preaching, moving instead to discussion groups as the primary vehicle for communicating the gospel to a community that has become suspicious of authoritarian proclamations. But such a shift shapes the very message we communicate: it moves us away from an authoritative declaration from God (through human "ambassadors"; see 2 Cor 5:20) that calls for joyful, humble submission and obedience. Instead, it turns our message into one of 'self-discovery', one that is open for debate.

Taking on the challenge

How, then, do we navigate our way through these competing dangers? The balance exists in the constant conversation between these two truths—the *danger* and the *necessity* of a passion for growth. Each truth operates as a word to the other side, depending on the pastoral context and setting.[1]

The fact is, some of us need one side, and some need the other. I'll address the two sides by referring to the dangers that (generally, not universally) threaten leaders at various stages of their ministry.

A word for younger leaders

Typically, younger leaders are more at risk of succumbing to the *dangers* related to a passion for growth.

The gospel is a challenge. It won't make leaders and churches popular. The church is indeed to be "a pillar and buttress of truth" (1 Tim 3:15). It must be a place where discernment is exercised, discipline enacted, and challenges issued that will cut people to the heart. It is a place where pastors can expect to be despised by the wider community and to face serious suffering. Younger leaders, in their zeal to see the gospel grow and bear fruit—a zeal that, in itself, is entirely right—can often lose sight of these truths.

It is necessary to drink deeply of the image of Jesus as the 'suffering servant', and of Paul, the one who imitated Christ, as a minister of the gospel who died daily and was widely despised. It is important to spend serious time reflecting on his last letter, 2 Timothy, where he calls on Timothy to "share in suffering for the gospel" (2 Tim 1:8) and to "share in suffering as a good soldier of Christ Jesus" (2:3)—by which he means that Timothy should share in *his* (Paul's) suffering. He testifies to his determination to "endure everything for the sake of the elect, that they also may obtain the salvation that is in Christ Jesus with eternal glory" (2:10). The whole letter drips with Paul's hardships. Or we could turn again to 2 Corinthians, where Paul compares himself to the so-called 'super-apostles' by describing the ways that he has been pummelled, literally and figuratively, in his ministry:

> Are they servants of Christ? I am a better one—I am talking like a madman—with far greater labours, far more imprisonments, with countless beatings, and often near death. Five times I received at the hands of the Jews the forty lashes less one. Three times I was beaten with rods. Once I was stoned. Three times I was shipwrecked; a night and a day I was adrift at sea; on frequent journeys, in danger from rivers, danger from robbers, danger from my own people, danger from Gen-

tiles, danger in the city, danger in the wilderness, danger at sea, danger from false brothers; in toil and hardship, through many a sleepless night, in hunger and thirst, often without food, in cold and exposure. And, apart from other things, there is the daily pressure on me of my anxiety for all the churches. (2 Cor 11:23–28)

We need to pray that God would enable us to resist, throughout our entire lives and ministries, the seductive call of the world to receive its respect or be its friend. The world, the city, the community will constantly tell you—actively and passively—that acceptance comes at a price: you cannot say this, and you must not do that.

What is necessary is *leadership character*—the kind that only comes through deep theological formation under leaders who 'get' these things, who have walked the path, and who can model and disciple younger leaders towards them. We need leaders who have 'suffering-servant values' so deeply embedded in mind and heart that they are alert to any small step off the right path and can see where such a step might take us. This pushes us very firmly towards top-quality theological education. But it also pushes us very strongly towards careful and thorough ministry training under men and women who have worked through the heat of the day and lived the life of sacrifice—men and women who know what it is to be unpopular, and yet continue to stand graciously but firmly for the truth of Jesus Christ. Such training also needs to take place under older men and women who have seen the outcome of various failed attempts to win the world, who have worked through these dangers in their own hearts and ministries, and who have witnessed how the dangers can ensnare other leaders.

But older, more established leaders are not immune to danger. In fact, they often face a different set of challenges: they can lose sight of the *necessity* of a passion for growth.

A word for older leaders

As we age, it is possible to get stuck. Our ministry has been hard, we're worn down, and we lose our zeal. We have battled for so long under the weight of small things that our vision has shrunk to become no larger than the day-to-day needs of the church. Our people—their needs, their problems, their requests—keep us busy, along with the routine of weekly preaching and the dreaded admin. "Think bigger? How? I can't cope with my current load! Besides, we're not doing too badly." We don't expect much. We keep things rolling along while the church around us dies or drifts into comfortable maintenance mode. We know God can do great things; it's just that we're pretty sure he won't do them in our context or time.

We tell ourselves stories and construct narratives to offer ourselves some comfort. The soil here is hard (perhaps it is). It isn't like the soil in that area where the church is growing (perhaps it isn't). If a church is large, it must be because it has compromised (perhaps it has). And so, to survive emotionally, we settle for less.

But leaders who settle into these ruts are confronted with the unsettling truth: the apostolic ministry was shaped by a burning ambition for the truth of the saving work of Christ to be not just known by the world, but *embraced* by the world. The apostles were prepared to pay whatever price was necessary to see that same world saved by the death and resurrection of Jesus. In this, they were following the example of Christ.

When we lead churches, we are not running book clubs. The church is the lifeboat in an ocean full of millions of drowning people—people "having no hope and without God in the world" (Eph 2:12). How often do we allow those who are already in the lifeboat to shape and limit our vision as we float past those who are drowning?[2]

It is urgent that we move beyond the 'just be faithful' line of thinking. To be like Christ, to be like the apostles, to be properly connected with the heart of God and the mood of God, we must actively work to see people won to Christ and grown to maturity in Christ. The more we return to this mood, the more we will be ready to pay the price necessary to get our churches moving forward—to change things that are broken in our ministries, and in ourselves. And leaders have a special responsibility to create a mood within the church where there is deep dissatisfaction with just going through the motions.

Satisfactory underperformance isn't possible if our vision is as large as God's: a vision where all things in heaven and on earth are united under the Lord Jesus Christ (Eph 1:10). It is a vision where "at the name of Jesus every knee should bow, in heaven and on earth and under the earth, and every tongue confess that Jesus Christ is Lord, to the glory of God the Father" (Phil 2:10–11). It is a vision in which the saved people of God—countless people "from every tribe and language and people and nation"—are gathered around the throne of "the Lamb who was slain" to sing his praises (Rev 5:9, 12). Satisfactory underperformance can't be an option when the realities of heaven and hell are fully known and deeply believed.

A passion for growth is very dangerous. But when you understand the nature of the gospel, the shape of the early church, the mood and tone of the apostles themselves, and the vision of God for his world, it isn't possible to live without a passion to see churches and gospel ministries grow. We must always live with the danger passion brings.

And so, how do we navigate these dangers? It is critical that we are more and more deeply immersed in the Bible and in thoughtful theological reflection within honest, Christ-centred community. Only these things can sustain us amid the pressures to compromise.

Passages for further reflection

- 2 Corinthians 10:3–5
- 2 Corinthians 12:7–10
- Philippians 2:9–11
- 2 Timothy 1:8, 2:3, 2:10

Questions for personal or team reflection

- Are you susceptible to the dangers that typically confront younger leaders? Are you susceptible to the dangers that typically confront older leaders?
- What are you doing to resist these various dangers and to keep moving forward in gospel ministry?

7

BEARING THE WEIGHT OF RESPONSIBILITY

The challenge of getting unstuck

The first part of this book might be described as aiming to 'build heat' around the topics of growth and change: acknowledging that change is painful, yet pushing us to reach the point where the pain of not changing is greater than the pain of changing. We need to generate the kind of energy that desires and welcomes change, because a longing to see growth in our churches and ministries is both necessary and biblical (while also being dangerous). A friend of mine refers to this as the push to reach 'escape velocity'.

We so easily fall into ruts in Christian ministry. As a four-wheel-driver on the beach knows, we are surrounded by ruts waiting to suck us in. And once you're in, it's very hard to get out. In fact, I want to suggest that bringing about change in the church is more difficult than in any other area.

Another friend works as a consultant among business leaders, while also engaging with church leaders from time to time. He has told me that when a business leader is presented with a list of necessary or helpful changes, at the six-month review he usually finds that the changes have been implemented. But when he has gone through the same process with church leaders, this is not the case. Necessary changes are identified and agreed to, but nothing happens.

There is something very significant within this observation. Why are business leaders generally better than church leaders at making necessary changes?

One major reason relates to different contexts. Business leaders manage employees, while church and ministry leaders operate in a volunteer environment. Managing volunteers and leading them through change is far more challenging than managing employees (most business leaders don't believes this, but it's true!).

What's more, churches are often relatively under-resourced compared to secular businesses, and a change process requires lots of resources. On top of this, church leaders are required to function across multiple spheres. While they run an organization of sorts, their core business is prayer and proclamation of the word of God. They work hard every week to produce what they hope will be a life-changing message, while dealing with pastoral issues that can be incredibly draining. This brings significant stress and forces leaders to expend large amounts of emotional capital. Leading change requires significant emotional, relational and creative energy, but most church leaders have very little in the tank (the rate of burnout among pastors is disproportionately high). Very few ministers jump out of bed on a Monday morning fired up to change anything in church life, let alone to change the world. There just isn't much left to give.

Having walked this path for many years, I'm very sympathetic. Ministry life brings unique challenges, and leaders deserve our compassion and understanding.

But we must change. And we must lead others to change.

So, how can it happen?

The biggest driver for change is the *desire* to change—generating the 'heat', hitting 'escape velocity', reaching the point where changing is painful but not changing is even more painful. That's where the deep truths that we've considered so far can transform our thinking and fuel our ministries.

But as important and foundational as this is, there's more. We need to consider a provocative and challenging aspect of this whole topic: the fact that we are responsible and even accountable for the fruit of our work (or perhaps for the lack thereof).

We'll think about this using the categories of 'inputs' and 'outputs'.

Inputs and outputs

In speaking of 'inputs' and 'outputs', I am very aware that these words are inadequate to describe and define the full picture of Christian ministry: it can easily sound like we're discussing the workings of a machine rather than the life of a real human being or an organic community. Moreover, I'm aware that countless Christian leaders have been godly, faithful, and thoroughly committed to gospel growth, all without using the language of 'inputs' and 'outputs'. This must not become a *shibboleth* to test someone's suitability for ministry. But just as Paul can sometimes compare Christian ministry with a field or a building, so we might find it useful to bear with this language for the limited purposes of this discussion.

In any activity, there are inputs (the things we do) and outputs (the consequences of our inputs). A teacher teaches (input), and the class learns (output); the police patrol, write tickets and make arrests (input), and law and order prevails (output).

Christian ministry, of course, is not identical to these parts of life, being a fundamentally spiritual activity. But it has enough similarities that we can make this part of our analysis. More importantly, the Bible teaches us to think this way.

We engage in various activities such as preaching, prayer, visiting the sick, rebuking and encouraging people, studying the Bible, gathering God's people together so that they can speak the truth of God's word to one another and love one another, and so on. These might all be described as inputs.[1] What is the output from all this work? Or, perhaps better, what *fruit* do we want to see from our *faithful* input? From everything covered so far, the answer ought to be clear: we want to see many mature disciples of Jesus, to the glory of God. We want to see people won to Christ and deepened in their walk with Christ. To return to Paul's expression in Colossians 1: "Him [Jesus] we proclaim, warning everyone and teaching everyone with all wisdom [our input], that we may present everyone mature in Christ [the great output of all our efforts]" (Col 1:28). Or, to use the Great Commission of Matthew 28, the desired output is that we see mature disciples of Jesus formed. Whether or not we like the language of 'inputs' and 'outputs', the point is the same.

But the crucial question then arrives: what is the relationship between our inputs and the spiritual output? What part do we play in presenting everyone "mature in Christ" and in "[making] disciples of all nations" (Matt 28:19)?

Our answer will have an enormous effect on the shape of our ministry. The leader who believes he or she is responsible for the outputs (the 'fruit') of the ministry, not just the inputs, will think about and likely even organize their ministry very differently from the leader who believes he or she is responsible *only* for the inputs.

This is, in part, why a secular business leader is prepared to go through the pain of change: she is very conscious of the connection between her 'inputs' and the success of the business; she is well aware that there is a direct line between the way she does her work and the company's outcomes. And so, if she fails to change, she will be seen as *the* reason for the failure of the business to produce good outcomes. That's a powerful driver. The Christian leader, meanwhile, may sever the direct link between input and output for theological reasons, and thus be slower or more reluctant to bring change.

But which attitude is appropriate for the Christian leader? Should he or she see the same kind of direct input-output connection that the secular business leader sees?

Many assume that the answer is no. It is often believed that the only proper Christian way is to work hard, tick enough boxes to 'be faithful', and leave the results to God. If there is fruit, it is his work. If not, it is still his work. A natural corollary of this thinking is that we have no responsibility for outcomes. A ministry shaped by this thinking has little drive to change much (so long as it is being faithful, broadly speaking), because what matters is the ministry intent, the sincerity of work, the godliness of the ministry leaders—in short, the faithfulness of the inputs. But the specific kind of work, how the work is done, and the ministry structures employed? These are all very secondary. God gives the growth. So, we just aim to be faithful.

But is this biblical?

As you may have worked out, the answer is yes and no.

The New Testament says much that focuses our attention on inputs. We might think of Paul's instruction to Timothy:

> I charge you in the presence of God and of Christ Jesus, who is to judge the living and the dead, and by his appearing and his kingdom: preach the word; be ready in season and out of season; reprove, rebuke, and exhort, with complete patience and teaching. ... As for you, always be sober-minded, endure suffering, do the work of an evangelist, fulfill your ministry. (2 Tim 4:1–2, 5)

Or we might consider Peter's instruction to leaders:

> So I exhort the elders among you, as a fellow elder and a witness of the sufferings of Christ, as well as a partaker in the glory that is going to be revealed: shepherd the flock of God that is among you, exercising oversight, not under compulsion, but willingly, as God would have you; not for shameful gain, but eagerly; not domineering over those in your charge, but being examples to the flock. (1 Pet 5:1–3)

"Pray without ceasing" (1 Thess 5:17). Proclaim the gospel. Suffer well. Be a godly example to others. Be true. Be faithful.

But is this all the New Testament says? Is there a direct connection between inputs and outputs?

Polar opposites?

We tend to function with what might be called a two-pole conception of this question—a black-and-white way of thinking.

At one pole is the thought that *we* are responsible for outcomes and the fruit of Christian ministry is, in effect, entirely up to us. If we work in a certain way and follow a certain pattern, we will see a definite and defined set of fruit. To use a theological label, this might be characterized as an *Arminian* way of thinking: human beings are in control of spiritual outcomes.

This way of thinking fits with what we might call a 'revivalist' mindset: if we can just understand and clarify the inputs that have been present in every revival throughout history, and then duplicate those inputs, we will see the output of revival in our time. Modern 'movement theology' takes the same approach. What inputs have facilitated fruitful gospel movements? Identify them and reproduce them—and, hey presto, a 'movement' will be born.

The problem is that neither the Bible nor Christian history fit with this way of thinking. Historically, revival doesn't fit neatly into any particular pattern. 'Revivalists' suffer from confirmation bias in that they find what they set out to find. But revivals aren't reducible to a formula. God won't allow it. Sometimes they were preceded by prayer, but sometimes they produced prayer. Sometimes they were preceded by unity among God's people, but sometimes they generated that unity—and sometimes a broad unity never really emerged. I dare say that the Lord acts differently in various times and places to remind us that he is in charge, and we are not.

More importantly, the Bible rejects this way of thinking. Scripture insists that, no matter who plants or waters, God alone gives the growth (1 Cor 3:6). Scripture insists that unless the Lord builds the house or watches over the city, the builder and the watchman labour in vain (Ps 127:1). Spiritual growth is, ultimately, God's spiritual work. His Spirit moves as he wills to bring people to new birth. We can't control the Spirit of God. He rules; we are at his mercy. He blows where he wishes (John 3:8).[2] The Holy Spirit is the real evangelist in the book of Acts, and only those "appointed to eternal life" believe and are saved (13:48).

And so, having noted all of the above and rejected the Arminian claim that human beings are in final control of spiritual outcomes, it is natural to rush to the polar opposite position: human beings have *no* responsibility for outputs, God *alone* is responsible for the growth of the gospel, there is *no* direct connection between our inputs and the outputs that follow, and therefore we are in *no* way responsible for the growth or decline of the church.

Centuries ago, Aristotle noted the human tendency to create simple systems of polar opposites. He used the simple example of cowardice and courage. Many assume that the way to reject cowardice is to be as far from it as possible. But as Aristotle noted, the extreme opposite of cowardice isn't courage; it's foolhardiness. Courage sits between these two polar opposites as the 'golden mean'.

We don't arrive at the truth by understanding an error and then adopting the opposite of that error. This will usually succeed only in producing a false antithesis.[3] Sometimes, maybe often, the truth sits between two extremes. That is certainly the case with biblical truth—including the truth of responsibility for outputs. The truth in this area, as in so many areas, is found in a complex interplay between two apparently contradictory ideas: God's sovereignty, and genuine human agency.

We see Jesus himself walking this line in Matthew 11, a chapter that records some of his most famous words. Verses 25–27 emphasize the sovereign choice of the Father:

"I thank you, Father, Lord of heaven and earth, that you have hidden these things from the wise and understanding and revealed them to little children; yes, Father, for such was your gracious will. All things have been handed over to me by my Father, and no one knows the Son except the Father, and no one knows the Father except the Son and anyone to whom the Son chooses to reveal him." (Matt 11:25–27)

But in the very next breath, he issues a call for his hearers to exercise their real moral agency in responding rightly to him:

"Come to me, all who labour and are heavy laden, and I will give you rest. Take my yoke upon you, and learn from me, for I am gentle and lowly in heart, and you will find rest for your souls. For my yoke is easy, and my burden is light." (11:28–30)

Acts 14 offers an intriguing mention of preaching that is worth our consideration. In verse 1, we are told that Paul and Barnabas entered a synagogue at Iconium and "spoke *in such a way* that a great number of both Jews and Greeks believed". This verse ties the output (the number of people who believed) to the input (the manner in which the evangelists spoke). In other words, the way Paul and Barnabas spoke is described as making a difference to the output produced.[4]

Or we could return to Colossians 1. Notice how Paul follows his great output-oriented statement with an intriguing insight about how this output is to be achieved:

Him [Jesus] we proclaim, warning everyone and teaching everyone with all wisdom, that we may present everyone mature in Christ. For this I toil, struggling with all his energy that he powerfully works within me. (Col 1:28–29)

Paul toils and struggles for the output; his own labours are an integral part of whether the output is achieved. And yet he acknowledges that the energy for this struggle is not his own, but God's energy working powerfully within him.

Perhaps the key New Testament text for assuring us that growth is God's work is a passage I have already quoted several times: 1 Corinthians 3:5–7. It has been said that if not for the life-giving power of God, we would be sowing stones. Paul can go so far as to describe himself and Apollos as mere "servants". But very quickly, Paul then identifies himself as "a skilled master builder" (v 10).[5] What's more, he ties the builder's future experience of judgement to the fruit of his work. The thing being 'built' here is the church (see v 9)—and "if the work that anyone has built on the foundation [the people served by the builder] survives, he [the builder] will receive a reward" (v 14). If not, the builder "will suffer loss" (v 15). In sum, Paul ties the judgement to come to the quality of a builder's output, not just their input.

Just a few chapters later in the very same letter, Paul writes of his determination to "become all things to all people, that by all means I might save some" (1 Cor 9:22). Note Paul's specific language: "that by all means *I might save some*". No doubt there is an element of rhetorical flourish about this, but some of us would feel more comfortable if we'd been able to edit this passage for Paul before he sent out his letter: "I've fixed it for you, Paul: 'I have become all things to all people, that by all means *God might use me* to save some'." But Paul, inspired by the Spirit of God, wrote as he did. His grasp of the sovereignty of God in salvation did not remove from him the sense that his actions made a very real difference in people's salvation.

In 2 Timothy, Paul plays with the complex link between inputs and outputs in the use of a series of analogies from various real-world endeavours: soldiering, athletics and farming.

Share in suffering as a good soldier of Christ Jesus. No soldier
gets entangled in civilian pursuits, since his aim is to please
the one who enlisted him. An athlete is not crowned unless he
competes according to the rules. It is the hard-working farmer
who ought to have the first share of the crops. (2 Tim 2:3–6)

The output of a farm is ultimately beyond the control of a farmer;
he can only plant and water. So many other events (storms, droughts,
disease, and the like) can impact the final output. And yet it is possible to see the difference between a lazy, foolish farmer and the
hardworking, wise farmer by the *output* of each farm. This principle
is so well established that Paul can use it as a picture of Christian
ministry. It is the hardworking farmer who should get the first
share. Similarly, a good soldier is single-minded; a good athlete follows the rules. In many ways, Christian ministry follows the normal
patterns of life that God has built into our world. Single-minded,
devoted work pays off. Paul takes these analogies and applies them
quite directly into the spiritual realm, urging Timothy to "think over
what I say" (v 7).

Put simply, Paul ties ministry inputs to ministry outputs—but
not in a simplistic way. That is, without *our work* of speaking and
toiling, people won't be saved and brought to maturity in Christ. Of
course, salvation and growth are *God's work*. But he has ordained
that he does his work through his instruments, or by his means—by
us, and by our preaching.

This brings to mind a conversation that is reported to have taken
place in the late-18th century between William Carey—missionary to
India and sometimes called the 'father of modern missions'—and
an older minister. As Carey was speaking to a large group and
making the case for the importance of overseas missionary work, he
was interrupted by the older minister, who rebuked him: "Young
man, sit down! You are an enthusiast [not a compliment in that con-

text!]. When God pleases to convert the heathen, he'll do it without consulting you or me."[6] Part of Carey's response was to write an important and now-famous paper titled 'An Enquiry into the Obligations of Christians to use Means for the Conversion of the Heathens'.[7] In this paper, first published in 1792, Carey argued that the Great Commission is still binding on all God's people, and called for "every possible exertion" to be made in order to see the lost saved.

Are we perhaps making the same mistake as that older minister with our failure to make changes in our ministries? Do we assure ourselves that God will save the outsider with or without us, and so leave things as they are and retreat to the security of 'just be faithful'?

James offers another important insight: "You do not have, because you do not ask" (Jas 4:2). If we lack some output, it could be linked to a failure on our part to focus on the 'input' of prayer. Positively, Jesus insists that "everyone who asks receives" (Matt 7:8). True, prayer is a different kind of 'input' than most others we might consider: it is faith in action, an expression of dependence on God rather than on ourselves, and an acknowledgement that we can't do things on our own. Yet it is still something we actively *do*. In his kindness, our heavenly Father does not leave us to sit by passively; he asks us and commands us to "pray without ceasing" (1 Thess 5:17), and he acts in response to our prayers.

The biblical complexity

It is important to recognize that I'm not saying—and certainly the Scriptures aren't saying—that there is a direct, one-to-one correspondence between inputs and outputs. I am not saying that if we pray, and if we pray in a certain way, then we will receive all that we ask for. We rightly reject such a notion on biblical grounds: three times, Paul prayed for the thorn in his flesh to be removed—no doubt praying with faith each time—but the Lord didn't remove it.

Instead, the Lord told him: "My grace is sufficient for you, for my power is made perfect in weakness" (2 Cor 12:7–9).

Many years ago, early in our church-planting experience, we had an extraordinary experience when our hot-water tank blew up one Saturday morning. I was consumed with ministry needs, I had no time and no money to fix the problem, and everything seemed overwhelming. I didn't know what to do. I suppose I figured we could heat water in the kettle and pour it over the kids for their showers, and everything would be fine.

That night, my wife happened to be in Sydney visiting her family for dinner. On a whim, they decided to walk to a restaurant. They finished their meal, and then on a whim decided to walk home by another route. As they walked home, they saw on the lawn in front of a large, well-appointed house (in a very wealthy part of the city) a hot-water tank. Cathie knocked on the door to ask if there was a problem with the system. The woman inside told her, "No, we just didn't like the colour". Cathie asked if we could have it, and the woman said yes. The next day, I took a borrowed trailer down to Sydney and picked it up. We had it installed, and it worked for seven years without a hiccup.

At no stage had I prayed about the situation. It was a wonderful reminder that God is sovereign. He gives even when you don't ask. And he doesn't always give when you do ask.

But here, once again, is the rub: it would be wrong to hear that story and conclude that there is no connection between our failure to have and our prayer life. For that would be to ignore the plain teaching of Scripture: very often, "You do not have, because you do not ask". Between the poles, between the false antitheses, there is a middle ground that is more complex.

What about the notion of perseverance in prayer? In Luke 18, Jesus tells his disciples a parable "to the effect that they ought always to pray and not lose heart" (Luke 18:1), using the illustration of a widow who is heard because she just keeps asking. Is it possible, therefore, that a lack of *persevering* prayer is one reason some ministries are not as blessed as others?

Similar principles are seen again and again throughout Scripture. Take parenting, for example. There is nothing I can do to *make* my child believe the gospel. I don't control their spiritual birth. But what I do (or don't do) as a parent makes a real difference to their responses to the gospel. The Proverbs tell us: "train up a child in the way he should go; even when he is old he will not depart from it" (Prov 22:6). Of course, the proverb isn't a *rule*. We can't conclude that the output is completely controlled by the input of quality parenting. But the Proverb is, at the very least, a warning that there *is* a connection.

As another example, Jesus promises that his heavenly Father will feed and clothe his people (Matt 6:25–34). He offers the example of God caring for the birds, even though "they neither sow nor reap nor gather into barns", and for the flowers, even though "they neither toil nor spin". The obvious implication is that we don't need to be anxious. If God provides for the birds and the flowers, he will surely provide for us. And yet, none of us ought to conclude that this promise will be fulfilled without us needing to sow, reap, store, toil or spin. The fulfilment of God's promise is, in some way, dependent on us doing what we do. If we don't toil, spin, harvest, cook, or even lift the fork to our mouths, we won't see God's sovereign promise to provide fulfilled. Does this make his promise dependent on us? Are we failing to trust God's sovereign provision by urging the lazy to heed the proverb that says, "A little sleep, a little slumber, a little folding of the hands to rest, and poverty will come upon you like a robber, and want like an armed man" (Prov 6:10, 24:33)? Was it right of Paul to say, "If anyone is not willing to work, let him not eat" (2 Thess 3:10)?

When Paul was sent as a prisoner to Rome, the ship he was travelling on encountered a severe storm, and an angel of the Lord appeared and promised him that everyone on board the ship would survive (Acts 27:22–24). But a short time later, when the sailors wanted to abandon the ship, Paul told the centurion and soldiers: "Unless these men stay in the ship, you cannot be saved" (27:31). He told everyone to eat because they needed strength (27:33–34). Was their survival dependent on the promise of God, or on their actions?

Again and again, the Bible presents a complex truth: our inputs aren't directly or irrevocably tied with outputs. But this doesn't mean we have no responsibility; there isn't *no* link between inputs and outputs. They are tied in some fashion.

What I'm wrestling to express is what theologian DA Carson has labelled 'compatibilism'.[8] It is the more complex middle ground between what might be called hyper-Calvinism at one pole and Arminianism at the other.[9] Perhaps a shorthand way of summarizing this is to say that while we don't *control* outcomes, we do *influence* them.

The conclusion that follows may be terrifying: the *way* I do ministry—my patterns of work, the structures I adopt, the skills and abilities that I have (or that I lack), the things I choose to emphasize, the amount of time I spend in prayer and the things I pray for—may actually be the cause (or at least *a* cause) of the fruit (or the lack of fruit) in my church or ministry. Where there is a lack of fruit, the problem may not be one of faithlessness, but of foolishness, or perhaps just blindness. Perhaps, under the guise of 'just being faithful', we have not paid sufficient attention to the things we've been doing and how we've been doing them. Work hard, we tell ourselves, and God will give the growth—but perhaps we have been working hard without working *smart* or working *effectively*.

Examining our patterns of ministry

If all this is true, it gives us a crucial driver for change: it may be that my failure to change is the reason I am not seeing more fruit. Maybe the patterns of ministry I've inherited or developed are harming the work. And my failure to notice and to act makes me complicit in the failure to bear fruit. I may be sincere, faithful and hard-working, but I am hurting the work.

This is certainly the considered opinion of church consultant Carl F George, who made this extraordinary statement some years ago:

> After almost two decades of careful investigation of the North American church, it is my growing conviction that the way pastors manage themselves as church leaders is the single most important cause for the failure of the churches to perform in the way God requires and in the way the Holy Spirit would empower them to accomplish.[10]

I would add my own small observation: within my wider ministry network, we have seen churches planted in regions where established churches were seeing no conversion growth, but within months these new churches were welcoming new converts. The numbers haven't been huge, but new people are being won to Christ.

In one instance, a godly pastor of an established church took his team of elders to visit the newly planted church. He sat his leaders in the building and drew their attention to what was happening: 'This church is seeing converts, but we aren't. They're preaching the same gospel as us in the exact same street as us. Why are they seeing fruit while we aren't?' It was a powerful moment of self-reflection, of asking hard questions, and of taking responsibility for the proper relationship between inputs and outputs. It empowered change.

Yes, of course, there are many other factors at work. It doesn't all depend on us as leaders. Paul's opponents sought to undermine his work by claiming he lacked impact. His letters to the Corinthian church remind us that there is more going on in the spiritual realm than can simply be explained by the pragmatics of ministry style and skill. The god of this age has blinded the minds of unbelievers, and there can be a determined judgement of God brought against a group, a nation, or a person. A recognition of these realities will help us to avoid the terrible dangers of technique-driven ministry, while also guarding us against pride. We must always remember where the power for our work truly lies. With Paul, we must always be able to say:

> I will boast all the more gladly of my weaknesses, so that the power of Christ may rest upon me. For the sake of Christ, then, I am content with weaknesses, insults, hardships, persecutions, and calamities. For when I am weak, then I am strong. (2 Cor 12:9–10).

But the complexity remains. And we must live and work within the complexity.

Practically, this boils down to the truth that we must take some responsibility for not just our inputs, but also for our outputs—in some fashion, and to some extent. It is simply wrong to say we have no responsibility for outputs. And in some contexts and situations, we will have to admit that at least part of the reason for the lack of impact and the lack of gospel fruit is our failures. It might be that we have failed to ask, or we have failed to plant and water, or we have failed to apply wisdom, or we have failed to work hard, or we have failed to be pastorally sensitive, or we have failed to preach effectively.

In Christ, we have the freedom to face these difficult possibilities, because our salvation—as well as our identity and our sense of self-worth—does not depend on being a perfect pastor. There is no such thing. Seeing our faults and failures is an opportunity to change, and to seek help and support. But in Christ, we also have a responsibility to face these difficult possibilities. There is too much at stake for us to avoid the hard questions.

What we do, and the way we do it, makes a difference—for better or worse. Yes, God is at work, and God is sovereign. Yes, we are just "jars of clay", and the Lord designed it this way "to show that the surpassing power belongs to God and not to us" (2 Cor 4:7). Yes, his power is made perfect in weakness. But his sovereignty operates in a far more complex way than a simplistic two-pole conception appreciates. Our inputs make a difference to the outputs, and we need to feel the weight of our responsibility in this work.

Passages for further reflection

- Matthew 11:25–30
- 1 Corinthians 3:5–15
- Colossians 1:28–29
- 2 Timothy 2:3–6

Questions for personal or team reflection

- What did you find most difficult or confronting about this chapter?
- Have you been so focused on inputs that you have neglected thinking about outputs? Have you been so focused on outputs that you have failed to remember the sovereignty of God? What steps will you take to correct any error?

Quote for personal or team reflection

"Damn all false antitheses to hell, for they generate false gods, they perpetuate idols, they twist and distort our souls, they launch the church into violent pendulum swings whose oscillations succeed only in dividing brothers and sisters in Christ." (DA Carson)

8

LIVING WITH
THE TENSIONS

Contented discontentment

As we allow the Bible to push us around and create an energy for change, the Christian leader is forced to live with a necessary amount of tension. Part of this is the tension that exists because of the dangers of a passion for growth that sit alongside the biblical necessity to be passionate about spiritual and numerical growth. There is also the tension of knowing that God is sovereign over everything and directly responsible for all that is good in the world, and yet also knowing that all my inputs make a real difference—for good or for ill—to gospel outputs. Ongoing tension is a normal part of Christian leadership. And tension produces pain. It becomes very difficult to be a 'relaxed' Christian pastor.

By nature, I am a relaxed kind of person. In fact, if it weren't for the truth of the gospel, I'd be living the life of a beach bum—drifting happily from one surf spot to another. But the five great theological realities 'plus one' drive me forward. The urgency of (spiritual and numerical) gospel growth drives me forward. Added to this is the growing realization that what I do and how I do it makes a difference to the spiritual outputs of people's salvation and their growth to maturity. I feel it. True, I feel it imperfectly—I feel it less than I ought. But it weighs on me. I don't sleep as well as I used to. I don't experience 'the sleep of the happy Calvinist'. But I notice that the apostle Paul endured "many a sleepless night" (2 Cor 11:27). Based on what he says in the very next verse, part of what kept him awake was his "anxiety for all the churches" (2 Cor 11:28).

I am sure Paul was a 'Calvinist'. He hadn't read the *Institutes*,[1] but he had a deep and abiding belief in the sovereignty of God. It's because of Paul's writings that Calvin was a Calvinist. And yet the apostle who commanded "do not be anxious about anything" (Phil 4:6) is the same apostle who experienced the "daily pressure" of "anxiety for all the churches". I dare say he lived with the pressure that came from being aware that his efforts made a difference to the outputs, and this weighed on him.

This is normal, gospel-hearted Christianity.

It is normal for a pastor to feel daily the pressure of their concern for their church, because they feel the weight of the difference their inputs make to the outputs. It may be far easier and more comfortable to retreat into a kind of hyper-Calvinism that imagines God's sovereignty negates the importance of everything we do. But the call to 'just be faithful' may hide an overly simplistic and lazy approach to ministry. It might cover over a heart problem, where there is little genuine and deep concern for the lost. Or it might hide a hardworking and passionate minister's inability to own the fact that he is working with bad ministry models, poor ministry practice, or a lack of skill in some important area.

If you are persuaded by the argument of this book so far, you may be starting to sense something painful, awkward and uncomfortable happening to you and in you. A deep and difficult sense of a burden for the lost, and for their salvation and growth to maturity, may be stirring within you. When this burden is present in a driving concern to take appropriate ownership and responsibility for outputs, it brings with it a deep sense of grief when these outputs are not happening. And this rests heavily on you. A lack of growth—both numerical and spiritual—in your ministry will cause you to keep examining yourself and your ministries. What am I doing (or not doing) that means so little is happening?

This is a powerful place to be. But it can easily drive a leader to a human-centred works theology when we should be God-centred. God is the power that makes this all happen; I am not the key to this work.

We keep returning to this crucial point: there is nowhere safe.

We want to avoid compromise, so we believe that if we are just 'Bible guys', everything will be okay. At least, we think, this means we will be theologically sound. But we can so easily fall into the danger of failing to share God's heart for the lost—at which point we are anything but theologically sound.

And so, convinced that our inputs really do affect outputs, we resolve to put our shoulder to the wheel, upskill ourselves, devour every possible resource on evangelism and church restructuring, and get all our ministry ducks in a row, confident that the growth must now follow. But we are now on the verge of embracing a human-centred theology that forgets it is God who gives the growth.

And so, we want to avoid compromise, so we believe that if we are just 'Bible guys' ...

We need to acknowledge that there is nowhere safe. And therefore, we need to learn to live the life of *contented discontentment*.

We need people who are living discontented lives: about the state of the church, about the relatively little impact we are making on society and on individual lives, and about the relatively little spiritual and numerical growth occurring among us. We need people who are deeply discontent that so many around us are going to hell. We need people who are discontent about how little we care, and who are therefore driven to pray persistently about these things. We are always so much less than we could be or ought to be.

Think of Paul's reaction when he arrived in Athens and saw that the city was "full of idols" (Acts 17:16). He didn't respond by saying "what an interesting cultural experience" or "isn't diversity wonderful?" He responded by being deeply distressed: "his spirit was provoked within him"—and it moved him to start preaching "Jesus and the resurrection", even though it meant that many of the cultural elites of his day dismissed him as a "babbler" (vv 17–18). This is the kind of discontentment we need.

But at the same time, we need people who live lives of deep contentment. We need to cultivate this deep contentment in at least three specific ways.

First, we need to be content in the present blessings of God upon us and our work.

What God has done among us is wonderful, and we should never despise or dismiss it. Be thankful. Count your blessings regularly. The church he has gathered in your corner of the world—though it may be small, full of weak and immature believers, and not everything that it could be—is a work of great power and a sign of the great and wonderful blessing of the Lord. God still rules, and he is perfecting his church as we preach Christ crucified and as his Spirit works among us. We are and will be his beautiful bride. And he saves us by grace, not by works, so that no-one may boast. Jesus loved me and died for me while I was still an enemy of God. How much more does he love me, and how much more will he give me, now that I'm his reconciled and adopted child?

Secondly, we need to be content in the sovereign power of God.

Yes, God is sovereign. He will build his church. I can rest at night because he will be at work sovereignly to gather a people to himself and to transform us into his image. As the '39 Articles of Religion'— which summarize the essential beliefs of the Anglican denomination —tell us, the doctrine of predestination and election "is full of sweet, pleasant and unspeakable comfort to godly persons". Remember

Jesus' parable of the growing seed (Mark 4:26–29): the man who scatters the seed "sleeps and rises night and day, and the seed sprouts and grows; he knows not how" (v 27). The sovereignty of God breeds contentment and comfort among the people of God.

Third, we should be content in our discontentment.

Discontentment is normal among people who truly embrace the truth of the grace of God and who long to see the word of the Lord "speed ahead and be honoured" (2 Thess 3:1). It is normal among people who embrace the complex reality of the sovereignty of God and our genuine responsibilities under him. We *are* influencing the outcomes, and even the lack of them. But the glorious truth is that God is intent on using even the weak and the frail to achieve his purposes. We are, after all, "jars of clay" (2 Cor 4:7). It is a struggle to be what we need to be and do what we need to do, but there is joy in the struggle and in our pursuit of knowing Christ.

Healthy gospel ministry and healthy gospel ministers are, in one sense, never balanced. The Christian life, and especially the life of gospel ministry, is never relaxed, comfortable or easy. But we aren't called to that life. We are called to die.[2] Our apostle was "poured out as a drink offering" (Phil 2:17; 2 Tim 4:6). Jesus told his disciples and the crowd around them:

> If anyone would come after me, let him deny himself and take up his cross and follow me. For whoever would save his life will lose it, but whoever loses his life for my sake and the gospel's will save it. (Mark 8:34–35)

There's a further consequence of embracing the life of contented discontentment: it positions me to look in the mirror and own the reality of what I see—in myself, and in my ministries. For I am upheld by grace. God loves me not because of my own merits, but because of the merits of Christ, and because in Christ I am adopted as his son. My joy and my identity are found not in what I can do for

God, but in what God has done for me in Christ. Our discontentment at the lack of gospel growth around us should never take away the contentment and the freedom that is ours in Christ.

"Leave no stone unturned": The 'Spurgeon Paradox'

There's a principle in the business world that goes by the name of the 'Stockdale Paradox'. It takes its name from Admiral Jim Stockdale, who spent eight years in a prisoner-of-war camp during the Vietnam War and survived through a combination of confidence for the future and honest assessment of the present situation. Author Jim Collins, who coined the term 'Stockdale Paradox' in his book *Good to Great*, summarizes it this way:

> Retain faith that you will prevail in the end, regardless of the difficulties AND at the same time confront the most brutal facts of your current reality, whatever they might be.[3]

The Stockdale Paradox is the idea that business leaders ought to be able to look honestly at the state of their business and own the problems, but to do so with confidence and optimism. I'm not sure why a business leader should be able to do that when there is no objective basis for confidence and optimism. A friend of mine joked that a Blockbuster video store in the early 2010s had very little reason for optimism, even if it adopted every leadership strategy in the world.

But if anyone can embrace the Stockdale Paradox with perfect assurance, it is the leaders of God's people. Yes, we influence outcomes. But our God is truly sovereign and endlessly gracious, and he has promised that he will build his church.

It is intriguing to see how the great preacher Charles Spurgeon thought about these things. He gave this advice to ministers who weren't seeing conversions in their churches:

I believe that the most of you, who have really tried, in the power of the Holy Spirit, by Scriptural teaching and by prayer, to bring others to Jesus, have been successful. I may be speaking to a few who have not succeeded; if so, I would recommend them to look steadily over their motive, their spirit, their work, and their prayer, and then begin again. Perhaps they may get to work more wisely, more believingly, more humbly, and more in the power of the Holy Spirit. They must act as farmers do who, after a poor harvest, plough again in hope. They ought not to be dispirited, but they ought to be aroused. We should be anxious to find out the reason of failure, if there be any, and we should be ready to learn from all our fellow-labourers; but we must steadfastly set our faces, if by any means we may save some, resolving that whatever happens we will leave no stone unturned to effect the salvation of those around us.[4]

Notice how Spurgeon urges serious engagement with ministerial responsibilities—he doesn't let leaders off the hook easily! But he urges them to operate within the context of continued hope. Begin again. Be aroused, but not dispirited. And rely on the power of the Holy Spirit.

Perhaps, instead of the 'Stockdale Paradox', Christians ought to refer to this as the 'Spurgeon Paradox'. After all, Spurgeon's insights came many years before modern business experts offered their thoughts.

A question of the heart

At this point, there is value in honest self-assessment by answering some diagnostic questions.

Do we grieve the fate of the lost as we should?

Do we truly hunger and thirst for a larger gospel future?

Are we driven by a desire to 'just be faithful' in presenting the food, or are we really concerned about whether people take it and eat it?

Why do so few of us take risks, throw ourselves out there, and push to see things happen?

Why do so few of us agonize over the lack of growth in our churches?

Why don't we hurt more for those in our church who are failing to be all that God intends for them, or for those outside the church?

Where is your heart?

If we are to see churches really growing in numbers and in depth of maturity, we will need to see leaders and leadership teams upskilled. But being upskilled is superficial and ineffective if it isn't accompanied by a burning gospel heart that weeps for the lost and grieves for the immaturity of so many.

Why is this heart so important?

It isn't because of some magical connection between that heart and the outputs—although, if such a heart leads us to persistent prayer, there undoubtedly *is* some kind of direct connection. The deeper reason that our heart matters is related to the big idea of this book: if our churches and ministries are to become more effective, they will have to change. *We* will have to change. And that change won't happen without cost. It may include financial costs, but it will certainly include costs to our comforts, our relationships, our respectability, and perhaps even to our health. And we won't be willing to bear that cost unless we are sold out to the urgent need for the gospel to bear fruit and increase.

~

Passages for further reflection

- Mark 4:26–29
- Mark 8:34–35
- 2 Corinthians 4:7–12
- 2 Corinthians 11:24–28

Questions for personal or team reflection

- Have you experienced a healthy 'contented discontentment'? Or have you only ever experienced one or the other? What would 'contented discontentment' look like for you?
- What place does prayer have in your life and ministry?

Quote for personal or team reflection

"We should be anxious to find out the reason of failure, if there be any, and we should be ready to learn from all our fellow-labourers; but we must steadfastly set our faces, if by any means we may save some, resolving that whatever happens we will leave no stone unturned to effect the salvation of those around us." (Charles Spurgeon)

THEOLOGICALLY PRINCIPLED PRAGMATISM

Proverbs and pragmatism

In all our thoughts about change—whether changes in us as leaders, or changes in our ministries—an important but often contentious concept will quickly rear its head: *pragmatism.* In many Christian circles, 'pragmatism' is a dirty word, something to be rejected and frowned on as one of the great evils of the church growth movement. The quickest and easiest way to condemn or discredit a Christian leader is to refer to him or her as a 'pragmatist'.

There is much that is both fair and necessary in a critique of pragmatism, which in many ways is akin to a consequentialist ethic. That is, we determine what is good and right solely by considering outcomes: if the output is good, then the input was good; if the output is poor, then the input was poor. In other words, the result is all that really matters; how you achieve that result is unimportant. The end justifies the means.

Unchecked, this approach is antithetical to the biblical pattern of gospel ministry. For the Christian leader, the end *never* justifies the means. Consider again Paul's description of ministry in 2 Corinthians 4: "We have renounced secret and shameful ways; we do not use deception, nor do we distort the word of God. On the contrary, by setting forth the truth plainly we commend ourselves to everyone's conscience in the sight of God" (2 Cor 4:2, NIV).

Yet we cannot entirely dismiss pragmatism quite so quickly. For it could be defined as simply 'doing what works'. People who love the Bible cannot be completely opposed to pragmatics, in part because an entire book in the inspired Scriptures testifies to the power and reality of pragmatism: Proverbs.

The book of Proverbs is largely a series of proverbial sayings reflecting on the reality of cause-and-effect in our world. That is, it notes the observable reality of doing 'thing A' which will bring about 'thing B'. For example:

> A little sleep, a little slumber, a little folding of the hands to rest, and poverty will come upon you like a robber, and want like an armed man. (6:10, 24:33)

> A soft answer turns away wrath, but a harsh word stirs up anger. (15:1)

> Train up a child in the way he should go; even when he is old he will not depart from it. (22:6)

> Whoever misleads the upright into an evil way will fall into his own pit, but the blameless will have a goodly inheritance. (28:10).

True, Proverbs also warns us against putting all our confidence in pragmatism: "There is a way that seems right to a man, but its end is the way to death" (14:12, 16:25). In a world that is corrupted by sin, and in which every *person* is corrupted by sin, 'the best-laid plans of mice and men often go awry'. We aren't omniscient, and therefore we can't know for certain which input will lead to what output. Circumstances and forces beyond our knowing will be at work. Yet the overall shape of the book, and proverbs like those listed above, tell us much about the nature of the universe. God has made a world in which certain causes generally produce certain effects with such regularity that we can discern a pattern to the world. Yes, the proverbs are general rules rather than immutable laws; there are many exceptions to the pattern. But there is sufficient predictability that generalizations are true and form an important part of God's word. To discern the God-given patterns in our world, and to live and act accordingly, is to be wise.

This reality grounds a healthy and biblical approach to the principle of pragmatics. That is, God has constructed reality in such a way that we can almost always predict certain outputs based on certain inputs. We can repeat the patterns with some predictability. Pragmatics works. This is the universe God has made.

In 1 Corinthians 9, an important passage to which I have already referred, the apostle Paul offers some measure of a pragmatic approach to gospel ministry. The context here is Paul's decision to lay down his rights for the salvation of others. Though he insists—just as Jesus insisted—that "those who proclaim the gospel should get their living by the gospel" (9:14), he has not made use of this right: "we endure anything rather than put an obstacle in the way of the gospel of Christ" (9:12). As part of his commitment to acting for the salvation of others, he embraces what could rightly be called a form of pragmatism:

> For though I am free from all, I have made myself a servant to all, that I might win more of them. To the Jews I became as a Jew, in order to win Jews. To those under the law I became as one under the law (though not being myself under the law) that I might win those under the law. To those outside the law I became as one outside the law (not being outside the law of God but under the law of Christ) that I might win those outside the law. To the weak I became weak, that I might win the weak. I have become all things to all people, that by all means

I might save some. I do it all for the sake of the gospel, that I may share with them in its blessings. (1 Cor 9:19–23)

Paul discerns that the ministry practice of 'like attracts like' works. A person is more easily able to engage with someone who shares their perspective and experiences; there are fewer barriers to connection and engagement. And so, Paul changes his ministry practice to best connect and engage with different audiences.[1]

In doing this—in laying down his rights for the sake of others, and making himself like others in order to win others—Paul was following the example of the Lord Jesus, who became human in order to save humanity. Of course, we cannot reduce the incarnation of our Lord to nothing more than an act of 'principled pragmatism'. There is much more going on, including the ontological need for God to become human to save humans (e.g. Heb 2:14–18). And yet in a sense, Paul was following the example of the God who became like us in every way (except that he was "without sin"; Heb 4:15) to save us. And Paul's way of doing this relied on observable human realities: the more we are like the people we are seeking to reach, the more we will be able to connect with them and see them saved; the more we do to adapt ourselves to their needs and their station in life, the more we can expect to see them respond to the gospel.

Pragmatism for those "under the law of Christ"

Even here, however, Paul observes critically important limitations to his pragmatism. He became "all things to all people" only in so far as he remained "under the law of Christ". What might be called 'rampant pragmatism' can never be the driving rule for those of us who are bound by Christ and his word. There are many things that are far more important than 'doing what works'. There are principles that must be observed and boundaries that must not be crossed. These principles and boundaries, laid down for us in the Scriptures,

control and constrain us. Perhaps it is more proper and more helpful to emphasize that these principles and boundaries serve to
empower and liberate us, for where the Bible places no boundaries
we are free to adapt ourselves to our cultural moment and to the
people we are seeking to reach. Yet the principles and boundaries
remain, and they rightly control and constrain us.

To take one of the most obvious examples, Paul wasn't 'free' to
behave in an ungodly fashion: he couldn't take on the sin of drunk-
enness to win the drunk. He couldn't engage in sexual immorality—
something about which 1 Corinthians has a lot to say—to win the
sexually immoral. Indeed, when it comes to matters of sin and righteousness, the New Testament's expectation is not that we will win
sinners to Christ by showing that we are just like them. On the contrary, it is when people see that we are *different from them* in our
patterns of behaviour and our holiness of life—not perfect, and not
smug or self-righteous, but different—that they will give glory to our
Father who is in heaven (see Matt 5:13–16; 1 Pet 2:12).

Even within the boundaries of the law of Christ, the word of God
gives texture and colour to our practice of ministry in ways that
will shape how we operate in our areas of freedom. Although Paul
can say he was free to be "all things to all people" in order to save
some, it is clear from 2 Corinthians that he didn't think this gave
him the right to become a self-obsessed power junky in order to
win a better hearing from the prestige-loving, triumphalist Corinthians. This is the point of the contrast he draws between himself
and the so-called 'super-apostles' (11:5, 12:11). Though he was free to
be all things to all people, some ways of being were out of bounds
for Paul, shaped and controlled by the very nature of the gospel
as he was. In 1 Corinthians, Paul was adamant that he would
"preach Christ crucified", despite knowing that the message was
a stumbling block to Jews, who demanded signs, and folly to
Greeks, who craved wisdom (1 Cor 1:22–23). He would rather be

seen as a complete fool in the eyes of the world than compromise on his message.

Jesus came as weak (in the world's eyes) to win the weak and to shame the strong. Gospel preachers, although free to be all things to all people, deny the very shape and character of the gospel we preach when we seek to become impressive to win the impressive, or 'cool' to win the 'cool'.[2] It will be effective, and relatively easy, to portray Christianity as a club for winners—the celebrity brand, the VIP seating, the clothes, the car, the language. And it will certainly achieve a growth output among a particular crowd of people—the successful, the trendy, the image conscious, and the powerful. But we will have portrayed a different Christ and undermined the very nature of the gospel. We will have proclaimed a message that ultimately cannot and will not bring about the true salvation from sin that Jesus desires. This is why Paul told the Corinthians:

> And I, when I came to you, brothers and sisters, did not come proclaiming to you the testimony of God with lofty speech or wisdom. For I decided to know nothing among you except Jesus Christ and him crucified. And I was with you in weakness and in fear and much trembling, and my speech and my message were not in plausible words of wisdom, but in demonstration of the Spirit and of power, so that your faith might not rest in the wisdom of men but in the power of God. (1 Cor 2:2–5)

Consider a specific example: it has often been observed that a person will connect into church more quickly and be more likely to stay if they are given a job fairly soon upon arriving. This is an observable cause-and-effect reality in human society: being asked to volunteer in service of a cause rapidly increases a person's commitment to that cause. As a result, some churches have embraced this pragmatic reality, and they have done so for very good reason: to see people established in church and to have churches grow.

Yet this approach communicates a very different sense from the gospel message we proclaim—a message in which membership precedes practice. That is, we belong to Jesus before we serve Jesus. We serve him out of a gratitude that grows from having been received into his kingdom without regard to our practice; we serve out of a desire to love our brothers and sisters in Christ and to use our gifts for the good of "the body of Christ", the church (1 Cor 12:7, 27). A church will (perhaps inadvertently) communicate the opposite pattern by building a sense of membership based on performance, rather than on grace. Church membership is properly based upon a person's shared life with Christ, not their acts of service. Service should certainly flow from the root of shared life together in Christ, but it should not precede it.

How, then, should we think about 'pragmatism'?

The biblical requirement for pragmatism

It is not just important that we are pragmatic—it is a biblical requirement that we are pragmatic. But our pragmatism must be rigorously theological at every point.

In 1986 and 1988, Phillip Jensen delivered two sets of landmark addresses to the Evangelical Ministry Assembly in the UK. One of these talks was provocatively titled 'The theological necessity for pragmatism'—or, in its shortened form, 'We must be pragmatic'.[3] Grappling with declining church attendance (which was already a big issue in the 1980s) and with the overwhelming number of unreached and unchurched people, Jensen called on pastors to change the agenda and priorities of church life to maximize opportunities to reach the lost.

"Pragmatism without theology is awful", Jensen said. "It is the awful tyranny of the church growth movement, which keeps arguing 'this works in growing churches, therefore we should do it'. On the other hand, theology without pragmatism is a tyranny that we're also under: traditionalism. ... On the one hand, we're being seduced into non-evangelical patterns of ministry; on the other hand, we're being constipated."

As Jensen suggests, there is an important place for pragmatics—but it must take second place to theology. Before and over and under our pragmatism lies a deeper truth: many things are good and right even though, from a human point of view, they don't appear to 'work'. It is possible to engage in 'theologically principled pragmatism'—a kind of pragmatism that is always subservient to theological truth, always bound by the revealed word of God, and always shaped and coloured by biblical principles.

And yet one of those biblical principles is that God has designed a universe with a pattern of cause-and-effect built into it (as already noted from the book of Proverbs). There is nothing inherently evil about being pragmatic, and much that is good and right about it. And that pragmatism is to be an expression of our passionate concern for the lost. We are not just free to embrace pragmatics; we *must* embrace pragmatics if we are to properly imitate Paul as he imitates Christ. As Phillip Jensen put it:

> The grace of the gospel is to be seen in our generous putting ourselves out to welcome others, laying aside our most treasured traditions for the sake of others. I have to see the priority of other people in salvation, and seeing the priority of other people's salvation requires me to be massively flexible.[4]

This is why Christian leaders must be theologians. It is necessary to know not only the theological and biblical boundaries to our practice, but also the range of freedoms within those boundaries. In other words, we need to know what the Bible says we can't do and what the Bible says we must do, and we must also appreciate the Bible's silences—the areas where it allows freedom of movement and action. Both dimensions are necessary to function effectively within a world where the revealed word of God comes first, but where God has also woven cause-and-effect into the very fabric of his creation.

The next two chapters seek to wrestle with these issues as they relate to the shape of church life and the role of a pastor.

Passages for further reflection

- Proverbs 6:10
- Matthew 5:13–16
- 1 Corinthians 2:2–5
- 1 Corinthians 9:19–23

Questions for personal or team reflection

- What is your instinctive reaction to the notion of 'pragmatism'? How does this chapter challenge that reaction (if at all)?
- "I have become all things to all people, that by all means I might save some": where and how has this principle shaped your life and ministry?

Quote for personal or team reflection

"The grace of the gospel is to be seen in our generous putting ourselves out to welcome others, laying aside our most treasured traditions for the sake of others. I have to see the priority of other people in salvation, and seeing the priority of other people's salvation requires me to be massively flexible." (Phillip Jensen)

10

FREEDOMS AND BOUNDARIES IN CHURCH LIFE

The extent of our freedoms

In the next two chapters, I want to consider two areas of Christian thinking and ministry: church, and pastors. There are a couple of reasons for doing so at this point. First, we may be thinking about these areas of ministry in a way that makes them 'heat dissipaters'. That is, we have, on some occasions and in some contexts, used certain ways of thinking to remove a proper sense of burden or responsibility in ministry—to dissipate the heat that should rightly be building around growth and change.

Second, we may have used our theological convictions about these topics to unnecessarily constrain the way we do ministry, placing limitations on our ability to lead and impeding the potential for growth. But I want to suggest that the Bible gives us greater freedom in the way we do our work than we might have assumed. Surprisingly for some, Calvin makes this point when he says, "we know that every Church has liberty to frame for itself a form of government that is suitable and profitable for it, because the Lord has not prescribed anything definite".[1]

Given the purpose (and the limitations) of this book, my engagement with the Bible's teaching on church and pastors won't be exhaustive; I will engage only to the extent that it helps us consider growth and change. Yet there are still important points to be made. In my view, the way we have conceived of these topics has contributed to our lack of impact in making more mature disciples. This is not immediately obvious to many, in part because of how deeply they hold their convictions about the nature of church or the nature of pastoral ministry. Of course, at whatever point the Bible draws the boundaries, we are bound to live within those boundaries, even if we believe it might limit our growth potential. More than this, we are to rejoice in God's good design and maintain an absolute trust in his word.

But if there is more flexibility than we have believed, and our failure to grasp this flexibility is limiting our growth, then our heart to see the lost saved will necessarily cause us to seek out more effective expressions and practices—always within biblical bounds—in each area.

Church: the fruit of gospel ministry

What is 'church'? How are we to conceive of it biblically?

Fundamentally, 'church' means 'gathering'. The Greek word most often translated 'church' is *ekklēsia*, the same Greek word used in the first century for an ordinary gathering.[2] Acts 19 uses the word for a great crowd of people gathered in the city centre protesting Paul's ministry. We are told: "Now some cried out one thing, some another, for the *ekklēsia* was in confusion ..." (v 32). That is, the 'assembly' or 'gathering' was in confusion.

So, when Paul writes to the *ekklēsia* in Corinth or the *ekklēsia* in Rome, he is most specifically referring to them as a *gathered* body of people—the *assembly* of God. But this isn't just any assembly; it is the one bought by the blood of God's own son. It is *his* gathered people. It is "the assembly of the firstborn who are enrolled in heaven"

(Heb 12:23). It is the gathering set apart to him, special to him.

This new thing called 'church' is anticipated in the Old Testament by the great gathering of God's people at Mount Sinai. Stephen, the first Christian martyr, uses the word *ekklēsia* to describe that gathering in Acts 7:38. For theological reasons, most modern English translations don't use the word 'church' in that context (the ESV uses "congregation"); it isn't the New Testament gathering we know as 'church'. But it was a gathering of God's people nonetheless, and it is the antecedent to the New Testament gathering founded in Christ.

This gathering at Sinai was a great moment in the history of God's people. God had rescued them out of slavery in Egypt, and now he was gathering them to receive his words. Moses commanded the gathered people:

> Only take care, and keep your soul diligently, lest you forget the things that your eyes have seen, and lest they depart from your heart all the days of your life. Make them known to your children and your children's children—how on the day that you stood before the LORD your God at Horeb, the LORD said to me, "Gather the people to me, that I may let them hear my words, so that they may learn to fear me all the days that they live on the earth, and that they may teach their children so".
> (Deut 4:9–10)

The essence of this gathering crosses over into New Testament times, for the essence of the Christian gathering today is for God's people to hear God speak to them.

More broadly, it can be said that being gathered is essential to being a Christian. Throughout the Bible, to be *scattered* is to suffer the *judgement* of God. From being cast out of Eden, through to being cast out of the land of promise in the exile, to be judged is to be scattered. But to be *gathered* is to receive the *blessing* of God. The reversal of the effects of sin brings about gathering. The cross is the key event in this reversal, as the (unconscious) prophecy of Caiaphas reveals in John 11:

> But one of them, Caiaphas, who was high priest that year, said to them, "You know nothing at all. Nor do you understand that it is better for you that one man should die for the people, not that the whole nation should perish." He did not say this of his own accord, but being high priest that year he prophesied that Jesus would die for the nation, and not for the nation only, but also to gather into one the children of God who are scattered abroad. (John 11:49–52)

Jesus has "broken down in his flesh the dividing wall of hostility" between Jew and Gentile (Eph 2:14); in himself and his death, he has created "one new man in place of the two" (2:15). So now, "there is neither Jew nor Greek, there is neither slave nor free, there is no male and female, for you are all one in Christ Jesus" (Gal 3:28). We are united to Christ and to one another, gathered as the people of God.

Here on earth, our local church gatherings are earthly expressions of the spiritual gathering that every believer has experienced as they have been gathered to Christ and into the heavenly assembly (Heb 12:22–24). Although we may only gather intermittently, spiritually we are always gathered. In the gospel, God's great purpose is to undo the effects of sin and to gather a people to himself and to each other, removing all barriers to our fellowship with him and with one another. We may only gather for a couple of hours each week here on earth, but we become identified as *those who gather*. And so, Paul can write of obligations and expectations which exceed the things church members can do when gathered physically. Being members of a particular church gathering tangibly affects our identity, our relationships, and our responsibilities in ways that go well beyond the actual gathering.

Church is a profound thing. Every gathering around the word testifies to Jesus' victory at the cross. God's people are gathered, chiefly because they are no longer "hostile to God" (Rom 8:7) or at enmity with him, but instead now enjoy "peace with God through our Lord Jesus Christ" (Rom 5:1). As a consequence, we are also gathered to each other by union with Christ through the unifying work of the Spirit, and we must be "eager to maintain the unity of the Spirit in the bond of peace" (Eph 4:1–6).

In this sense—and very importantly for our purposes here—church is an end in itself. In other words, church is the *outcome* of all our inputs, rather than simply one of the inputs. The apostles didn't go throughout the Mediterranean planting churches *per se*. They simply went around preaching the gospel, which properly and naturally produced gatherings—churches. Church was one of the outcomes of their disciple-making activity, the fruit of gospel ministry. This is not to say that 'church' was a thing of little consequence; it was an intentional fruit of their gospel ministry. That people are gathered together in 'church' reflects a deeply important part of who we are as Christians: we are gathered to Christ and to each other, assembled as God's new community.[3]

This is important in helping us to appreciate some proper 'boundaries' that we apply to church life and practice. Church is not merely one step on a ministry pathway or a tool for the task of achieving gospel purposes.[4] As leaders, we need to help our people see that 'gathering' is what we do as the saved, redeemed people of God. The very experience of gathering for church glorifies God: "through the church the manifold wisdom of God might now be made known to the rulers and authorities in the heavenly places" (Eph 3:10). We gather to reflect the power of the gospel to create a new people—a people who now long to praise and honour the one who has saved us.

It is certainly true that church performs an edification function, and that role is crucial (1 Corinthians 14). In fact, one of the changes we might need to make is a greater attention to the church gathering as a place that empowers and enables effective edification—through better preaching, singing, prayer and interaction as we each speak the word to one another and build one another up. But church is far more than merely a location for efficient edification. It is far more beautiful than that.

Church life and the shape of our gatherings

In chapter 2 of the book of Acts, we have the first description of the experience of the gathered church:

> They devoted themselves to the apostles' teaching and the fellowship, to the breaking of bread and the prayers. And awe came upon every soul, and many wonders and signs were being done through the apostles. And all who believed were together and had all things in common. And they were selling their possessions and belongings and distributing the proceeds to all, as any had need. And day by day, attending the temple together and breaking bread in their homes, they received their food with glad and generous hearts, praising God and having favour with all the people. And the Lord added to their number day by day those who were being saved (Acts 2:42–47)

It is a beautiful and wonderful picture. But what do we do with the picture today? What does it say to us now? Is it the description *and* the prescription of the perfect church? The aspirational model for what all our churches should be? The proper basis for our 'vision statements'?

At the very least, Acts 2 shows that something profoundly new has arrived in the religious landscape. Christ died, has been raised, and has been exalted to the right hand of the Father. Now, the Spirit has been poured out in fulfilment of centuries of prophetic hope (see

Acts 2:1–21). Finally, God has now taken up residence by his Spirit in the hearts of men and women. The age of the Spirit has dawned, and with it has come the end of ritualistic religion. No longer do people need to perform sacrifices to cleanse themselves. No longer do they need earthly priests to mediate the holy God to sinful humans. No longer do they need temples within which all of this occurs. Something profoundly new has come. It is a new kind of relationship: people are able to live as sons and daughters of the eternal King. It is a new kind of status: saints. It is a new kind of freedom: freedom from condemnation, guilt and the curse of the law, and freedom to serve one another in love. And in all this, God himself is with us— dwelling in each believer and in us together as his church. This wonderful newness is pictured in glorious shorthand in Acts 2.[5]

It is a beautiful picture of a spontaneous and egalitarian group. No-one is higher or lower than another. All are together, and all share the Spirit and enjoy equal access to God the Father through the Lord Jesus. The life of the Spirit shows itself with a spontaneous sharing of everything, and in a devotion to the word of God and prayer. And every day, new people are being saved and gathered into the church.

Any believer with a heart for the things of Christ and a sense of the glory of the new covenant can't help but thrill to it. And it is easy to see how Christians might draw certain convictions about church life today from these verses.

One application drawn by many, for clear and obvious reasons, is the need for today's church to return to this New Testament ideal. In fact, some would say that until the church expresses its life just like these early Christians did, it is falling short of its calling.

This was the ethos of the 'house church movement' of some decades ago. It made much of the 'spontaneous' nature of the picture in Acts, and therefore it was often an anti-institutional movement. It intentionally turned away from the 'organizational', the 'structured', the 'programmed' and the 'strategic', and sought instead to return to the beauty of a spontaneous, Spirit-filled Christian life where everyone held things in common—a place where God's people don't just meet to 'do Bible study', but to 'do life' together in all its diversity.

But is this what we are supposed to glean from Acts 2 (and we might also include Acts 4:32–37)? Is this why these Spirit-inspired words were given to us?

In the end, though they may have the best of intentions, those who read the Acts passages in this way over-read the Bible and its meaning: they take one part and make it into the whole, without proper regard to other aspects of the biblical testimony.

Within Acts itself, the picture from chapter 2 is significantly modified. By chapter 6, the new community has lost some of its shine. Prominent Christians have deceptively misused the church for their own glory (5:1–11). And the spontaneous sharing of resources isn't done so beautifully, which leads to tension and division between the Greek Christians and the Hebrew Christians (6:1). While this latter problem is effectively resolved and the church keeps growing (6:2–7), it must be noted that the beautiful spontaneity and generous love which characterized the very early church has given way to the need for appointed officers to supervise and oversee the new community. Structure was necessary so that the fledgling church could properly express its life as a Spirit-filled, gospel-shaped community. Little mention is made at this stage of a further order of ministry such as 'eldership', but it is soon evident that this leadership structure was part of the life of the early community.

We'll return to some of these ideas below, but what is clear from the early chapters of Acts is that organization and structure, planning and programs, are not antithetical to the life of a truly Spirit-filled, gospel-shaped community. The apostles didn't chastise the early Christians for failing to fulfil their spiritual life as loving servants of one another; they recognized that the beauty of spiritual community life needs to be lived in the reality of a fallen world, and they provided appropriate structure and process to ensure the church could be protected and encouraged.

It's worth noting that in 1 Timothy, Paul gives instructions for how widows should be cared for in the Christian community: he writes of the need for a "list" (5:9, NIV), and gives specific criteria to ensure that only appropriate widows are put on this list (vv 9–11). It sounds a lot like an early form of an Excel spreadsheet—yes, Paul was telling Timothy that the churches should maintain a database! And Paul shows no embarrassment about creating a structured system to care for those in need. This wasn't an oddity within a loving, spiritual community. What's more, it suggests that the churches were large enough that it wasn't possible to keep track of the widows by simply knowing them personally (not surprising when people are being saved and added to their number every day!). This kind of organization was a proper expression of healthy love among God's gathered people.

There is a saying about socialism and conservatism: If you're not a socialist at twenty, you have no heart; if you're not a conservative at forty, you have no brain.[6] I have often thought that saying has some applicability to the life of the Spirit community. If you aren't drawn to the picture of the Spirit community being beautifully spontaneous and having everything in common without the need for structure and organization, then maybe you don't share the Spirit's heart. Surely this is the glory of God's purposes and of Jesus' disciples having heartfelt love for one another (John 13:34–35). Surely this is what it should look like when Jesus' disciples, changed by the Spirit under the new covenant and having the law of God written on their hearts (Jer 31:31–34), are being all that God intends for them to be.

And yet, if you remain wedded to the notion that this Spirit community can be all that God intends without order, structure, officers, organization and programs, then maybe you have no brains. Or maybe it's nicer to say that you haven't yet been fully "transformed by the renewal of your mind" (Rom 12:2). Our new life in the Spirit is lived out in a fallen world with fallen people who still carry around in them the "body of death" (Rom 7:24).

Six conclusions about church life

Once we grasp the nature of the church and the New Testament's parameters for how church life can (or should) be ordered, six conclusions may follow.

1. Organization, systems and structures are healthy and important aspects of life in a Spirit-filled church

A friend of mine describes an anti-institutional approach to church and ministry as 'beads-and-sandals Christianity'. That is, some people's attitude reflects a preference for anti-establishment, anti-organization approaches—almost like a hippie dropout thing.

I should hasten to add that I love hippies. I think it's part of having grown up on the beach. When this attitude is simply bound up with a love of nature, an enjoyment of the more earthy things in life, and a laid-back, relaxed approach to people and relationships, it is refreshing and enjoyable.

But when it is part of a larger idealism that imagines institutions and organizations are enemies of the truly healthy life, then it is foolish and always fails.

It is only possible to run the organic, freewheeling, share-every-thing-with-each-other kind of church while it is small and young—and even then, it is hardly easy! The Acts 2 church needed someone to be in the kitchen preparing the food and someone to look after the kids. It didn't 'just happen'. Add in the complexities of growth in size and age, and it just isn't possible, nor is it desirable. We will confront too many of the Acts 6-style complications.

This might not matter if our task is to simply enjoy being small.

But the commission Christ gave us has never been described as the 'small commission'. We have always recognized it for what it is: the *great* commission. We may love small and organic, casual and anti-establishment. But small and organic is never biblically required. What *is* biblically required is that we must be willing to lay aside our personal preferences for the sake of the salvation of others.

Acts seems to indicate that the very earliest Christian community gathered in a large group to listen to the apostles' teaching (see 5:12). They may have also broken out into smaller groups, but their practices appear largely to have been driven by practicality rather than by theological necessity. And recall the need for widows to be properly and thoughtfully "enrolled" from 1 Timothy 5, which suggests a community operating on a size and scale where it was impossible for the leadership to informally keep track of the needs of others.

The ideal presented in Acts 2 needs to be lived in reality. And reality requires structure, systems and management.

2. Systems and structures are not the ideal—they serve our pursuit of the ideal

The purpose of organization, systems and structures in church life is to maximize the opportunities for the ideal to be realized within a fallen world. This insight protects us from an inappropriate and unhealthy focus on structure, management, officers and administration.

The fact that Acts 2 and Acts 4 come before Acts 6 (extraordinary insight, I know) suggests very strongly that the appointment of 'deacons' in chapter 6 was simply a step towards organization and structure to help foster and nurture the ideal of chapters 2 and 4. I would suggest that the so-called 'diaconate' was simply the scaffolding that was a necessary aid in pursuit of the ideal amid the hard realities of life.

The organization, the administrative structures and the diaconal officers appointed within church life only properly exist in so far as they serve the ideal. They themselves are not the ideal. In other words, they are the means to the end, not the end.

Acts 2 contains a vitally important observation about church: it is an expression of a climactic moment in God's plans of salvation. Finally, this new reality has arrived—the Spirit of God has been poured out and now dwells in the heart of each of his people. There has been a profound transformation of heart and mind, fulfilling the promises of Ezekiel 36:

> I will sprinkle clean water on you, and you shall be clean from all your uncleannesses, and from all your idols I will cleanse you. And I will give you a new heart, and a new spirit I will put within you. And I will remove the heart of stone from your flesh and give you a heart of flesh. And I will put my Spirit within you, and cause you to walk in my statutes and be careful to obey my rules. (Ezek 36:25–27)

Every believer is now a 'priest', where all equally have access to the Father (see 1 Pet 2:5). All men and women can prophesy (see Acts 2:17–18). And the cleansing from sin because Christ has died, risen and ascended to now pour out his Spirit on all flesh means that love from the heart can be our experience. *These* are the ideals, the ultimate gospel realities that we should be pursuing in church life. These are the kinds of outcomes we are seeking.

We don't run church to have neat structures. 'Success' isn't implementing a great administrative process that works wonderfully. This isn't our desired output. It may well help us to achieve our desired output, but it is only good inasmuch as it helps us to see the gospel grow and bear fruit—which is seen most wonderfully in lives of love.

This is perhaps the key insight from Colin Marshall and Tony Payne's influential book *The Trellis and the Vine*:

> The basic work of any Christian ministry is to preach the gospel of Jesus Christ in the power of God's Spirit, and to see

people converted, changed and grow to maturity in that gospel. That's the work of planting, watering, fertilizing and tending the vine. However, just as some sort of framework is needed to help a vine grow, so Christian ministries also need some structure and support.[7]

This is what Marshall and Payne call the 'trellis' of ministry—the kinds of organizational and administrative support structures I've been describing. But the authors then warn how easy it is for the trellis—the institutions of church and ministry life—effectively to swamp the vine:

> Trellis work ... tends to take over from vine work. Perhaps it's because trellis work is easier and less personally threatening. Vine work is personal and requires much prayer. It requires us to depend on God, and to open our mouths and speak God's word in some way to another person.[8]

Ironically, a passion to be biblical can lead a church to focus on its structures rather than on God's mission of making and growing mature disciples of Christ. It is possible to read the New Testament's teaching on elders, deacons, bishops, 'lists' and membership, and then to imagine that the church—if it is to be the true church—must contain each and every piece of this puzzle. Once this happens, church can easily slide into functioning for the sake of facilitating these structures. From here, these structures come to identify the church as the church. Church is the business meeting, the budgets, and the incorporated association. We can easily confuse the legal and observable structures of our organizations *with* the church. The result is that we run church so that everything is as easy as possible for our church leaders, rather than expecting our church leaders to make the life of the Spirit community flourish and grow.

If this happens, the tail is wagging the dog.

At our church, we have worked hard to make it very clear that our legal Constitution (the legally incorporated dimension of our community life) is *not* the church. The rules contained within that Constitution simply describe the operation of a necessary legal structure that enables us to run the church in our part of the world. The church is properly understood, in the famous words of the 39 Articles of Religion, as "a congregation of faithful men [and women], in which the pure word of God is preached, and the Sacraments be duly ministered according to Christ's ordinance". It is a spiritual body defined by Christ and his word, not an institution defined by the law of the land or accountable to human rulers. It intersects with those things and so must organize itself to properly engage within them, but it isn't defined by them. In many contexts it might not need (or be allowed) to legally constitute itself, yet it remains the church of God.

Offices, structures and systems aren't the church. We don't run church *for* these things. We adopt whatever structures are needed and most helpful to build the biblical thing called 'church'.

3. Appropriate structures can preserve our evangelistic mission and outward focus

Every 15 years or so, another prophetic leader or another innovative group comes along and seeks to call us back to 'the Acts 2 ideal'. They will often bring with them a rejection of organization, structure, 'lists' and the like. Many idealistic young men will flock to them, as will many jaded old men. It is often the best of us, those with a true heart for the purposes of God, who are drawn to a naïve 'beads and sandals Christianity'. But it doesn't work in the context of the real world, just as Acts 2 gave way to Acts 6.

Moreover, the pursuit of this ideal often impedes evangelistic effectiveness, especially in Western settings. When people gather out of a desire to create 'intimacy' and 'community'—to be 'authentic' and to 'do life together'—this squeezes out the gospel imperative to grow by adding new members. Every new member changes the social dynamic, which threatens the very intimacy the group hoped to create. And so, perhaps subconsciously and despite having good intentions, such churches often create an intense and inward-looking culture that is hard for new people to penetrate.

A smaller and more intimate style of church can be outward looking and can grow well in a context where necessity, rather than a desire for intimacy, drives the strategy of 'smallness'. This has been true among house churches in places such as India and China, where small community wasn't the aim; gathering as the people of God was the aim, and small communities were the only option. But growth was still built into the culture and shape of church life.

Of course, it needs to be said that many older, more traditional churches and denominations have wedded themselves to forms that have become more important than the pursuit of gospel growth. For example, leaders and their followers cling to robes, vestments, choirs and organs, even when these things hinder their ability to reach new people. Many modern evangelicals look on from the outside, bewildered and frustrated that one specific form of church has become more important than the mission of the church.

But if we're not careful, we modern evangelicals can end up just as powerfully wedded to forms and structures that have come to be seen as biblical requirements, but which should properly be seen as matters of pragmatic freedom. We can buy into a way of doing church which becomes more fundamental than the effectiveness of the church in achieving its primary goals of making disciples and deepening them in the faith. It is possible that a church hasn't seen any converts for years, but it is sure it is doing church *the* right way—the way that it thinks most closely resembles the 'pure' New Testament church—and so consoles itself that its lack of fruit must be for other reasons.

4. We have a large degree of freedom in our church structures

Closely related to the last point, we should note that the 'diaconate' of Acts 6 came into existence because of a pragmatic need. It was a response to the needs of the time, not an eternal and ubiquitous form that is necessary for every church to truly be a church. Can church be church without this specific structure? Of course.

Owning and accepting this brings much-needed freedom. Structures can shift and change to serve the purposes of the local church in its place and time. There is no necessity, for example, to have a specific structure called a 'diaconate' if that structure doesn't serve the needs and the purposes of the local church.

This is true even though the office of 'deacon' appears more established in some of Paul's letters. The fact that Paul addresses deacons in Philippians 1, and that he gives qualifications for them in 1 Timothy 3, doesn't necessarily mean that they have now become essential elements in every truly biblical church. It is better to see the qualifications in 1 Timothy as a description of who may fill the role of deacon *if* a diaconate is needed.

We have a significant amount of freedom with respect to church structures. Principled pragmatism can drive our decisions without necessarily undermining our biblical heart.

5. Leaders must not think too highly of themselves

Yes, "if anyone aspires to the office of overseer, he desires a noble task" (1 Tim 3:1). To lead within the people of God is precious and valuable—but not in any absolute sense. A leader is still just one member of the body of Christ, one piece in the larger thing that is the church—the church over which Jesus Christ alone is the "chief Shepherd" (1 Pet 5:4). A leader leads, not because they are closer to God or uniquely endowed with the Spirit, but because they have been given one 'grace gift' (see Rom 12:6) which is "for the common good" (1 Cor 12:7). They lead with a desire to facilitate the new-covenant ideal of a beautiful equality of all the members of Christ's church. They lead "to equip the saints for the work of ministry, for building up the body of Christ" (Eph 4:12). History is littered with failures in this area—whether it be Roman Catholic, Anglican, the modern Charismatic movement, or independent church leaders who see themselves as indispensable to their church or movement.

6. A proper understanding of church helps us to remain clear on the outputs we are pursuing

What is the measure of how well things are going? Are we seeing more people bow the knee to Jesus and receive the salvation that he offers? Are we seeing people grow in the grace and knowledge of their Lord and Saviour Jesus Christ (2 Pet 3:18)? Are we seeing more people grasp what it is to be part of this new community that is saved by grace and endowed with the very Spirit of the living God? Are we seeing people transformed to become people of love? We will no longer measure 'success' by asking whether all our organizational ducks are in a row. Instead, we'll see organization as an input that can help us achieve our desired gospel outputs.

We ought to take care not to naively buy into 'beads-and-sandals Christianity'. It's appealing, but it isn't the whole picture. The Spirit-filled church needs to be lived out in the context of the realities of life. But once we accept those realities, we will find a large amount of freedom within which our churches can operate in pursuit of gospel growth.

Passages for further reflection

- Acts 2:42–47
- Acts 4:32–5:11
- Acts 6:2–7
- Ephesians 2:14–18

Questions for personal or team reflection

- Are there any points at which you are tempted to transgress the biblical boundaries that define what church must look like? Are you rejoicing in these boundaries and trusting the word of God?
- How can you better use the biblical freedom and flexibility to reform church life so that you might better fulfil your God-given mission?

Quote for personal and team reflection

"We know that every Church has liberty to frame for itself a form of government that is suitable and profitable for it, because the Lord has not prescribed anything definite." (John Calvin)

11

FREEDOMS AND BOUNDARIES FOR PASTORS

Shepherding the flock of God

Just as it is possible to unnecessarily constrain the shape and style of church, so it is possible to unnecessarily constrain our understanding of the role of 'pastor'. The result can be a view of pastoral ministry which impedes growth in any number of ways.

This isn't to say that a proper view of 'pastors' and 'pastoral ministry' will in itself produce growth, nor is it to say that the only important measure of pastoral ministry is whether it produces growth. That would be rampant pragmatism. Once again, we must embrace biblical patterns of ministry whether we believe they will produce growth—and we should do so gladly and joyfully! But it is possible to *think* we've adopted a biblical model when we've misread the Scriptures, and in so doing to unnecessarily hinder our ability to reach more people. Great care is needed here.

According to the New Testament, what is it to be a pastor within the people of God?

It is possible to focus on certain texts in the New Testament and adopt a very skewed position.

For example, in 1 Thessalonians 2, Paul expresses the deep

personal engagement that he and his colleagues (Silvanus and Timothy, see 1:1) had with the Thessalonian Christians:

> But we were gentle among you, like a nursing mother taking care of her own children. So, being affectionately desirous of you, we were ready to share with you not only the gospel of God but also our own selves, because you had become very dear to us.
>
> For you remember, brothers, our labour and toil: we worked night and day, that we might not be a burden to any of you, while we proclaimed to you the gospel of God. You are witnesses, and God also, how holy and righteous and blameless was our conduct toward you believers. For you know how, like a father with his children, we exhorted each one of you and encouraged you and charged you to walk in a manner worthy of God, who calls you into his own kingdom and glory. (1 Thess 2:7–12)

Paul and his colleagues were "like a nursing mother" and "like a father" to the Thessalonians. They weren't just messengers who preached with cool detachment, but they shared their "own selves". Add to this Jesus' language in John 10, where he describes himself as "the good shepherd" who, unlike the "hired hand", knows his sheep, cares for his sheep, and lays down his life for his sheep. From here, it is a short step to shaping the pastoral office in this way. Take, for example, these comments from Eugene Peterson reflecting on his own ministry:

> There are a lot of different ways to serve the Lord: evangelism, missionary work, organizational work, etc. A pastor has a unique place in all of this. I realized I needed to stick to what I was called to do. The way I understood the uniqueness of the pastoral vocation is that it is insistently personal. You cannot do pastoral work in a programmatic or impersonal or organizational way.
>
> You've got to know the names of these people, know their lives, be in their homes. The unique vocation of pastor is to

know those people. And at the same time, to know the scriptures, the whole world of scripture, so that stories of those people get integrated to the stories of scripture.[1]

In this view, to be a pastor equals knowing people's names and being in their homes. It is incompatible with an "impersonal" or "organizational" approach to ministry. We will all know people like this: godly people who elicit comments like "Isn't he a lovely man?" or "he's so pastoral!"

But is this right? Is this the essence of what it means to be a 'pastor'? If Peterson is right, it will shape the pastoral ministry in very strong directions and rule out many current practices. But if he is wrong, or if he has overstated the case, it will unnecessarily constrain the role in ways that will damage the mission and the task. It is critical to get this right.

Understanding New Testament terminology

To properly understand the meaning of 'pastor' according to the Scriptures, it is necessary to know that it has the same meaning as the word 'shepherd'; the two words are effectively the same—just different versions of the same idea with different linguistic backgrounds.[2] This observation opens up the larger canvas on which the meaning of the term can be painted.

The ancient near-east was very familiar with shepherds. The place was riddled with them. Importantly for our thinking, it was common for the word 'shepherd' to be applied metaphorically to *leaders* and *rulers* in many ancient near-eastern cultures; Israel wasn't alone in this. This helps to 'demystify' the word: 'shepherd' (or 'pastor') was in common use in all kinds of contexts, and its meaning within the Scriptures trades heavily on its meaning *outside* the Scriptures. That is, the term was applied to rulers and leaders, based on the assumed knowledge of what it meant to be a literal shepherd (or pastor). In particular, the use of the word relied on the fact that a literal shepherd didn't just lead his sheep; the best shepherd also *cared for* his sheep. He guided them, protected them, and fed them.

The Lord himself embraced this metaphor to convey the richness of what it means for him to be our God. This is captured perhaps most vividly in Psalm 23, which David opens with the breathtaking declaration, "The LORD is my shepherd" (Ps 23:1). But it was particularly apt for the God of Israel to embrace this language given that Israel was, in a sense, born in its wilderness wanderings. God led them through the wilderness as a shepherd leads his flock (e.g. Ps 77:20, 80:1; Isa 63:11).[3] So many features of the shepherding role come to mind with the use of this image: God went before them, directed them towards rich pastures, carried them when they struggled, and protected them from their enemies.

Extraordinarily, God appointed 'under-shepherds' who exercised shepherding leadership. Numbers 27 refers to Moses functioning as the shepherd of God's people, to be replaced by Joshua after his death "so the LORD's people will not be like sheep without a shepherd" (v 17, NIV). The sovereign Lord of the universe conveys such status to his creatures: responsibility (under him, of course) to guide, protect and nurture his people. Later, the kings of Israel assume this role, most explicitly David, who "shepherded [God's people] and guided them with his skillful hand" (Ps 78:72).

The use of shepherd language establishes a movement between Old and New Testaments. Shepherding leadership establishes a wonderful ideal, but one that isn't fully realized within the Old Testament. In the end, the Old Testament leaders of God's people failed to properly shepherd the people, seen most notably in the sustained prophecy "against the shepherds of Israel" in Ezekiel 34. These shepherds have fed themselves, but not the sheep: "The weak you have not strengthened, the sick you have not healed, the injured you have not bound up, the strayed you have not brought back, the lost you have not sought, and with force and harshness you have ruled them" (v 4). They may have ruled over the people, but they did not 'shepherd' the people. The prophecy ends with the stunning idea that the Lord himself will rescue his people *from* the shepherds— and he will do so by becoming their shepherd:

> I myself will be the shepherd of my sheep, and I myself will make them lie down, declares the Lord GOD. I will seek the lost, and I will bring back the strayed, and I will bind up the injured, and I will strengthen the weak, and the fat and the strong I will destroy. I will feed them in justice. (Ezek 34:15–16)

The New Testament is God's answer to the need and longing and promise of the Old Testament. The Gospel writers make this link explicit when they tell us that Jesus had compassion on the crowds when he saw that they were "like sheep without a shepherd" (Matt 9:36; Mark 6:34). Most vividly, Jesus himself makes this fulfillment obvious in John 10, where he refers very directly to the failures and the hopes expressed in Ezekiel 34, before declaring himself to be "the good shepherd" who "lays down his life for the sheep" (John 10:11, 14). Elsewhere in the New Testament we read that Jesus is "the great shepherd of the sheep" who equips his people with everything good so that they may do his will (Heb 13:20). He is "the Shepherd and Overseer of [our] souls" (1 Pet 2:25), the chief Shepherd from whom all new covenant 'under-shepherds' will derive their role (1 Pet 5:2).[4]

The links between testaments go even further. Alongside the promise that God himself would come to lead and shepherd his people, the Old Testament also includes the anticipation of the coming of multiple shepherds—'under-shepherds', who would mediate God's rule to his people:

> Then I will gather the remnant of my flock out of all the countries where I have driven them, and I will bring them back to their fold, and they shall be fruitful and multiply. I will set

shepherds over them who will care for them, and they shall fear no more, nor be dismayed, neither shall any be missing, declares the LORD. (Jer 23:3–4)

Peter is the most direct and vivid example of the fulfillment of this promise, when Jesus pointedly tells him, "tend my sheep" (literally "shepherd my sheep") and "feed my sheep" (John 21:16–17).[5]

So then, there is great unity of thought across the testaments with respect to the concept of 'shepherd': the New Testament trades on the language and ideas of the Old Testament, and carries those thoughts forward to their fulfillment in Jesus. But as these thoughts are brought forward into the New Testament, the language of 'shepherd' somewhat recedes into the background. It is still present, to be sure, but other important titles now emerge—titles such as 'elder', 'overseer' and 'leader'.

Yet the function and shape of the shepherding role never disappears. Although 'elder' and 'overseer' function as synonyms in Titus 1, for example,[6] 'shepherd' is what the elder or overseer does and who he is. When addressing the Ephesian *elders* (Acts 20:17), Paul exhorts them: "Pay careful attention to yourselves and to all the *flock*, in which the Holy Spirit has made you *overseers*, to care for [literally '*shepherd*'] the church of God, which he obtained with his own blood" (20:28). Peter exhorts the *elders* to "*shepherd the flock* of God that is among you" and to be "examples to the *flock*" (1 Pet 5:1–3). In Ephesians 4, where Paul describes the foundational gifts that the risen Christ has given to his church, one of those is the role of the '*shepherd-teacher*' (Eph 4:11) or 'pastor-teacher'.[7] Grammatically in the original language, this is clearly one gift.[8] This means that the role of shepherd-teacher corresponds to the role of 'elder-teacher', because the elder (or overseer) is responsible for teaching within the household of faith (see 1 Tim 3:2; Titus 1:9).

All this is to say that the terms 'shepherd' (or 'pastor'), 'elder' and 'overseer' are essentially synonymous in the New Testament. But they remain culturally charged synonyms.[9] And given the roots of the New Testament church within the confines of the Jewish world, it is unsurprising that 'eldership' emerges as the most natural term for leadership in the early stages of church history (see Acts 11).

Critically, each of the words used for the leader suggest just that: that they *lead* or *rule*. The 'elder' is the older man who carries authority within his sphere of influence.[10] This function was well established in the Jewish setting, with an eldership body often leading within the Jewish community. The language of 'shepherd' carries this same sense: David, as the king of Israel, *"shepherded* [God's people] and *guided* them with his skillful hand"* (Ps 78:72); the Lord *"led* [his] people like a flock by the hand of Moses and Aaron"* (Ps 77:20). Joshua succeeded Moses as Israel's shepherd by leading the people, so they would "not be as sheep that have no shepherd" (Num 27:17). First Peter 5 brings this notion of leadership into the New Testament role.

This leadership is chiefly exercised through the word of God. In the Old Testament, this happened through the process of leaders "inquiring" of the Lord (e.g. Exod 18:15; Judg 18:5), but in the New Testament it happens through the process of bringing the very word of God to bear on the life of the community. This is why being "able to teach" is essential to the qualification of elder or overseer. God is a speaking God who has breathed out his written word for us (see 2 Tim 3:16–17), and Christianity is a word-based system of belief where we are called to hear the "living and active" word of God and respond in trust (see Heb 4:12–13). Teachers, therefore, take on a critical role (see Jas 3:1).

So, what emerges as the essence of the shepherd's (or elder's, or overseer's, or pastor's) task? *The shepherd is to lead, rule, protect and tend the flock of God by feeding them with the word of God.* This is the essence of the task.

This isn't to suggest for a moment that the shepherd is to dominate or control the sheep. It is so easy for the sinful heart to take hold of words like 'lead' and 'rule' in such a way that we justify mistreating the people of God. Peter perfectly captures the essence of the way the shepherd should conduct himself as he fulfills this task (using many of our key words along the way):[11]

> So I exhort the *elders* among you, as a fellow *elder* and a witness of the sufferings of Christ, as well as a partaker in the glory that is going to be revealed: *shepherd the flock* of God that is among you, exercising *oversight*, not under compulsion, but willingly, as God would have you; not for shameful gain, but eagerly; not domineering over those in your charge, but being examples to *the flock*. And when the *chief Shepherd* appears, you will receive the unfading crown of glory. (1 Pet 5:1–4)

Those who are "younger" are then urged to "be subject to the elders", but *all*—whether elder or younger—are to show "humility toward *one another*, for 'God opposes the proud but gives grace to the humble'" (v 5). While shepherds rule and lead the people (by teaching the word of God), they must never do so for their own gain (remember the fate of the shepherds who fed themselves in Ezekiel 34).

Many have attempted to capture these concepts with the phrase "servant leadership".[12] As good as this phrase is when properly understood, I'm afraid it often tends towards a denial of any exercise of leadership and lands with a sense that shepherds are always and only to do as the congregation directs—a kind of servant that never actually leads. The 'servant' adjective effectively negates the 'leadership' noun.

The point is that the biblical shape of pastoral leadership is somewhat different from many popular descriptions. The 'shepherd' is to lead, rule, protect, feed and direct, caring for the sheep as he feeds them by the word.

GROWTH AND CHANGE

Shepherding for growth and change

Having summarized the essence of the task of a shepherd or pastor—albeit briefly—let's consider three implications for pastoral leadership, especially as it relates to how shepherds can keep a passion for growth and lead God's people into change.

1. The importance of being insistently personal

Eugene Peterson is certainly correct to note that the role of pastor/shepherd must be "insistently personal". Even a cursory appreciation of the role throughout the Bible reveals how profoundly personal it is (and was). The language of leadership and authority is coloured with strong notes of care and tenderness. The shepherd is to "pay careful attention ... to all the flock", knowing that danger is never far away (Acts 20:28–29). Leading God's people is never a matter of just 'managing the business'. It is highly personal, with focused care for each member of the flock. The tone of Peterson's comment quoted above is exactly right. A shepherd who lacks intense, personal care for the flock of God, and for each of the sheep, is likely to be a disaster.

2. Maintaining a vision for growth

But while it is right to note that the task is "insistently personal", we should also note what we might call the 'limits' of a shepherd's personal care—not that we could ever place limits on how much we care for people, of course, but that we may limit the requirements for exactly how this care must be exercised.

As we have noted, leaders like Moses and David were designated as 'shepherds', which means that we cannot conflate "insistently personal" with knowing everybody's name and being in their homes. If Moses or David took to heart Peterson's definition of being 'pastoral', it is hard to see how they would have survived in the role![13]

For all Paul's closeness and warmth with the people he shepherded, he moved on to new locations. He handed people over to the care of others. That is, his "insistently personal" concern wasn't antithetical to his larger vision. His care for people didn't prevent him from stepping back, delegating, and expanding his work.

Paul's words in 1 Thessalonians 2, and Jesus' comments about knowing his sheep in John 10, should colour our understanding of the shepherding role. And while these passages don't constrain a true shepherd to pastor a group that is small enough for him to know everyone personally, the Bible's language drives us away from impersonal leadership models. The shepherd of God's people can never operate as a kind of CEO who uses the people for his own purposes, remains distant and aloof, or is cold and demanding as he runs the 'business'. Rather, pastors must be "examples to the flock" under their care (1 Pet 5:3). A pastor must serve people willingly, without lording it over the flock. These images should have a huge influence on our exercise of pastoral authority. The truly biblical pastor must exemplify the normal Christian life, which is one of love and care.

The church and its members must never become fodder for a zealous and driven pastor's machine. The people of God must never be abused and manipulated by insecure leaders who cannot see beyond their own ego. In our day and age, far too many of Christ's beloved sheep have been bullied and mistreated by leaders whose passion for growth—often the growth of their own empire rather than the growth of God's kingdom—has led them to treat people as a means to an end, or as 'collateral damage' in service of their empire-building efforts, rather than as precious members of the flock of God to be nurtured, defended and loved. This is another great danger for leaders who have a passion for growth.

And yet we mustn't throw out the baby with the bathwater. We mustn't set up a false antithesis where we either care for people or lead them forward to make sacrifices for the sake of the gospel. What's more, we don't guard against an impersonal CEO model of ministry by embracing an unnecessarily narrow conception of shepherd/pastor. This profoundly reduces a leader's ability to grow the work and impact communities.

There is a very real possibility that our traditions of ministry practice have inadvertently collapsed the 'deacon' role into the 'elder' role, thus creating a job that allows no real room for leadership. But it is striking that in the book of Acts, two of the seven men named as 'deacons' in chapter 6 are immediately seen exercising word ministry: Stephen delivers a long address before the Jewish ruling council and becomes the first Christian martyr in chapter 7; Philip preaches the gospel in Samaria and leads the Ethiopian eunuch to Christ in chapter 8. There is also some evidence that the 'deacon' was to be the 'minister of the word' in the context of a closer, more personal ministry.[14] That is, they didn't just 'wait on tables' as some kind of exalted administrator, but expanded the ministry of the word into the context of individuals and families. They were likely the ones who visited homes and engaged with the individual needs of church members. This is one of the reasons why many have suggested that women were appointed as deacons:[15] they could properly and appropriately minister in the homes of widows.[16]

3. Titles aren't sacrosanct, but clarity in roles is vital

Titles for church leaders shift according to the cultural setting (Jewish contexts preferring 'elder', but Gentile contexts preferring 'overseer'). There was and is no necessity to use one word over the other. Paul and Peter, being Jewish, may have preferred the term 'elder', but given the flexibility in New Testament usage it is impossible to insist that there is only one way to designate the leadership of a church.

What matters much more than terminology is that leaders are identified within the community as having a particular role, and that they perform the functions of a shepherd—leading, caring, feeding, protecting and guiding. What does an elder/overseer/pastor/shepherd/minister *do*? Remember, the essence of the task is to lead and

rule the people of God by teaching and exemplifying the word of God
—the attributes required of 'elders' and 'overseers' in 1 Timothy 3
and Titus 1 are elsewhere required of all believers.

But further to this, what is implicit in the requirement to manage
his family well is made explicit in the use of 'overseer' for the role of
leader. The use of the word in its contemporary setting carries an
important sense of management and organization. As DA Carson
notes, "'Overseer' conjures up administrative and ruling functions".[17]
He continues:

> As important and central as is the ministry of the Word of God,
> the thoughtful pastor/elder/overseer will devote time and
> energy to casting a vision, figuring out the steps for getting
> there, building the teams and structures needed for discharg-
> ing ministry and training others, building others up, thinking
> through the various ways in which the gospel can be taught at
> multiple levels to multiple groups within the church, how to
> extend faithful evangelism and church planting, how to engage
> the surrounding world as faithful believers, and much more.[18]

Carson is getting at an important truth here: biblical oversight
should not be limited to the Sunday sermon, as though this is the
extent of a shepherd's leadership. Of course, this is *essential*, but it is
not *enough*.[19] A pastor's theological leadership is seen not just in the
pulpit, but also in every decision that he makes and in the overall
direction that he leads the church. Carson says:

> Just because a person is an able preacher does not necessarily
> make him an able pastor/elder/overseer. Indeed, if he shows
> no propensity for godly oversight, then no matter how good a
> teacher he may be, he is not qualified to be a pastor/teacher/
> overseer. It is not for nothing that Scripture applies all three
> labels to the one office.[20]

Which model? Balancing boundaries and flexibility

The nature of a pastor's role raises an important issue: Is pastoral leadership best seen as a form of solo leadership, or does it happen as part of a group? Our answer to this question relates to the wider issue of maintaining an appropriate balance between observing biblical boundaries and employing biblical freedoms in the way we structure our ministries.

This is no doubt a hotly debated issue, and I don't intend to try and resolve such a longstanding question in a few short paragraphs. I'll offer just a few brief comments in keeping with the purpose of this book.

There are some indications that a normal pattern of church leadership included plurality (e.g. Acts 14:23; Titus 1:5; Jas 5:14). But many throughout history have suggested that it goes beyond the intent of these passages to insist there *must* be a plurality. For instance, commenting on Titus 1:5, John Calvin says:

> It is a point which ought to be carefully observed, that churches cannot safely remain without the ministry of pastors, and that consequently, wherever there is a considerable body of people, a pastor should be appointed over it. And yet he does not say that each town shall have a pastor, so that no place shall have more than one; but he means that no towns shall be destitute of pastors.[21]

In a similar vein, DA Carson has written about the care that should be taken to avoid overreading the biblical material (while also suggesting that churches are wise to err on the side of a plurality of elders):

> As far as I can see, there is no absolute biblical rule requiring that a certain number of elders is necessary for larger churches, or that a percentage of the congregation must be elders. Of course, one might reasonably argue that there is safety in

numbers; even more reasonably, one might argue that one should not appoint as elders those who are unqualified. Probably it is true to say that in the New Testament there is a bias towards a plurality of elders in the church, but instantly one recalls that the New Testament local "church" might have numerous "house churches" or assemblies comprising it.[22]

There is some evidence that suggests many churches in the ancient world functioned with a single elder. And it has long been the case that wherever there is a plurality of leaders, one overall leader emerges (think, for example, of James in the Jerusalem church). This is an almost-universal reality of humans organizing themselves into community. At the very least, groups need a 'chairman' or 'first among equals' to provide direction, while at the same time recognizing the wisdom of plurality and operating with a strong gravitational pull in this direction.

The key point is that we must be careful not to mandate one leadership structure if the clear teaching of Scripture doesn't require it, especially if it would constrain our biblical freedom to adapt ourselves for the sake of mission and ministry. If it is true that the Bible offers us greater flexibility in the structuring of church life than we have assumed, then we are wise to notice this and to allow the appropriate freedoms. In certain situations or during certain seasons, there may be wisdom in not appointing a plurality of elders; I would argue that this is never a good idea over the long haul, but this conclusion owes more to pragmatics and to biblically informed wisdom than to any firm biblical injunction. Further to this, 'pastoring' need not require intense engagement with every person 'pastored', but it should include a higher level of concern for management and organization than has often been thought. And it need not demand plurality, though there is much wisdom in operating together with others.[23]

Many good and godly people enter pastoral work because of a desire to be personally involved in people's lives. We can easily bring our own personalities into our reading of the biblical evidence, or perhaps we look at slick megachurches and react against the apparent loss of the "insistently personal" facet of pastoral care. Perhaps we reject the 'Pastor as CEO' model that seems to emerge from these kinds of churches. We are right to push back on many abuses. But we must take care not to overreach and so create church structures and patterns of leadership that ultimately—and without proper biblical warrant—stifle possible growth.

For example, I've noticed that many leaders simplistically use the language of 'family' for church life. Church is certainly a family—or better, "the household of God" (1 Tim 3:15). But we can import our own experience of family, whatever that may be, and assume that church life should therefore follow corresponding patterns. Many today are choosing smaller families with the thought that it gives each child 'more of the parents'. This is surely wrong-headed and fails to appreciate that there is more to the health of a family then intense parenting. Likewise, there is much more to the health of a church than intense pastoring. A very large family may need a great deal of order, structure and discipline to function, and each child may get relatively little intense one-on-one time with Mum or Dad— yet the family can still thrive. If the church is "the household of God", we need to acknowledge that there are many healthy ways for a family or household to function.

To take another example, some are tempted to import a model of 'pastoral ministry' that took shape in the 'age of Christendom'—a model that was perhaps more chaplain-oriented. Think of the 'village pastor' or the 'country parson'—the kind of spiritual leader who exercised their role in a context where everyone in the parish was part of the church. This pastor was highly engaged in the inner life of the wider community. Accordingly, he would see it as his task to work with each of his members—which meant every person in the general vicinity.

Today, with the collapse of Christendom (or perhaps with the realization that it ceased to exist long ago), the leader needs to be far more than the 'community chaplain'. We should be slow to extrapolate from this model, or from the 'church as family' model, or from any single model of church life, to a far-reaching model for how every pastorate must function.

We need leaders of churches who are first and foremost shepherds, not business managers or CEOs. The leader's 'default setting', his instinct and fallback position, will profoundly shape the culture of the church. If the leader is a business-minded thinker who assumes the role of pastor, the church community is very likely to be coloured as a business that looks a bit like a family. But if the leader is a biblically minded shepherd who has also learned some management skills, or who also brings gifts of leadership to bear, they will keep dripping biblical, pastoral colour into the life of the church community. Their 'default setting' will be to care for, guard and lead the flock by the ministries of the word and prayer, rather than relying primarily on structure and strategic management resources.

But again, this sense of pastoral 'colour' doesn't narrowly control or define leadership. So much of the shape of the offices of church life is pragmatically driven (though not all of the shape, of course). Leaders are a gift that God has given to his church, and they are to lead. Exercising leadership—so long as it is shaped by servant models, as exemplified by Christ—is a blessing for God's people. And leading an organization, even a unique organization like the church, necessarily entails consideration of how to manage resources wisely, how to steward what God has given, how to mobilize and delegate, how to provide for the present and future needs of the organization, and so forth.

There is a grave danger that we run from a 'pastor-as-CEO', business-style model and instead embrace the 'beads-and-sandals' conception of Christian leadership that makes a hero out of being non-managerial, non-directive and non-strategic. Ironically, embracing this model can create either a controlling and centralized form of leadership or an entirely problem-centred leadership. Both errors fail to 'unleash' the church community for ministry because leadership is conceived in very tight and specific forms: it is all about the pastor being heavily invested in the lives of all the sheep, because that is what a shepherd does. This can *feel* biblical. But it becomes pastor-dominated and fails to create an Ephesians 4 church where all God's people are equipped for works of service and genuinely mobilized for ministry. This kind of shepherd will probably notice a lack of ministry initiative among the 'flock', but is unlikely to notice that the way his leadership is being exercised is the cause of this problem.

God gives shepherd-teachers to the church for a purpose: they are given, under God, to lead a Spirit-filled community where every member serves so that the body is built up. This is the Ephesians 4 model. But this won't just happen because there is a shepherd who 'teaches' regularly from the Bible. In the real world of Acts 6, more thought is required to get communities of people to become all that God longs for them to be.

The flock of God needs to be led. Pastors need to lead—pastors whose core concern and conviction is that the members of their church community are under their care, not a resource to be managed or utilized. And a pastor's greatest concern for those under his care will be the spiritual development of each and every person. Notice again Paul's emphasis in Colossians 1: "Him we proclaim, warning *everyone* and teaching *everyone* with all wisdom, that we may present *everyone* mature in Christ" (Col 1:28). This means that the life of the pastor as a model and exemplar of the faith is absolutely critical. What matters more than his management skills is his life with God, which flows out into everything else that he does.

Passages for further reflection

- Ezekiel 34:15–16
- Acts 20:17–38
- 1 Timothy 3:1
- 1 Peter 5:1–5

Questions for personal or team reflection

- (For those who are leaders.) Are you leading God's flock willingly and eagerly? Are you being a godly example to the flock?
- How can you better use the biblical freedom and flexibility to reform the shape of your ministry and enable more effective mission and ministry to happen?

Quote for personal or team reflection

"As important and central as is the ministry of the Word of God, the thoughtful pastor/elder/overseer will devote time and energy to casting a vision, figuring out the steps for getting there, building the teams and structures needed for discharging ministry and training others, building others up, thinking through the various ways in which the gospel can be taught at multiple levels to multiple groups within the church, how to extend faithful evangelism and church planting, how to engage the surrounding world as faithful believers, and much more." (DA Carson)

12

LEADING WITH OUTCOMES
AT THE CENTRE

Taking aim—but at what?

With many pieces of my argument now in place, I want to suggest the one major change that should follow in our leadership activity: a shift from being input-focused to being output-focused.

What emerges from the pages of the New Testament is a style of leadership among God's people that is focused on achieving certain outcomes, and even taking some measure of responsibility for achieving those outcomes.[1] In other words, church leaders must be output-focused, rather than simply input-focused.[2] The pastor is the leader who not only takes responsibility for doing their task faithfully and well; he also takes some responsibility for the care and growth outcomes for the sheep under his care (one set of outcomes) and for leading those people into making more disciples—seeing more and more men and women won to Christ (another set of outcomes).

Pastoral leadership must be output-oriented.

In one sense, this is just an expression of a basic principle of leadership. Because it is a complex activity, it is difficult to offer one simple definition. But surely, at the most basic level, a leader is a person who *takes responsibility for leading*, which must surely involve *seeking to move an individual or group towards achieving an outcome that they otherwise would not have arrived at on their own.*

In other words, leadership is not just facilitation. A facilitator helps a person or group get to an outcome they were already moving towards. This is a good thing to do, and it might be one activity a good leader does, but it is not the core idea of leadership. A leader is responsible for the more fundamental task of moving a person or a group of people towards something they wouldn't have achieved on their own, *and may not even have wanted to pursue on their own.* This will sometimes involve elements of facilitation, but it will sometimes involve redirection—encouraging someone towards a goal that they weren't previously heading towards. The commander of a platoon of soldiers who gets his platoon to attack a well-entrenched hill is a highly successful leader. Without leadership, they weren't going anywhere near that hill. Of course, a better leader enables them not just to attack the hill, but to take the hill.[3]

This brings us back to the often-unnoticed element of leadership: integral to the task is a *focus on outcomes*, and even on taking responsibility for achieving those outcomes. The leader is intent on achieving an outcome and will move a person or a group towards achieving that outcome. They lead people *towards* something, which necessarily means leading them away from other things.

The French revolutionary Alexandre Auguste Ledru-Rollin is reported to have said, "There go my people. I must find out where they're going so I can lead them." It turns out that the quote is probably apocryphal, but it is often repeated because the sentiment being expressed is not uncommon. A leader who isn't actively leading people *towards something* is not, in fact, a leader; they are just another member.

This may seem like an obvious insight, but sometimes it is the obvious things that need attention. And the burden of the previous chapters has been to demonstrate that this is integral to the Bible's presentation of leadership among God's people. And in my experience, for many people this is not so obvious after all. It's just not how they think about churches or church leadership.

Let me use a classic illustration: how does an archer fire an arrow? They set up a target, pick up the bow and arrow, carefully take aim at the target, ready themselves to shoot, and release the arrow. If the arrow misses the target, they adjust their aim and fire again.

How does the church fire its arrows? All too often, we pick up the bow and arrow, ready ourselves to shoot, and just fire away. Then we proceed to draw the target wherever the arrow has landed so the arrow sits neatly in the bullseye.

This is a lovely, friendly way to do archery, because you never need to worry about missing. And you certainly never feel any pain— except perhaps about the quality of your stance and technique, or about whether your arrow wobbles violently or sails smoothly and gracefully through the air on its way to landing in a bush.

But when you start with an output in mind, when you are trying to hit a specific target and achieve something, and when you take seriously your responsibility for hitting the target, you start feeling the pain if you miss. But you can also reshape what you do. You can correct, learn, adapt and change, so that your work starts to achieve the outcomes you're seeking. You have a clear basis on which to critique your performance and strive to do better.

It is crucial for the life of a church that the leader (whether we call him 'pastor', 'elder' or 'minister') is clear about outcomes and lives and breathes outcomes, *while also being deeply concerned with inputs*. And it is crucial that the leader brings others with him in pursuit of these outcomes.

Inputs are vital

I am very aware of those who would critique these assertions by insisting that Christian leadership is about being focused diligently on inputs. The thinking goes something like this: we can't control outputs—only God is in charge of those—so surely we ought to focus all our attention on what we *can* control: the inputs. We should focus on setting and meeting targets around the number (and length) of gospel conversations we have, the number (and length) of sermons we preach, the number of evangelistic events offered, the number of hours spent in prayer (both privately and in prayer meetings), and so on. It is said that we can control these inputs, and so we are properly held accountable for them. Taking this approach is thought to separate our part in the work from God's part in the work.

But it must be noted that, if we are to be consistent in our biblical thinking, we are not in complete control of the inputs. Calvin discusses this issue when commenting on 2 Peter 1: "Scripture ... plainly testifies, that right feelings are formed in us by God, and are rendered by him effectual. It testifies also that all our progress and perseverance are from God." He adds that when Peter demands certain qualities in us, "he by no means asserts that they are in our power, but only shews what we ought to have, and what ought to be done".[4]

Paul raises these very same issues in Philippians 2:

> Therefore, my beloved, as you have always obeyed, so now, not only as in my presence but much more in my absence, work out your own salvation with fear and trembling, for it is God who works in you, both to will and to work for his good pleasure. (Phil 2:12–13)

We only work out our salvation because God is at work in us, which means it is simplistic to suggest we can take responsibility for inputs because they are somehow under our control. The very faith through which we are saved is a gift of God (Eph 2:8). Paul assessed his own ministry by saying, "I worked harder than any of them, though it was not I, but the grace of God that is with me" (1 Cor 15:10). He toiled and struggled with all *God's* energy that powerfully worked in him (Col 1:29). Jesus told his disciples, "apart from me you can do nothing" (John 15:5). Under the sovereign hand of God, we 'control' nothing in any absolute sense.

Even so, the sentiment around this input-based thinking has much to commend it. And I must confess to feeling a great deal of sympathy towards this position. It helps to protect us from human-centred ministry thinking and from unfettered pragmatism (though it doesn't fully secure that protection). It seeks to glorify God by emphasizing the centrality of his power and purposes. And the Bible certainly places a heavy emphasis on leaders being committed to certain inputs. The pastoral epistles speak about this at length. For example:

> First of all, then, I urge that supplications, prayers, intercessions, and thanksgivings be made for all people, for kings and all who are in high positions, that we may lead a peaceful and quiet life, godly and dignified in every way. This is good, and it is pleasing in the sight of God our Saviour, who desires all people to be saved and to come to the knowledge of the truth. (1 Tim 2:1–4)

> Until I come, devote yourself to the public reading of Scripture, to exhortation, to teaching. (1 Tim 4:13)

> I charge you in the presence of God and of Christ Jesus, who is to judge the living and the dead, and by his appearing and his kingdom: preach the word; be ready in season and out of season; reprove, rebuke, and exhort, with complete patience and teaching. ... Always be sober-minded, endure suffering, do the work of an evangelist, fulfill your ministry. (2 Tim 4:1–2, 5)

> But as for you, teach what accords with sound doctrine. ... Show yourself in all respects to be a model of good works, and in your teaching show integrity, dignity, and sound speech

that cannot be condemned, so that an opponent may be put to shame, having nothing evil to say about us. (Titus 2:1, 7–8)

Certain inputs are fundamental and must remain in the foreground. Pastor-teachers are bound to them, and we should regularly take stock of our effectiveness and faithfulness in delivering these inputs. Are we being diligent in prayer? Are we working hard at our preaching? Are we sharing the gospel with unbelievers? Are we creating new opportunities—or reinvigorating old opportunities—to engage people with the word of God? In all our areas of responsibility, are the ministries fit for purpose?

Inputs are vital, but are not enough

But a focus on inputs from leaders isn't the only drive through the New Testament. We can't control outcomes (just as we don't ultimately control inputs), but we do influence them. And at certain times and in certain ways, we are held responsible for outcomes. Recall, for instance, Paul's discussion in 1 Corinthians 3: alongside his emphatic declaration that only God makes things grow (vv 6–7), he discusses the importance of the quality of one's work. Some will "receive a reward", while others see their work "burned up" (vv 10–15).

In the Great Commission, Jesus doesn't say that we should make it our ambition to preach the gospel (though this is a biblical expression; see Rom 15:20). The charge is to "make disciples"; it is focused more on the output than the input. Further to this, Paul models a ministry that is deeply devoted to outputs—even though he knows he doesn't control them. Remember Colossians 1:28–29, where Paul mentions inputs—the message he proclaims—but retains a dogged and determined focus on outputs—what the inputs are meant to achieve. Remember 1 Corinthians 9, where Paul is flexible about everything (except the gospel) in order that he (not just God) might save some.

As Bible-believing pastors, we must be deeply concerned for and committed to biblical inputs. But in all that we do, we must be driven and shaped by a focused concern to see outputs achieved, owning our responsibilities in leading the church towards them.

Making the shift

This shift to a more output-focused leadership is hard for many church leaders. It is hard because of the theological issues raised throughout this book. It is hard because we know that the outputs depend, at least in some measure, on our inputs, but we don't always know how to change our inputs in order to achieve the desired outputs. And it is hard because of our ministry training and backgrounds, and because of the contexts within which we work.

Our training can be heavily focused on 'getting the Bible right'. This is good—vital, in fact! But this good thing can cast a negative shadow: it can tend towards developing leaders who stop at thinking about the inputs. What's more, our work context is one where it isn't always easy to be clear on the outcomes we're seeking—how do you measure 'outcomes' when the aim is maturity in Christ? And in any case, who will hold us accountable? A leader in an established church is paid a regular salary, which can mean that there is no enforced 'feedback loop' to help us reflect on whether we are missing the mark or failing to see any outcomes. Often, the only area in which we are forced to confront the reality of outcomes is church finances: we set targets (we call them 'budgets') and, despite not being able to control the money, we sense a degree of responsibility for hitting these targets. Most of us have no choice, because if we don't hit this target, we don't eat.

Yet we can feel awkward about this because we refuse to set specific targets for anything else. We persuade ourselves that it is wrong to set targets on things we can't control, despite having just done so with money.[5] This means that we can live in a confused and inconsistent world, which many in our congregation find strange and bizarre (although they too appreciate being 'let off the hook').

For all these reasons and more, we are drawn back to largely focusing on inputs—on the daily and weekly tasks that need doing, the preparation of sermons, the regular prayer times, the pastoral visitation, the management meetings, and so on. And for most of us, there is plenty of this to be focused on—our lives are kept very full just worrying about the inputs.

But while the shift from input thinking to output thinking is very difficult for ministry leaders to make, I cannot see how we can avoid it—both biblically and practically.

Output-focused leadership brings with it great strengths and benefits, but it also brings some dangers and potential downsides. And yes, in describing and analyzing these strengths and weaknesses we are moving once again into the realm of pragmatics. But these can (and must) be theologically principled pragmatics that operate within biblical boundaries.

So, let's think about these strengths and dangers, starting with the strengths.

Focus, intentionality and results

Generally speaking, an output-focused ministry gets better results. It is an observable fact that church plants tend to see more people converted than established churches. Why should this be? In my experience, it is because of a difference in the way both kinds of church view outputs.

In a church plant, there is an almost-unavoidable focus on taking responsibility for outputs. This is so not just with the leadership, but also among the core members. The leader is focused on outputs, for he knows that if he doesn't secure that new visitor or win that slightly interested outsider, his church is going to crash. And so, he chases every lead with enthusiasm. He borders on stalking to get that new person connected.

But this isn't just how the leader operates. The congregation members are intuitively focused on outputs. The leader doesn't have to say much to encourage a group of people to focus on the output of seeing people converted and changed when they turn up to church each week and see a group of only 30 or 40 others. Every week, they can't avoid the fact that they will need to devote themselves to getting new people to come, or getting that first-time visitor connected. Every new person who comes close to church is surrounded by a crowd of congregation members like bees to honey. If we don't do these things, we fail. It's that simple. This brings focus, which brings intentionality, which produces growth.

But after a time, the growth slows. This usually happens around the time a church hits 'viability': the point where it is now paying its own bills and feels like an established reality—a 'going concern'. At this point, the regulars can turn up to church without being confronted by anything that screams 'focus on outputs'. This produces a drift towards input thinking, at least in the congregation. A new person can walk into church and go almost unnoticed—a few keener people will still take an interest, but the rest will no longer go the extra mile. We can now turn our attention to 'just being faithful'. We can settle into comfortable ruts.

This dynamic plays out in so many areas of life, not just gospel ministry.

When I was growing up, my father would task me with mowing the lawns. I did it (not as often as I should've), but it was just a task to tick off the to-do list so I could get back to relaxing as quickly as possible. My focus was entirely on the input of mowing the lawn.

But now, as a man who owns his own lawn, I mow with an output mindset. I'm focused on the difference that the inputs make because

I want the yard and the house to look nice. I complete the task, but I do it with a different type of energy and enthusiasm. I am motivated; I appreciate the value and purpose of the task. I go the extra mile because I'm invested in the outcome.

Think of the steps a student will take to get an assignment finished when they know they will be judged not just on the sincerity of the attempt or the amount of time spent on the task, but on the quality of the material they produce. Think of the weight of responsibility a parent feels for their children—the sense that, in some way, their parenting could make or break their child's eternity—and the way this will motivate them to action. I know that if I fail to model a Christ-centred life to my children, if I fail to bring the word of God to bear on their lives, if I prioritize my own comfort, I will influence them *away* from Christ and not towards him. This sense of the intimate connection between my input and the output of faith in their lives moves me to action.

Examining our preaching and our ministries

To return to the specific theme of Christian leadership, consider our evangelistic preaching. In his essay 'Christian Work', Charles Spurgeon addressed a young evangelist who was concerned about the lack of response to his preaching:

> Above all, we must work for God with confident faith in him. "We have not because we ask not." We have not success because we have not faith. A young brother said to me once, "I have preached in the streets, and I have seen no converts." I said to him, "Do you expect people to be converted every time you preach?" He replied, very humbly, "No, sir." When I said, "That is the reason you do not succeed, because you do not expect to do so. According to your faith so be it unto you."[6]

When you preach for response (output), you preach slightly differently than if you are merely preaching to present truths faithfully (input). This is true whether you're preaching evangelistically or to a congregation mostly comprising Christians. You follow the apostolic example and "exhort", "implore" or "teach and urge" your hearers to respond rightly to the word of God (see Acts 2:40; 2 Cor 5:20; 1 Tim 6:2). You work hard not just at exegeting your text and getting your passage right, but at understanding your hearers and applying the Bible to their hearts and minds.

Paul Grimmond is Dean of Students at Moore College in Sydney, where he also lectures in Mission and Ministry. His doctoral thesis is on equipping students at Moore "to develop biblically faithful, relevant application in preaching". Grimmond says that the College possesses great strengths in helping students to hone their skills in exegesis and theology—in "getting God's truth right from the Bible".[7] Few who know the College well would dispute this assessment, and it is essential—and cause for great rejoicing—that any Bible college would possess such strengths. But Grimmond also writes with honesty and penetrating insight about what he calls the program's "downside":

> Because their exegetical skills are finely honed, and because of the value placed on the truth, students tend to spend most of their preparation time exegeting the passage and writing the sermon, rather than on reflection and application. The resulting sermons sound like a verbal commentary. Anecdotally, people from the churches where our students minister report a lack of connection between the students' preaching and real life.
>
> In response, we have begun trying to emphasize application in the proclamation workshops. But the effect has not always been positive. As one colleague described these groups recently, "It's like they got the exegesis spot on, then closed their eyes, fired an arrow randomly into the air, opened their

eyes to see where it landed and said, 'That looks like a good place to do application!'" While the students can see the need for relevant and faithful application, apart from a few notable exceptions they do not currently possess the skills required to move from the text to application.

What has become increasingly apparent is that while Moore College is providing a framework and methodology for exegesis, it is not necessarily providing a framework and methodology for application. Given that many of our students move to roles involving significant preaching ministries post college, and most of our students will be involved in ministries where biblical application is crucial, the need for training in biblical application is vital. ...

Our students' sermons are often perceived as dry, or in reaction to this, the student majors on application without sufficient connection to the exegesis of the passage in question. Neither option is helpful or fruitful. If churchgoers hear those who have been to theological college preaching sermons that don't feel grounded or practical, it reinforces an unhealthy distinction between head Christianity and heart Christianity. This can lead either to mysticism, for those who react against the dryness of the preaching, or to a doctrinaire formalism that values truth without its substance. It is important for the growth of the kingdom and for the discipleship of God's people that the College improves its training of preachers in developing application.[8]

The solution, as Grimmond rightly explains, is not *less* biblical rigour, but *more* biblical rigour. Preachers young and old need to see that properly "declaring ... the whole counsel of God" (Acts 20:27) requires them "to engage sound hermeneutical methods and deep theological reflection".[9] Truly biblical preaching is always about 'getting the passage right', but it is also about more than that: it is about applying the truth of God's word to people's hearts and lives. We don't just preach the Bible; we preach it *to people to change their lives for eternity.*

The same kind of principle will apply to all aspects of our ministry. The output-focused leader will work a little bit harder, and a little bit smarter, for they are forced to engage in an important feedback loop, just like the archer who misses the target. If you are clear on outcomes, missing those outcomes forces the review questions: What went wrong? Why did we miss? What can we change so that we hit the target next time?

This doesn't mean that making changes to our inputs will come painlessly and easily. On the contrary, change is—as I've stressed many times by this point—almost always painful. It may require trial and error, coaching from an experienced and trusted colleague, an investment of time and money into some training resources, some difficult self-reflection, or a combination of all these things. It will certainly require much prayer, and it may be a slow and arduous process. But the critical thing is the mindset. Are we willing to engage in the process for the right reasons? Are we willing to ask the hard questions and pursue answers, with God's help?

By contrast, the input-focused leader tends to commit to a set of inputs and stick to them, whether or not they are producing results.

The failure of early Aboriginal mission in Australia is a case in point.

In the early years of European settlement in Australia, many Christians felt a great burden to bring the gospel to the nation's original inhabitants. This very largely failed, but not for lack of effort. The work of many of the early missionaries in Australia is a testimony to the courage, resilience and dedication of godly men and women. The stories of their devotion are extraordinary.[10] Many concluded that the lack of response was simply because the indigenous people weren't suited to the gospel. But note this reflection:

Two abiding impressions which I gain from reading about the Wellington mission, impressions identical to those gained from reading of any one of dozens of nineteenth century missions. The first impression is the missionaries' deep concern that the Aboriginal people should come to faith in Christ. The second impression is the manner in which *the missionaries' beliefs and consequent actions frustrated that very purpose towards which they believed themselves to be working.*[11]

One problem was the missionaries' conviction that peasant farming was a Christian lifestyle, which "wrongly tethered the gospel to the arbitrary and ethnocentric social change".[12] But some missionary contemporaries even suggested the real problem was the way they presented the gospel itself: "[John] Bulmer [a missionary and pastor in the 19th century] saw that the message that they did present to the people was incomplete, concentrating as it did on sin and punishment, rather than hope".[13]

Too few of the early missionaries paid attention to the impact that their inputs were having on the outcomes, and as a result they were not sufficiently self-reflective or flexible enough to change their practices to pursue better outcomes. In many ways, their ministry backgrounds blinded them to certain problems with their inputs. They were sure that the way they were doing things was the best way—which led them to conclude that the problem must be with the hearts of those they were trying to reach.

We would be wise to appreciate that we are just as vulnerable to the same error as those zealous early missionaries. We have formed certain practices within evangelical ministries that we believe are theological principles, not just pragmatics—practices that have been with us so long that to question them is to leave many others questioning our theological pedigree.

Keep asking questions

Further, being focused on outputs helps us to assess what might be called 'intermediate output targets'. It is wise and healthy to set input targets—such as the number of conversations, the number of visits, and the number of prayer times. This helps us to take appropriate control of the things we know we can control (bearing in mind the earlier discussion about whether we truly have final control over inputs), and allows us to compare our stated priorities with the reality of how we spend our time. But being output focused enables a leader to keep assessing whether these inputs are genuinely serving the outcome that we seek—namely, more converts and greater maturity in Christ. As painful and difficult as it can be, keeping a larger focus on outputs gives shape to all I do.

If there is no conversion growth, or no discernible growth in maturity among those under our care, we need to take responsibility for this; we need to look at our own work and ask the hard questions: what am I doing, or not doing, that means so few are being saved and that there is so little growth in maturity?

The output-focused leader will communicate their vision more clearly and more naturally. They will necessarily keep asking the 'why' and 'what' questions that are so important to clarity: 'Why are we doing this? What is this meant to achieve? What is the outcome we're seeking or expecting with this activity? What difference is this meant to make to our work?'

Again, consider our preaching as an example. Why do we preach? Is it to ensure that the word of God is spoken, whether or not people respond in faith? No, we preach in order to see lives changed. That is our purpose. We preach to bring about conversion and maturation in our hearers.

In this, our preaching is somewhat different from that of Isaiah, who was tasked with a preaching ministry that was intended to make people's hearts dull, their ears heavy and their eyes blind (Isa 6:10). Under the new covenant, *this isn't our model*. With the death and resurrection of Jesus, a new salvation-historical timeframe has emerged: we are now in the age of salvation, the age of the Spirit. Even though Paul uses Isaiah 6 to explain his lack of fruit during various phases of his ministry to the Jews near the end of the book of Acts (see Acts 28:23–27), the book finishes with these wonderful words: "Therefore let it be known to you that this salvation of God has been sent to the Gentiles; they will listen" (28:28). Notice the last three words: *they will listen*. This is the age of reaping, the age of all the nations being gathered to the Lord Jesus for the forgiveness of sins and for salvation. Our preaching is to be focused on this positive response. We do it to see lives changed and people grow. This is the target on the wall.

Another set of questions naturally follow: Are we hitting the target? Are we seeing the outcome that all our inputs are directed towards? If not, why not? Is it the way I'm preaching? Is it my skill, my style, or my technique? Sure, it may be that the soil is hard. But an output-focused leader won't rush to this conclusion too quickly. They will be prepared to sit with the hard questions and consider a range of possible answers, even where those answers are confronting.

Measuring the things that matter

All this presupposes that we can know whether we are hitting the target, which assumes some kind of measurement. This seems so obvious, but is often ignored or perhaps even passionately resisted—largely because, as already mentioned, it feels crass. It feels human-centred and ungodly. It feels like the sin of David in 2 Samuel 24, when he ordered a census to gauge the strength of Israel's army. We've probably all seen numbers measured, or leaders obsess over numbers, in unhealthy and ungodly ways.

But properly understood, David's problem wasn't counting per se.

After all, an entire book of the Bible is called *Numbers*; God is not opposed to his people being counted on principle. David's problem was pride and misplaced trust—a failure to trust the God who can win any victory with any number of people. David counted to boast and to draw confidence in his strength. Yes, it is possible to count or measure with this same sinful attitude. But it need not be so. And the fact is that almost everyone is prepared to use output-based measures in some form or another (think again about the budget).

There are two basic ways to measure: numerically (specifically), and anecdotally (generally). Money is the most obvious example of a numerical measure. We would never measure income and expenditure anecdotally, which is good! A careful numerical count is part of responsible stewardship of the resources God has entrusted to us. But if we care about other outcomes—people's salvation, and their growth in maturity—it is proper to keep a clear sense of how we are going. This means we can give thanks to God for positive outcomes, and we can review our practices to see *what* we are doing and *how* we are doing, which will enable and inform change where necessary to see a better outcome.

The notion of numerically (specifically) measuring our ministry will quickly raise a question for gospel workers: how are we supposed to numerically (or specifically) track a disciple's growth in maturity? How do we get a proper handle on something so nebulous?

Some indications of discipleship can be measured numerically— or at least specifically in some way. For example, is the person regular in attending church (or a small group)? Are they faithful and generous in giving? Have they invited someone to church, or led someone to Christ? Are they saying their prayers and reading their Bible? Are they making themselves available to serve in ministry and to be trained and equipped for works of service?

But beyond this, it's right to acknowledge that there is much that is intangible and unmeasurable about the task of presenting everyone mature in Christ. All God's people—leaders included, in case it needs to be said—are works in progress; none of us can ever be said to have 'arrived'. Even the most output-focused Christian leader should accept that there is much about his or her work that will remain unknowable until "the Day" discloses it (1 Cor 3:13).

That said, the importance of anecdotal (general) measurements should not be overlooked. Those who are discipling God's people will (or at least should) be able to give some account of whether the people under their care are moving forward in the faith. Almost every pastor I meet is doing this in some fashion. We have ways of measuring how our people are going. We have answers to these kinds of questions: Are they growing in the grace and knowledge of their Lord and Saviour? Are they displaying the fruit of the Spirit? Are they renouncing ungodliness and worldly passions, living self-controlled, upright, and godly lives in the present age, and waiting for their blessed hope, the appearing of the glory of their great God and Saviour Jesus Christ?[14]

The even bigger point is that an awareness of the limits of numerical measurements should not be used as a pretence for abandoning all kinds of numerical measurements. We should persevere with determination in the open-ended, lifelong task of discipling God's people, while also embracing specific measurements in appropriate areas. Leadership that is output-focused will find ways to measure the things that matter.

How many fish? Sharing the vision

In addition, focusing on outputs enables a leader to share the vision more naturally. An output-focused leader will speak more spontaneously of what matters. This becomes contagious. God's people are stirred when we talk about the essence of Christ's mission and our plans and desires for making disciples of all nations. This is the greatest possible cause—winning the nations to Christ, forming Christ in people, and seeing all of this expand our sense of God's greatness and goodness, to his glory. This is far more motivating, far more contagious, than seeing our lives and ministries as being about the inputs, where I lead groups, I preach, I sort out problems, I share my life, and I run an organization. I do all of this very largely for the sake of the outcomes—knowing God, and having him known by more and more people. The greater our clarity on *why* we do what we do, the more readily we will spontaneously speak to these things. The great cause of Christ will ooze from us in every setting and situation. And our people will inevitably catch the vision.

Early in the life of our church, we ran a missionary interview that has now become somewhat infamous (given that I've shared the story in various contexts). We organized a video link with a missionary family in Europe (before the days of Skype and Zoom, so we thought ourselves quite advanced to have a live video interview with a family on the other side of the world during church). One of our key leaders was running the event. He connected with the family and ran through a series of questions: What is the weather like? What can you see from your window? How are the kids going? Schooling? Transport? And so on. It was hugely helpful to put our missionaries in a proper context for us to understand the setting they were operating in. But one absolutely crucial thing was missing: they were never asked about the 'success' of the mission. There was no discussion of the fruit they were seeing from their labours.

Later, I drew the interviewer aside and offered my best attempt at a Nathan-before-David moment. I put to him this scenario: "Imagine we are both mad keen fishermen, and you have gone to the Northern Territory to fish for Barramundi. Now imagine that I call you—what would be my first question?" Straight away, with no more prompting from me, my friend answered: "How many fish?" In an instant, the penny dropped for him. He knew he'd blown it. But he dusted himself off and learned the lesson. To this day, he continues as a great blessing among us and brings an output mindset to much of his ministry.

Clarity is key. Why did we send a missionary overseas? *To win people for Christ.* If we are clear on that, and if we burn for that to happen, it will ooze from us in every conversation. We will spontaneously and repeatedly speak of the larger vision for all our work—to see the world won for Christ. We won't need a vision statement to make us speak it; we won't be able to help ourselves.

We have a reciprocal relationship with all our church's mission partners: we want to support strategic missionary endeavour, but we also want our mission partners to strengthen our own mission activity locally. I want them to want to tell us about how many fish they've caught. In fact, I want that to be the first thing they want to share. The clearer they are on why they are overseas, the clearer they will be in their communication with us, and the more their mission will strengthen our focus and our effectiveness in mission. Being output focused becomes a vision multiplier.

The dangers of focusing on outputs

For all the strengths, there are certainly a series of dangers or potential downsides that go along with being output focused. Four immediately merit comment.

1. Stress and grief

When we care about achieving something through our ministries, and we appreciate how much our inputs influence the outputs, we will be more fully engaged in the successes and failures of our work. This won't bring health into our lives!

An input-driven ministry will make us feel better. We will be able to contain the work to a healthy balance. We won't live with the roller-coaster ride of being bound to the people we work with and their ups and downs. There is a great health benefit in not feeling any sense of responsibility for outcomes. But this is surely a secular principle that has been inappropriately brought over into the spiritual realm. Paul certainly never received the memo:

> You are in our hearts, to die together and to live together. (2 Cor 7:3)

> Apart from other things, there is the daily pressure on me of my anxiety for all the churches. Who is weak, and I am not weak? Who is made to fall, and I am not indignant? (2 Cor 11:28–29)

> For to me to live is Christ, and to die is gain. If I am to live in the flesh, that means fruitful labour for me. (Phil 1:21–22)

> For now we live, if you are standing fast in the Lord. (1 Thess 3:8)

Here is a man who is so concerned about the outcomes in the lives of those around him that he stands or falls with their ups and downs, even though he couldn't control their progress.

Yes, a challenging aspect of being output focused is an unhealthier and less-balanced life. But we didn't sign up to live a healthy balanced life; we signed up to give ourselves over to death every day! "Death is at work in us ..." (2 Cor 4:12).

2. Possible negativity

Imagine that your church invests heavily in running an evangelistic event, working towards running the event for over six months. The event itself goes off brilliantly, and all those present have a great time. There is only one small downside to the whole thing: no non-Christians were present. An input-focused congregation will think it was brilliant. An output-focused leader will be the only one who's disappointed! And that will put something of a dampener on the whole event. "No, it's not good enough that we all had a great time of fellowship! We aren't going to just draw a new target on the wall wherever the arrow landed."

This 'negativity' may not play well among those who had such a good time.

3. Rampant pragmatism

As noted in an earlier chapter, a good amount of pragmatism is entirely warranted. But *rampant* pragmatism, unchecked and unformed by theology, is a grave danger. We must always be shaped and controlled by biblical boundaries and by the text of Scripture.

The fact is, however, like the other tensions explored throughout this book, the answer to rampant pragmatism isn't *no* pragmatism, but a closer walk with the Scriptures to be clear and firm on both the boundaries and borders *and* on the areas of true freedom that exist for our ministries and the way we conduct them. There are no shortcuts here.

4. 'Whatever the cost ...'

This is the first cousin of rampant pragmatism. Output-focused leaders become very, well, output focused. And they exude a greater drive to see things achieved rather than just 'being'. This can sometimes result in relational fallout. To put it more starkly, the output-driven leader can sometimes trample over others in the pursuit of what they perceive as a grander, more glorious goal.

This is a problem for many reasons, including that it is a failure to appreciate the full range of outputs. The outputs we are called to produce are more than merely a set of impersonal results. Our task is to produce a family of people who love one another as Christ has loved them. One of the central outcomes of the gospel is *relationship*—relationships of mutual love and support. Hurting and damaging the very people he is seeking to nurture to full maturity in Christ is a grave failure on the part of an output-focused leader. The problem of 'whatever the cost' isn't so much that a leader is output focused, but that he or she is not properly output focused.

These four dangers, and others like them, should not be brushed over too quickly. We're all sinners, and we're all susceptible to the potential downsides of output-focused ministry. But an awareness of the dangers, and of our weaknesses, allows us to move forward—prayerfully and carefully—in seeking to become the leaders that God wants us to be.

Examples of output-driven leadership

Because the shift to being an output-driven leader is difficult in any number of ways, it will help at this point to offer some examples of the way in which both kinds of leader, input-driven and output-driven, engage. I've already talked at some length about preaching—about the output-driven preacher not being content to simply 'get the passage right', but also working hard to apply the truth of God's word and to preach with specific outcomes in mind. Let me offer two more examples.

Vision statements and reports

An input-focused leader will offer a vision statement such as: "Our purpose is to see our church active in mission, holding out the gospel to the world around us".

An output-driven leader would instead offer something like this: "Our purpose is to see people converted and to see people actively serving in mission". These are both very simple examples, but notice that the output-driven statement has two outputs: seeing people saved (conversion); and seeing people actively serving in mission (part of maturity).

Or consider this report from a ministry leader to the members: "Five years ago, we had nothing. Now, we have five staff members, a budget of $600,000, and an office." In this case, the leader has reported on progress with respect to inputs. In many ways, this is perfectly understandable. When a ministry starts with nothing and works hard to build itself up to become viable and effective, it is hard for the leader not to feel a great sense of satisfaction in the progress made on inputs. "We had nothing"—you can empathize with the pain of those words. To now have a machine in place that can do some work is hugely pleasing.

But the danger with this focus on inputs is that the ministry can feel as though it's arrived because of the input results—after all, five staff, a budget over half a million dollars and some infrastructure is not nothing! Yet the edge is so easily lost for the output work—the work of saving and maturing people. The vision that is subtly being cast is for a growth of inputs rather than a burning desire to see the lost saved, the immature grown, and the mature going from strength to strength. It is hard for those hearing the report to not become muddled in their own thinking.[15]

An output-focused leader would certainly notice the growth on the input side—in fact he *must* notice it, for without that growth it is hard to build a ministry that makes a difference. But he notices it without fixating on it. The inputs, cause for rejoicing though they are, are just the tools for doing the job. And the job is saving people and growing people. The output-driven leader's first and last thought each day is about outputs: how are we going in seeing people saved and built up in Christ? This means that his first instinct is to report on outputs, which in turn casts further vision in a way that is easy for others to catch.[16]

Staff and leadership positions

The output-driven leader will think very differently about staffing, and indeed about any ministry position, whether paid or unpaid.

Typically, churches and ministries appoint people to 'oversee' input structures. We build a small-group network, for example, and we raise up or employ someone to 'oversee small groups'. What we've done is embed a strategy for attaining an output—small groups—as *the* key piece of our work, and appointed someone to just look after it. This may or may not work, depending on the quality of leader.

By contrast, an output-focused leader will remember the outputs that the small-group structure has been set up to achieve, and will therefore appoint a leader *to take responsibility for achieving those outputs by using the small-group structures.* This is a very different role. In fact, built into this role from the outset is a far more powerful dynamic: the person appointed is responsible to achieve certain outcomes. They are clear from the outset that the thing called 'our small-group structure' is only there to achieve those outcomes. The structure itself isn't sacrosanct; there is always flexibility. If it isn't achieving or can't achieve the outcomes we're seeking, we'll change it or drop it.

Our use of language here is important: making a leader *responsible for* small groups (or for the outcome), rather than appointing a leader to *oversee* small groups, is a significant shift. For it nurtures a focus on getting the right things happening and on taking responsibility. The word 'oversee' tends towards creating leaders who just watch over something without specific, passionate regard to the outcomes.

Many years ago during my driving test, my instructor asked me what I should do when approaching a pedestrian crossing. I replied, "slow down and watch for pedestrians". The instructor responded, "What—and just run them over slowly?" It isn't sufficient to just watch over a ministry; it must be clear from the outset what that means. An output-focused leader is responsible not just to watch over a structure whether or not it is achieving anything, but to achieve certain outcomes by using a particular input structure.

This is all part and parcel of the shift to becoming leaders who properly own our responsibility for outcomes. It brings pain, but also greater clarity and resolve.

The values of life and ministry

It is my longing that we would breed many more men and women who are restless—restless not just to preach and teach and leave the outputs to God, but restless to be whatever they need to be and do whatever they need to do (within the bounds of God's word, of course) to see our churches make disciples.

This book is about promoting growth and change in our churches and other ministries. But long before any discussion of leadership technique that might be used to help that happen, there is much thought needed on the values we bring to life and ministry.

The ministry of the gospel isn't a work for gentlemanly scholars—quietly studying, reflecting on deep things, drinking endless cups of tea with old ladies. We don't run philosophical societies. There is an urgency that is meant to permeate everything we do. People are going to hell all around us. And our failings are contributing to that fact.

A big part of getting growth and change happening is *us*. It might be that we as leaders and core congregation members are carrying around within us a deep spiritual problem that is inhibiting God's work among us and through us—not because God *can't* work unless we fix ourselves up, but because we are the ordinary means he uses to work out his sovereign purposes. And getting us sorted out is a core part of his agenda and program. He wants to mature *us*, the leaders of God's people.

Once again, of course, the burden isn't all ours. It isn't our burden alone, and it isn't our burden independent of anyone or anything else. Yes, God is sovereign. No, you are not the Messiah. The burden isn't meant to be *too* great. But it *is* meant to be great. The man or woman who lives with a relentless focus on and concern for outputs will certainly live a more disturbed life than the man or woman focused only on inputs. They won't sleep as well, either; they will live daily with their anxiety for the church, and they will live with a certain grief that the gospel is not making more progress.

And yet they will also live with a powerful confidence and trust in God for their work and their people. For it is ultimately *his* work, and they are ultimately *his* people. These leaders will rejoice in being privileged to share in the sufferings of Christ and to be part of the most important work that anyone could ever do. It is true that the future isn't up to us. But neither do we have no influence over that future or no responsibility for that future.

Passages for further reflection

- 1 Corinthians 3:5–15
- 1 Corinthians 15:10–11
- 2 Corinthians 11:28–29
- Philippians 2:12–13

Questions for personal or team reflection

- Are you leading people where they wouldn't necessarily have gone on their own? Or are you only facilitating the operation of the ministry?
- Is there any sense in which you find yourself resistant to becoming a more output-focused leader? Why?

Quote for personal or team reflection

"There go my people. I must find out where they're going so I can lead them." (attributed to Alexandre Auguste Ledru-Rollin)

DEALING WITH THE
PRESSURE OF MINISTRY

Handling the burdens of being output-driven

As I've acknowledged throughout the book, the approach to ministry that I'm advocating—and the attitude of the heart that fuels it— can leave us feeling overwhelmed. Leading God's people with an output-driven mindset is hardly a ticket to an easy life. An input-driven ministry will still be stressful—there are sermons to prepare, meetings to organize, and countless other people and events clamouring to fill our diaries—but this leader just won't feel the pressure in the same way. Heavy lies the head that accepts responsibility not just for delivering the right inputs, but also—to some extent, within the bounds of celebrating God's sovereignty—for the outputs produced by those inputs.

Yet an output-minded leader is not just a meaningless vessel to be flogged to death in service of the gospel. He or she is a beloved child of their gracious heavenly Father and a follower of the Saviour who delivered this precious promise:

Come to me, all who labour and are heavy laden, and I will give you rest. Take my yoke upon you, and learn from me, for

I am gentle and lowly in heart, and you will find rest for your souls. For my yoke is easy, and my burden is light. (Matt 11:28–30)

Because pressure is an inevitable part of leading for growth and change, and because God cares for us and wants us to serve in a joyful and sustainable way, it is imperative that we find healthy, nourishing, God-honouring patterns of life.

In this chapter, I want to offer brief answers to two important questions: How do we deal with the pressures of an output-oriented ministry? And how should we approach the question of our work hours? Whole books are devoted to answering these questions, so this will be a very brief overview—but hopefully a step in the right direction.

Three lessons to learn

1. Learning to trust God and look to eternity

This book is written from within a theological framework that has often been labelled 'Calvinist'. That is, I hold firmly to the truth that God is sovereign in all things. But I also hold to the truth that humans are responsible moral agents under God's sovereign rule. Both things are true, even though they may be hard to reconcile intellectually.[1] This is Calvinism.

The emphasis of this book is the 'human agency' side of things (combating a kind of 'intermittent hyper-Calvinism'). This is because I so often engage with pastors and leaders who seem to have too low a view of human responsibility. And, as I've argued, this quenches any drive to grow and change. Too often, the great and wonderful truths of God's sovereignty are used as a 'get-out-of jail-free card'. We often don't pause to consider what we're bringing to our task. We often don't feel any great weight of responsibility such that we are willing to vigorously pursue growth and go through costly change because, well, God is sovereign and will just do what he does.

But although I've focused on human responsibility, I need at this point to say more about God's sovereignty. Because it is essential that we affirm the comfort this truth brings.

While we are not puppets, we also need the joy and peace that come from a proper and profound appreciation of the sovereignty of God. He is utterly sovereign! He is at work in his world, bringing all things together according to his eternal plan (Ephesians 1). He cannot and will not be thwarted. He will do as he pleases "among the host of heaven and among the inhabitants of the earth", who are "accounted as nothing" next to his "everlasting dominion" (Dan 4:34–35). He has chosen and elected a people for himself (e.g. Matt 24:31; Romans 9; 2 Tim 2:10). He *will* build his church (Matt 16:18). As many have said, we've read the final pages of the Bible and we know how the story will end.

All of this is deeply comforting. As mentioned in chapter 8, the 39 Articles say that "the godly consideration of Predestination, and our Election in Christ, is full of sweet, pleasant and unspeakable comfort to godly persons". We are right to draw deeply on this soul-reviving truth. In a very real sense, we cannot fail. God's work will prevail. We serve the omnipotent, all-knowing Lord of the universe. We are merely servants. He gives the growth. Even when we have done all that God asks of us, we should happily declare, "We are unworthy servants; we have only done what was our duty" (Luke 17:10).

Yes, it is true that we can rush too quickly to the sovereignty of God. But we can also go there too slowly. There are massive limitations to our lives and ministries. We aren't omniscient or omnipotent. We are not the Saviour of the world. These are emotional and theological realities that every one of us needs to accept *and* celebrate.

Paul spoke of the pressure he felt in his ministry, but he also spoke of the wonderful delight of finding comfort in not only the sovereign hand of God, but also in God's grace and mercy and in the future hope of rest. In 2 Corinthians 6, the apostle offers a rapid-fire set of contrary experiences. He ministered:

> Through honour and dishonour, through slander and praise. We are treated as impostors, and yet are true; as unknown, and yet well known; as dying, and behold, we live; as punished, and yet not killed; as sorrowful, yet always rejoicing; as poor, yet making many rich; as having nothing, yet possessing everything. (2 Cor 6:8–10)

There is so much complexity here, and much that is wonderfully instructive. Paul experienced sorrow. He lived with stress. And yet he was sustained through such things and continued to talk of his joy and hope in Christ. In the first chapter of this letter, he wrote of sharing so "abundantly in Christ's sufferings" that he and Timothy "despaired of life itself" and felt they had "received the sentence of death" (1:5–9). He had been in dark places. He knew what it was to run the full gamut of emotional experience and response. His life wasn't one of stoic steadiness. And yet in the gospel he had the resources that were necessary to manage and to process the struggles. God's grace was sufficient for him. The hardships came "to make us rely not on ourselves but on God who raises the dead" (1:10). His very sense of weakness was evidence of God's empowering strength, for God's power is made perfect in weakness (12:9). When we are weak, then we are strong (12:10). This didn't remove the demands on his life, but it upheld him through those demands. Even as Paul carried a strong sense of responsibility, he readily fled to the comfort of the sovereignty of God.

All things *are* in God's sovereign hands. We don't need to despair. He is building his church, through frail vessels, "jars of clay", like us (4:7). Let the sense of need and our part in it push us, yes, but let us also carry a strong sense that God's power is over and above all things. Paul asks the rhetorical question: "Who is sufficient for these things?" (2:16). The sense of responsibility weighs on him. Yet what is his final answer? Our sufficiency is in God, who has made us ministers of the gospel of Christ. God is at work in putting us where we are and making us who we are. We therefore look for strength to him who can carry us through any trial.

What I'm about to say may seem obvious, but the obvious things are often the most important. Spend time in the word of God such that you let the word preach to your own heart and soul. Be in prayer regularly. Be quick to use what others have called 'the preacher's prayer': 'Dear Lord, help, help, help, help. Amen.' There are times when any meaningful content is beyond us. In those moments, pray in whatever pay you're able. Cry out. The Lord hears and answers. He knows of what we're made. He is not far from the one who is "humble and contrite in spirit" and who trembles at his word (Isa 66:2). He does not despise "a broken and contrite heart" (Ps 51:17). In his kingdom, "the poor in spirit" are blessed (Matt 5:3). His Spirit sustains the weak. Even—or especially—when you are at your lowest ebb, expect his supernatural empowering. Learn to trust him.

And reflect often on the future hope that is ours. This world is not our home. There is an eternal rest. And there is salvation, even for those who might escape "as through fire" (1 Cor 3:15). No matter what we have said or not said, done or not done, no-one will snatch us out of the hand of the one who died for us and gave us eternal life (John 10:28).

Jesus is the friend of sinners (Matt 11:19; Luke 7:34). He invites us not to rejoice in what we can do for him, but in what he has done for us (Luke 10:20). When we labour and are heavy laden, he invites us to come to him to receive rest; "Take my yoke upon you, and learn from me, for I am gentle and lowly in heart, and you will find rest for your souls" (Matt 11:28–29). He is a gracious and gentle master who calls me into his service and upholds me through it all.

Preach these things to your heart.

2. Learning to understand yourself

Part of our challenge is the many other things we bring to the burdens of ministry. This is not a book on psychology, and I'm no expert, but very few of us come into our work without any baggage. We might bring issues around identity and the need for significance and 'self worth'. We might bring the clamour of unmet needs that constantly brings us down. Inner voices will critique and condemn. There is some evidence of a generational shift, where younger pastors struggle more with this kind of baggage when compared with earlier generations. Whatever the details of our experience, this kind of baggage can colour our ability to hear the Bible as it speaks of a leader's responsibility for outcomes: we find any focus on our responsibility demoralizing, even crushing.[2]

But is it possible that such a reaction is an overreaction, where our rejection of responsibility is really our own fear of what it might do to us given the many negative voices in our heads? Is it possible that we might then project our own struggle onto everyone else, and perhaps even onto the biblical testimony?

It is certainly true that there is great variation among pastoral leaders in their ability to carry the weight and load of responsibility. This, in itself, isn't a problem: we each have our gifts and our struggles. Where it can become a problem is if we measure what is appropriate against the most fragile among us. Some of us need more time off; others need to press on in the work. Further, the answer to these issues isn't to reject any sense of output thinking. The answer is to deal with our inner demons. When we feel a crushing burden—our insufficiencies and inadequacies, our awareness of poor practice—how much is simply the weight of eternal things, and how much is our personal need to succeed?

There is much we need to do in healing brokenness and past hurts so that they don't intrude on what is already a challenging path. This process is important for another reason: there is a spiritual being who seeks to play on our weaknesses—the evil one.

It has been said that Satan works his schemes by singing to our weaknesses and sharpening them. Apparently, there are some singers who are so skilled that they can pitch their voice so it causes a piano string to resonate to the note. Satan, who is nothing if not crafty (Gen 3:1), functions with our weaknesses in just this way. He plays on them. He sings to them. He seeks to fan into flame any weakness that is already in us so that it brings us down.

How do we deal with our inner hurts? Pause to reflect on your reactions to things. The key here is underreaction and overreaction. What circumstances cause you to overreact? What causes you to underreact? Interrogate these responses. We carry a sense of responsibility, but we do this under the sovereign hand of God. What might make it hard for you to know the joy of that upholding power of God? What might make it difficult for you to draw on the resources of God's grace in the midst of carrying genuine responsibility for outcomes? Do you carry a secret sense that you are unworthy? Are you operating as though God accepts you based on the quality of your ministry, rather than on the gracious gift of the merits of Christ?

It is possible to sometimes get to the bottom of these things by exploring the worst of our fears. What if I fail? What if my ministry fails to produce the fruit I long for it to produce? What emerges as I consider this kind of outcome? Is my deepest longing for me and my reputation? Or is it truly a sincere desire for the glory of God and the salvation of souls?

At this point, it is tempting to simply leave and find an easier path. But the more difficult path has many blessings. As Jesus said, "It is more blessed to give than receive" (Acts 20:35). There is so much opportunity for personal growth as we walk this path with our compassionate and kind God. The challenges can enable a healthy internal review of our lives and our hearts. This can only be good when done within the loving hands of a gracious heavenly Father who loves perfectly and unconditionally, not because of our own worth and effort, but because of the merits of his beloved Son.

3. Learning to take the Sabbath seriously

There are various reasons for taking a day off each week. One day off in every seven-day week is not a command for those living under the new covenant, but it is the pattern that God reveals in his word (more on the six days of work later in the chapter). But more than this, it reminds us that we live to rest, not to work—not 'rest' in the worldly sense of endless leisure, but rest properly understood on God's terms. We were made for rest with God, not for the burden of work in the weeds.

When we rest, we are reminded that heaven is our eternal home. We are reminded that knowing God matters more than the work we do. We are reminded that we aren't indispensable. I take a day off each week to live the very real experience that I'm earthly and mortal. I can't be everywhere and everything to everyone. The world can turn without me. My work and ministry must do without me so that it knows—and so that I know—that ultimately it is God's work. His work alone is decisive. I can stop. I can rest in him. My weekly sabbath day reminds me of this in a vivid way. Turn off emails. Avoid social media. Get away and enjoy God and his creation. Take time off with the wife or husband of your youth, with some good friends, or just by yourself. Enjoy. And recharge.

Holidays sit in the same category. We need holidays, not only so we can continue to work effectively after our time off, but also to remind ourselves that *it isn't all about us*. Yes, we play a part, as I've argued repeatedly. But we aren't everything. Take long breaks. Again, enjoy and recharge. Learn that it is God's work before it is your work. Invest in family and in the joy of life together.

Let me offer a few practical tips on managing work and learning to rest well. Wherever possible, take the night off before your day off.

You'll go into your day off ready to relax and enjoy it, rather than feeling frazzled. If you're a pastor, don't take Monday as your day off. After the intensity of Sunday at church, you won't have the emotional reserves to enjoy it properly. Don't do more than two nights out in a row. Create healthy sleep patterns, and learn about what helps and hinders sleep.[3]

Pay attention to your physical health. Stress builds up and gets pushed down into the systems of the body. Exercise releases these processes and brings relief. Eat well. Find out what refreshes and invest appropriately in those things.

Don't be like Scottish pastor Robert Murray M'Cheyne, who died at the age of 28, shortly after saying: "God gave me a message to deliver and a horse to ride. Alas, I have killed the horse and now I cannot deliver the message". Look after yourself because you matter to God and to the people who love you, *and* because it will allow you to be fruitful in ministry.

Thinking about work hours

Any discussion of work hours is a challenge for many reasons, but especially because we're all so different. Even if we desire to take the point of this book seriously and embrace a sense of responsibility for outputs, that can't mean we simply add more and more hours to our working week. How do we make decisions about how we spend our time and take a more nuanced position?

Work hours have also become an issue of concern in recent times because of the heightened incidence and awareness of burnout among ministers. The experience of burnout varies, as do its causes and its treatment. At a very basic level, burnout can be understood as simply a feeling of exhaustion—the kind of exhaustion where a holiday helps. But there is also a far more serious kind of burnout that has long-lasting and potentially serious consequences. This second form can be hard to come back from, and it drives many discussions of a pastor's work hours. Burnout can be so severe that it leads some to a suggestion that I regard as radical: a pastor should work no more than 40 hours a week.

This more serious kind of burnout is complex; it isn't simply the result of long work hours', but often involves other stressors in life and ministry. Therefore, it is too simplistic to address this (very real) problem by making broad rules around shorter hours. Much more attention needs to be paid to personal issues. Long hours will likely trigger burnout, but only if there are other factors at work. Therefore, it is better to consider some broader principles (biblically and practically) around hours and then work backwards to individual needs and circumstances.

Work hours in the Bible

The immediate impression given by much of the New Testament's language is that the pastor's task is a challenging one, and is properly described as 'hard work' (see Acts 20:35; 1 Cor 4:11–12a; 2 Cor 11:23; 1 Thess 2:9). Paul honoured Epaphras for this style of ministry (Col 4:13) and expected this to be the pattern for all pastors (1 Thess 5:12). When he taught Timothy about the life of pastoral ministry, he used three illustrations that speak to the need to be controlled (the soldier), focused (the athlete) and hard-working (the farmer; 2 Tim 2:4–6).

We could add to this the many warnings throughout the book of Proverbs that condemn the lazy and commend the hard worker (e.g. Prov 6:6–11, 13:4, 20:4, 21:25–26). God has designed a world in which hard work is rewarded and laziness brings suffering. Hard work is the pattern for the pastor just as it is for all healthy, able-bodied people.

Of course, the challenge here is that 'hard work' and 'laziness' are relative terms. Some people have been raised in an environment where 'hard work' means nothing less than a 70-hour work week. Others will have been raised as indulgent teenagers who were always able to pursue leisure; for them, anything over 40 hours a week will seem oppressive, perhaps even offensive to a lifestyle that honours God, who gives us all good things to enjoy (1 Tim 4:4–5). Our cultural and family backgrounds will shape our perception of effort and sacrifice.

There is no simple biblical command that speaks to the number of hours a person ought to work. But we can find some direction.

Made to rest and to work

Within the context of work being a good gift from God (Gen 2:15), though now lived in a world where it is hard and painful (Gen 3:17–19), we are given a command about the weekly work pattern: the very well-known pattern of six days of work and one day of rest (Exod 20:9–10). We were made for rest, where 'rest' is not only rest from our hard work, but also a deeper experience of relationship with God through the merits of Christ (see Hebrews 4). Some workers, especially some pastors, need to hear this very loudly. If that's you, go back and re-read the section on the sabbath rest above. It is right to enjoy the many good things of creation: stop working, and go and enjoy! Give thanks. Deepen your walk with God and your rest in him. Fill up your spiritual tank and rest.

But we were also made to work. And the Bible's obvious pattern (though not a direct command to new-covenant believers) is a six-day working week. This need not mean six days of paid work outside the home; it can certainly include the work required in household and family chores. But it is a striking message in certain cultural contexts.

Assessing these things can be difficult. In our Australian context, we get mixed messages. There are increased pressures to work because of financial strain. More women are working. But the average number of hours worked is declining, particularly for men, with fewer and fewer people working longer than 45 hours per week. And in many respects there is a strong cultural push to pursue more leisure. In my region, albeit a beach culture, advertisers explicitly promote a six-day weekend as the ideal lifestyle. It's effective because it strikes a chord among so many, not just because they're stressed and tired and need a break, but because for many leisure is the aim of life.

While personal circumstances differ, many people share an equal horror at the thought that a working week ought to be six days long This is understandable, since we have removed any sense of a life beyond this one and an overarching purpose for our lives. Why would we spend this life working when it is the only life we might ever live? Much better to say, "Let us eat and drink, for tomorrow we die" (Isa 22:13). 'Flourishing' is now the great aim, even in many Christian circles: 'Live your best life now'.

The Bible is countercultural, even more so when its assumptions about a daily routine are considered. Both Psalm 104 and Matthew 20, although written centuries apart, assume a dawn-to-dusk pattern of work. This is a long way from a law, but it gives an insight into the culture of the Jewish world. Both passages would have made sense in a world where there was no electric light bulb: you worked when it was light, for as long as it was light, and you did this six days a week.[4] Again, all this may be heard differently depending on your culture and family history. But it is important to notice where the biblical culture is different from our own and allow the biblical culture to speak to our own in some way. As a counterpoint, the Jews had various festivals that broke this pattern and provided a rich balance of work and rest. But these kinds of days were also possible because people had developed resilience and learned to cope with hard work.

Overall, then, the impression given is of a working week that is around ten-hour days, six days a week.

As noted, for many today this is an awful suggestion and a horrifying prospect. In those parts of Western culture that are leisure-soaked, we need to reclaim not only the Bible's teaching on the importance of rest, but also the value that Scripture puts on work as a good thing, given by our good God, who himself is working to this very day (John 5:17). If Paul can say "Whatever you do, work heartily, as for the Lord and not for men" (Col 3:23), how could we not approach gospel ministry this way? If Paul can urge God's people to be "always abounding in the work of the Lord, knowing that in the Lord your labour is not in vain" (1 Cor 15:58), how could we opt for a comfortable lifestyle or settle for an 'average work week'? How could we make it our aim to 'abound' in leisure time?

And yet we are also to be resters! We should work hard and work well, but we should also rest well. Our ability to do both well, and to do both in right measure, is a powerful testimony to the world.

Lazy workers, people shaped by our culture of ease, don't adorn the gospel. But neither does the workaholic pastor who can never down tools and rest, who cannot find joy in the people around him or in God's good creation, and who runs himself and everyone around him into the ground.

How many hours?

So, does this mean we should do six ten-hour days a week for a total of 60 hours?

When it comes to the nitty gritty of landing on the number of hours we should work each week, there are so many factors to consider. We could ask: How many hours does the average person in your church work, and how much time do we expect them to spend in church activities on top of this each week? What about the time they spend commuting (when you may work from home or from a nearby office)? How do we compare our work to the work done by stay-at-home mums? How do the demands of other workplaces, or of full-time child-rearing, compare to the pressures of pastoral work? What unique demands are placed on us? What unique freedoms do we enjoy? Is a pastor working when he shares lunch with church members who are also friends? What about when you're reading a Christian book—are you working right now?

And we could go on.

If I were forced to land on a number, I would suggest that 50 hours a week is a good starting place for most young leaders. This equates to roughly:

- Four weekdays working 8am to 5pm (with a lunch break)
- Half a day at some other point during the week
- An eight-hour Sunday (two church meetings, preparation time, plus hospitality over lunch)
- Two or three nights of work in a typical week.

Fifty hours a week is the 60 hours mentioned above minus ten, which allows for factors like the challenges of living in our hyper-connected internet age, the unique pressures on a pastor, and the importance of investing in home and family life. But because there is just so much to do, I think it's unwise to subtract more than ten hours from the 60-hour baseline. Our congregation members need to be led by people who model hard work.[5]

We should also acknowledge that, because there are different ways to do pastoral ministry, hours alone are not an adequate measure. Some pastors do their jobs in such a relaxed way that they could 'work' 70 hours a week and be left feeling relaxed and refreshed; others push themselves so hard, in a very pressured and hostile environment, that 45 hours feels a far greater burden than the CEO doing 70 hours. Working life is very hard to quantify between pastoral roles, let alone across entirely different professions.

What cannot be disputed, though, is that ours is a difficult lifestyle. In independent analyses, pastoral ministry is regularly found at or near the top of the 'most difficult job' list. The level of 'burnout' among pastors is among the highest of any profession. A 2023 survey of around 200 Protestant pastors in Australia found that 35 percent "had given serious consideration to quitting the ministry in the past 12 months", while a 2022 US-based survey found that 42 percent of American pastors had considered leaving.[6]

"The appointed time has grown very short"

In navigating these issues, it is critical that the pastor has been captured by the love of Christ and by our world's great need for the gospel. If the heart is captured in this way, all our work will be done willingly, not because of external demands or rules (see 1 Pet 5:2–4). The pastor must be genuinely eager to serve. Guilt, fear, personal needs, internal baggage that creates an unhealthy drive—all these will kill a pastoral ministry. A pastor must desire to be a pastor and to bear the burden of ministry. He must desire to work hard for the people under his care, out of concern for their wellbeing and love for God.

'Working hard' doesn't demand a specific number of hours. But at the very least, there is something dreadfully wrong with a pastor who has chosen the role as a 'lifestyle choice' or who is concerned to ensure he 'maintains a balanced lifestyle' so life can be as full and rich as possible. This is very far not only from the pattern of biblical ministry, but also from the pattern of Christian living in these last days. As Paul says in 1 Corinthians, "the appointed time has grown very short" (1 Cor 7:29). Christ will return. People will die apart from Christ. How can we prioritize 'balance' and 'health' when there are so many lives to save?

Our task is a noble one (1 Tim 3:1), but also a profoundly important one. There is no more important task in the world. We don't do what we do as a lifestyle choice; we do it out of a desire to make a difference for Christ. The love of Christ compels us. Woe to me if I don't preach the gospel.

Passages for further reflection

- Psalm 127:1–2
- Proverbs 6:6–11
- Luke 12:15–21
- 2 Timothy 2:3–6

Questions for personal or team reflection

- How many hours will you aim to work each week? How will you structure your work week?
- Are you at risk of being seduced by 'this-worldliness' in your thinking about hours? Is the way you spend your time a proper reflection of what you believe and of what is most important to you?

Quote for personal or team reflection

"God gave me a message to deliver and a horse to ride. Alas, I have killed the horse and now I cannot deliver the message." (Robert Murray M'Cheyne)

CONCLUSION:
DO NOT STOOP

Any leader who wants to lead for change needs to grapple with inertia. For inertia is a powerful dynamic.

When you scratch beneath the surface of a church, you often discover that many in the congregation don't really want growth. Maybe they want to be in a small or medium-sized church. Maybe they want 'Cheers Church'—a place where everybody knows their name.[1] Very often, it is only the leaders who want the church to be larger. And even then, many leaders secretly *don't* want the church to grow, because it's already hard enough to handle the many demands on their time and energy within the current church. It's easier to just plug away without a specific plan, see what God does, and avoid the pain of change.

No wonder we aren't growing more.

At EV Church, it took less than ten years for us to establish patterns that brought resistance to change. A certain amount of inertia had set in. We have had to keep working at cultivating an ongoing desire and expectation that church will be different each year. This creates the attitude that change is normal and allows us to provide room for more people to join us. It's hard work. I'm not suggesting it is as hard as shifting a longstanding traditional church. But if a church that was less than ten years old found the forces of inertia at work, how clear is it that these forces will be at work in all churches?

And if a new church needed to keep breaking things and pushing past a change-resistant culture, how much more will this be necessary in a long-established church? Getting church into a place where there is a burning desire among everyone—not just leaders—to see growth and change happen *and keeping it there* is a constant work— even more so in long-established churches.

In seeking to promote a culture of ongoing growth and change, one thing that has served our church well over the years is the metaphor of a lifeboat. I have used this image at every monthly newcomers' night, from the very first year of our church's life until now (I must have used it well over 200 times by now). I ask people to picture church as a lifeboat in an ocean full of drowning people. The gospel is our God-given means to rescue people from drowning, and they are rescued to come aboard the lifeboat.

But what happens when most of the seats in the lifeboat are taken and someone expresses reluctance to rescue more people from certain death by pulling them into the boat? What if someone in the boat started saying that the boat was full enough and urging us to not fill it up any further? "If we do that, I won't know everyone on the boat. It could become uncomfortable."

What would we say to a person like that?

Almost every time I share this story, someone in the group inevitably suggests we should solve the problem by throwing out the person who's complaining! Everyone laughs—and the point is made.

The church is certainly more than just a metaphorical 'lifeboat'. It is at the heart of God's redemptive plan to remake humanity, to gather together a people who are united in Christ, remade in his image, and exist for his glory (see God's vision in Ephesians, outlined in chapter 3 of this book). But the lifeboat metaphor captures a big part of who and what we are. In the gospel of the Lord Jesus Christ, we have the words of eternal life. Where else are we to go? Where else are our lost and perishing neighbours to go? If there is any truth at all to the lifeboat metaphor, and if people truly are perishing without the gospel, then church cannot be about our comfort. It is a place for more and more people to find a home and a welcome and to hear the gospel. And if church isn't about the comfort of those who are already in the boat, we must keep pushing for more. We must never be content with our current numbers. We must be ready to embrace growth and its inevitable consequence—change. We cannot remain as the cozy community group where everyone knows everyone.

It is possible as churches and leaders to be entrusted with great resources—property worth millions of dollars (in crass human terms), the even more valuable human resource of God's people, and the most valuable resource of all: the gospel, the divine dynamite that can explode its way into even the hardest heart and bring salvation and eternal hope. Are we marshalling these resources as well as we can? Is it appropriate that a ministry with so many resources might touch the lives of only a few? Sometimes, perhaps. And certainly every life is precious. Those 'few' need to be loved, nurtured in the faith, and matured. Praise God for faithful pastors serving their people and keeping them to the end.

But we need to keep this in perspective: those people are surrounded by hundreds of thousands of unreached people who have no hope and are without God in the world. Even with so many perishing around them, the church is so often run as though the lifeboat is full—or at least full *enough*—which means hardly anyone will ever be brought to Christ in that place. The evangelistic side of the ministry will only become effective again if large swathes of people—especially the leadership—take to heart the deep concern we are to have for the output God is seeking, and if they then own the fact that we as God's people bear some responsibility for seeing these outputs happen.

Without these deep concerns, there will never be the necessary changes that allow the church to fulfil its God-given mission. But with these deep concerns, the church can be revived and reshaped so that it can fulfil its mission to reach a dying world.

The burden of this book has not been to lay out every detail for how to manage growth and change or how to lead yourself and your ministry through a process of change. This leaves space for leaders and teams to work through these issues in their local context. It also keeps the book from being twice as long! The main reason for mostly sidestepping such a level of detail is that it would distract from the book's main burden: to create a passion for growth and a heart that is willing to bear the pain of change. That said, I have included an appendix that will help you get started on considering the practicalities. But don't fall into the trap of rushing to the *how* of ministry before you've devoted deep, prayerful thought to the *why* of ministry.

I hope this book has helped you to contemplate the *why* of ministry and the *why* of your life. I hope it has helped you to grasp the magnitude of the task that lies before us. I hope you feel the weight of the responsibility that is ours. Perhaps Paul's words are ringing in your ears: "Who is sufficient for these things?" (2 Cor 2:16). Who, indeed? I hope you appreciate the need to dedicate yourself to the task so that you can lead with faithfulness, clarity and skill.

Yet more than any of that, I hope you've been gripped once again by the gospel of God's grace. I hope you share God's heart for the lost. I hope you're driven to sacrifice your comfort for the salvation of sinners and for the glory of God.

Gospel ministry is not easy. But there's no great merit in being good at things that are easy. And leading God's people for growth and change is a challenging but noble task. Our labour in the Lord will never be in vain. And I love it. I absolutely love the challenge. I hope you love it too, and that you will abandon your life to the service of Christ and his glorious, life-changing gospel.

Do not stoop from being a preacher to become a king. Don't ever give up. Why would you dedicate your life to anything else?

APPENDIX:
FIVE FOUNDATIONS
FOR MINISTRY

In this appendix, I will share five foundations for ministry that can help us to analyze and organize our ministries. But before coming to these foundations, we'll begin with some examples that show output-focused leaders in action. These are imagined composite scenarios, based on real-life situations, which I've put together to offer a glimpse of where you might need to channel your energies in your local context.

Scenario 1: 'Fierce conversations'

Consider a pastor who arrives as the new leader of an established church. There are many ministries already in place, so he decides to spend the first six months observing how everything operates. But one thing constantly confronts him: the music at church on Sundays. It is painful to his newly-arrived ears. The choir sings poorly, but the biggest issue is the piano player: he finds it hard to keep time, and often misses the beginning of each song—perhaps because he is very hard of hearing. But these people 'own' these roles. The piano player has made it quite clear that this is his thing. The congregation bears with it, hanging on in quiet desperation.

They've come to believe that this is just the way it is. This is what church is like, and church wasn't meant to be easy.

What should the new leader do?

Now imagine that the pastor and a group of others in the church have considered the issues raised in this book. During that time, a question is put to the leader: Is the music ministry impacting our ability to achieve your desired output of conversion and maturity? Yes, of course it is. It is almost impossible to bring anyone to church because, unless you've grown up with us, the music is terribly off-putting.

So, the next question comes: what are you going to do about it? The answer: we'll pray.

That's a good answer, to be sure. As noted earlier, "you do not have, because you do not ask" (Jas 4:2). One of the chief pieces of evidence that we are gripped by God's deepest concerns for his world and by our failures as churches is heartfelt and persevering prayer. Prayer ought to bubble forth from us at all times. It is right that we live in a state of constant groaning before God over the lostness of our world and over the impediments to reaching the world for Christ.

But prayer, as important as it is, is sometimes the pain-avoidance answer. For this prayer usually takes the form of asking God to make someone miraculously appear—someone who will make the difficulty go away without anyone getting hurt.

So, the discussion returns to the leader—the person most responsible for the church's present failure to achieve its mission and maturity outcomes: Aside from praying, which is essential, what are you going to do about the problem? The cavalry isn't coming. It's up to you, the leader. What are *you* going to do about it? Someone raises the notion of 'fierce conversations': how do we initiate them, what should be said, and how does this form part of the task of discipleship?

After some time, the leader determines to do something. The pain of not changing becomes greater than the pain of changing. In particular, he begins to feel the pain of seeing so many people in the local area unable to come and hear the gospel, because his church is repelling everyone except for those who are already committed. In other words, he sees a direct connection between the shape of his church meeting and the failure to reach more people in his area. People are going to hell because his church is poorly run. He has been driven and empowered to embrace the pain of change.

So, he has the 'fierce conversation'. What's more, he comes to appreciate that this difficult conversation was a crucial moment of discipleship for the pianist. This isn't a case of needing to treat his musician as 'collateral damage' so the church could grow; this is the pastor taking responsibility for the growth outcomes of the church *and* for the Christian maturity of his musician! Seeing this conversation as part of discipleship casts it very differently. It's not just some kind of 'sacking'; it's about everyone's movement towards growth and change.

Thanks be to God, the conversation goes very well. It's the first time someone has really pushed this musician in his life with Christ and in what it looks like to be truly sold out to Jesus and to die to self. It is an opportunity to bring real growth and change in the man's life. This, in turn, enables change in the church's life. Things have now turned around dramatically, and the church has begun to grow numerically. Within two years, it has grown by 50 percent, with many people being converted.

Scenario 2: New building

Imagine a church that meets in a very old building that has served its purposes well in years gone by. But the building is regularly full, and there is no room for congregational growth. It's satisfying for the pastor to preach to a full building, but he wants to set his vision by the fields, not by the barn. He begins to feel the immense pain of so many people around them going to hell. And he realizes that the church's failure to reach any new people is because of the way they're doing church—*where* they're doing it, and *how* they're doing it. And as the leader, he realizes that he bears significant responsibility for the church's failure to make any changes that mean it might reach more people.

As it happens, a nearby building has room for many more seats, and is also a little closer to the city centre—potentially an ideal space. But it will cost a lot of money, and will mean a massive move from a very familiar space. And yet the pain of not changing has pushed the leader out of his stupor. He is resolved to make more space, and so he embraces the pain of change.

He begins by taking his people through a discussion of the 'five truths plus one'.[1] He presents them with the vision of the rescue crew seeking to save people from the ferry-boat disaster.[2] He talks about their collective responsibility for outputs. And, slowly, he wins people to the need to embrace change.

Now, some years later, they are in that new space. In fact, within just a few months of moving, they grew by 20 percent. The change of venue, plus several other changes, has meant that the church is seeing a steady stream of converts. There is energy and momentum.

Scenario 3: Resources redeployed

A pastor leads a busy church that runs numerous activities, but he has come to recognize that these activities leave little in reserve to invest in building the church's energy for mission. Church members are highly committed to their respective groups and activities, but not all these activities are part of the church's core business of making disciples. People's busyness is making it practically impossible to reach their community with the gospel. The pastor knows the burning desire of God's heart is for people's salvation, but thousands are being lost without an effective witness from this local church. He's begun to feel that this lack of effectiveness is his responsibility.

So, he decides to act. In the first instance, this means starting to say 'no' more often. It also means taking the difficult but necessary step of shutting down ministries that aren't serving the mission. He does this in a context of also teaching and preaching about the larger purposes of God. He works with the elders and other leaders, patiently and deliberately taking them through the various principles of a passion for the lost, leadership responsibilities, and the pain of people's visible needs versus the pain of their invisible needs. Gradually, he shifts the church's resources. Now, they are seeing growth and new converts. There is a renewed sense of purpose and focus. Things have changed dramatically.

———

I hope these three scenarios show that leading the church through a deliberate process of growth and change *is* possible. It's not rocket science. But I also hope that the scenarios don't give the false impression that it's easy. It's hard work. Not every real-life story ends in obvious 'success'. Leading through these kinds of changes can be exhausting, demanding, and very painful. The examples are easy to read on the page, but they represent months—or sometimes years—of hard and determined work. That's why leading for change is not primarily a matter of techniques and skill sets, but of deep conviction—of being fuelled by a heart that pulsates with the gospel, with God's love for the lost, and with God's love for his people.

Once again, step back and ask the big questions: If somebody cut you, would you bleed the gospel? If we pricked your finger, would God's love for his world ooze out? Yes? Then you're ready to lead the church to the changes that are needed.

With these scenarios under our belt, let's turn to our five

foundations. These foundations are not so much a precise blueprint for how to structure your church or ministry. Rather, they aim to capture an overall philosophy of ministry and can help leaders to analyze the steps that need to be taken and the areas of a ministry that need to be resourced. The five foundations are:

- Clarity is king
- Be faithful in inputs
- Take responsibility and build responsibility (in others)
- Break down the big things
- Understanding the ecosystem

The first two of these have been covered earlier in the book and so will be addressed very briefly here.

Foundation one: Clarity is king

One of the great dangers of pastoral ministry is that we get so caught up in the hurly-burly of church life that we just lose focus. As the days and weeks roll by, we can lose sight of our God-given purpose. Why are we here?

As I said in chapter 3, clarity is king for leaders. Get clarity on your purpose and your role, and keep hold of that clarity at all costs. We're here to make mature disciples of Christ in ever-increasing numbers. That's the bottom line. Don't lose your clarity.

Foundation two: Be faithful in inputs

I've urged you to become an output-driven leader, but even the most output-driven leader cannot bypass or ignore inputs—it's the inputs that produce the outputs! And God has told us what the key inputs for any gospel ministry must be. Preaching and teaching the word of God, prayer, and the community, people together are all central to our ministry. Whatever else you do, never lose sight of these inputs.

Foundation three: Take responsibility and build responsibility

Leaders in every other area of life are expected to take responsibility for the results of their work. Yet within the world of Christian leadership, there is so much that conspires to take away any sense of personal responsibility for outputs. We have the get-out-of-jail-free card of saying, "God gives the growth". We can become conditioned to just turn up and go through the motions, with little or no expectation that our ministry might experience growth and change.

But as we've seen, this attitude is incompatible with Scripture. As leaders, we must take responsibility for the fruitfulness (or lack thereof) of our work, and we must instill our congregation with a sense of responsibility.

But *how* do we exercise responsibility? You want to make a difference, and you're ready to start taking appropriate responsibility (still under God, of course) for outputs. What do you do? And how do you build responsibility in others? This is where we need to get a little more practical.

A good place to start is with what we might call *leadership levels*. I want to describe four such levels. The first three sit well under this 'foundation', while the fourth may sit more naturally under a later heading. Understanding these different levels of leadership will help us embrace our role in bringing growth and change.

1. Learn to lead yourself

When it comes to your growth as a person and your growth as a leader, you must take responsibility for your own life. In other words, you have to be proactive, not just reactive. And that starts with knowing what you're trying to achieve. What is your life for? Why did God put you here? What do you want to achieve in the few short years that he has put you on this earth?

I am thoroughly convinced—by the word of God—that the purpose of my life is to make mature disciples of Jesus Christ in ever-increasing number, to the glory of God. That's where I really want to make a difference. It's as simple as that.

Once you've worked out what you want to achieve, this will begin to work itself out in your life in all kinds of practical ways. And one of the chief ways to take control of your life is to start saying 'no'.

In truth, this is not quite the right way to say it. Because even though we usually don't realize it, we're all saying 'no' to things all the time. Every time you say 'yes' to something or someone, you've said 'no' to using that time for anything else. If you're married, when you said 'yes' to your spouse, you were also "forsaking all others" and saying 'no' to every other person on the planet.

So, it's not just a matter of starting to say 'no'; the key is taking charge of your 'no' by working out where, when and why you will give your 'yes'.

In the first chapter of Mark's Gospel, everyone is looking for Jesus because they've heard about his power and they want to be healed. But Jesus says 'no'—he must move on to the next towns to preach, for that is why he came. He had a larger priority, a larger concern that demanded his devotion.

There are only so many hours in a week. There are only so many weeks in a year. There are only so many years in a lifetime. How will you use them to influence gospel outcomes? Of course, if you're working in a team ministry there will rightly be expectations from others in that team, especially the team leader. But wherever possible, be proactive. Lead yourself. Take control of your diary—before anyone else can fill it up, *you* should fill it with the things that matter most and add the most value to your disciple-making endeavours. Take charge of what you do on a day-to-day level.

2. Learn to lead others

It's important that we don't just lead ourselves, but that we learn to lead others so that they will contribute to gospel outputs. This is a skill that needs to be learned. Just being sincere and passionate as a Christian is not in itself going to lead others forward.

There are two different aspects to this: leading others in their spiritual growth and formation, and leading others in ministry tasks. The two things are connected, but are slightly different, and require different skills.

Learning to lead others spiritually is about preaching the word of God—whether through sermons, one-to-one ministry, or leading small groups—and teaching others to live the Christian life. This is the bread-and-butter work of discipleship, and learning these skills—learning how to preach, how to meet with people, how to teach them about personal growth in Christian maturity—is incredibly important. For this is where we see people grow and change in the most fundamental ways.

But we must also *learn to lead others into ministry*. This can only happen if we are leading others spiritually, for spiritual growth is the fuel of ministry growth. But leading others into ministry is a slightly different skill. If you don't develop this skill, you won't grow your work.

This involves a raft of new things.

To begin, it involves vision setting, or a kind of Bible teaching that builds a fire in the belly such that a person wants to devote themselves fully to the work of the Lord (see 1 Cor 15:58). This is the kind of preaching that does something more than merely explain the Bible passage (as fundamental as that is). It is the kind of preaching that presents the 'five foundational truths plus one', along with many other biblical pieces, to help people see the big picture of God's plans for the world and for our lives. It applies the Scriptures in such a way that listeners long to "seek first the kingdom of God and his righteousness" (Matt 6:33).

From there, it includes the skills of active recruitment, delegation, management and review.

Some people hear the word of God and just 'organically' want to give more of themselves to disciple-making activities (or so it seems from a human perspective, though we know this is the work of God's Spirit). We pray for this and preach with this aim. But this will only take us so far. If this is as far as our ministry goes, we have fallen into what might be called the 'maturity myth': the idea that if we just preach and pray, then people will mature and they will naturally and spontaneously want to step into informal and formal ministry roles. While this will happen for some, there are many for whom it won't happen, *even though they are growing in gospel convictions*.

This is the key thought for us to grasp. People are in such different places. Many will carry a great deal of insecurity and baggage, and will find it very hard to volunteer for roles and responsibilities. 'What if the leadership of the church doesn't think I'm ready? What if I fail?' So, they sit quietly, wanting more but not knowing what to do. In my experience of observing many churches, combined with research in this area, I would safely estimate that at least 40 percent of people in a typical Bible-believing church sit in this category. They *want* to serve, but they don't know *how* to serve, or they are too nervous or insecure to put themselves forward.

Everything changes if a leader initiates a conversation. When a key leader sits with a person, gains insight into their life, and helps them find a path into fruitful formal ministry, so many more people will step up and serve.

In our church context, we call this a 'serve chat'. It may not be the most imaginative name, but it is a critical piece of our discipleship plan. We aim to sit with every new person (once they've begun to be established in other ways) and every disconnected regular, talk with them about their life, their struggles, their hopes and their longings, and then work with them towards finding a role that will enable them to more deliberately become a contributing part of growing their own church.

Organizing and having these conversations is a skill. It requires clarity around the ministry possibilities that are available and needed in the church (which itself involves understanding the organizational system of church—more on this below), and around what each role might involve. It requires an ability to help a person see how their contribution could truly make a difference to the larger purpose of glorifying Christ. And it requires the ability to follow up and manage people so that they are supported and helped to grow in whatever role they've stepped into.

It also requires a shift in values—a shift from leaders who love doing the ministry to leaders who love ensuring that the ministry is done. This is harder than it seems, because it is a matter of personal growth and change for a leader. So many leaders want a church full of people who are active in ministry, yet so many bemoan the lack of participation. One of the most common reasons is that so many of us struggle to let go of doing the work ourselves and to delight in the work being done. We must shift to celebrating the success of others and embracing something of a loss of personal connection to the entirety of the coal face.

The key is to build the *desire* to serve, then to actively recruit. Match the right people to the right roles. Learn to delegate. And learn to manage and grow people as they serve. Learn to rejoice in the fact that the work is being done, not in doing all the work yourself. In this you start to build a sense of partnership and responsibility for ministry in others.

This is just the beginning of what can be said on this point, but at least it's a start.

3. Learn to lead leaders

Leading ourselves and leading others are obviously important, but this third level is where it becomes possible to achieve real multiplication. If a leader can learn to lead leaders, there is the possibility of expanding the work far beyond the ability or capacity of one leader. Now, many more people will be labouring and serving to grow and develop the work. Rather than just adding to the ministry, we can multiply the ministry.

Given the scale of the need around us, it is critical that we learn this level of leadership. One pastor can only do so much; many more leaders and elders can expand and grow the work far beyond the abilities of one leader. Imagine a church where there are many men and women who take on the burden of leadership among the people of God. Imagine a church where a growing team of leaders work together to mobilize the saints so that their gifts and energies are directed in effective and fruitful ways.

The key here is a leader who knows how to raise up other leaders *and* lead them. Again, this is not as straightforward as it seems. Some have described this as the shift from being a 'shepherd' to being a 'rancher'—perhaps one of the most profound changes a leader could ever make. It means shifting from being the pastor/shepherd of every person, at least in a close, one-to-one way. It means raising up and leading other shepherds who do this close work. It therefore means rejoicing in the fact that others are now doing the close pastoral work, rather than needing to be the person who is needed by everyone in church. And it means leading those leaders so that they are equipped and empowered to do the work and to start leading others for themselves.

This is a very difficult shift to make. And so, to return to one of the core theses of this book, we will only make this shift if the pain of not changing is greater than the pain of changing.

Together with this emotional change and this shift in values, we also need a shift in the kind of skills required. Much of this is simply growing more adept at the kinds of skills needed in level two—delegation, management, review, and so on. But there are other elements as well.

One critical factor is the ability to cast an outcome-oriented vision. One way to understand the difference between *doing* the ministry and *leading* the ministry is that the leader has taken responsibility for achieving an outcome and leading others towards that outcome.

This is the difference between rosters (also known as rotas) and teams. Churches often function with a series of rosters: people are added to a list to come and serve in a particular area of ministry—perhaps teaching the kids on a Sunday morning. Such rosters cultivate (and in fact operate on) an input mindset. People turn up to do a job; they perform a function, then they go home. If something else comes up, they drop out. After all, they're just filling a slot or doing a job.

But now join this person together with a team of other people, with everyone invested in achieving a specified outcome—in the lives of the children they teach, in our example. Give them responsibility for achieving that outcome, under the care of a leader particularly charged with that responsibility, and church life is transformed. Now there is real energy and commitment. People invest far more deeply and wholeheartedly. Instead of casually dropping out and calling the team leader to have someone fill their gap, they make every effort to be there. There are now more people lying awake at night thinking about the progress of the work—which is a sure sign that the ministry is maturing.

How does a leader raise and lead these kinds of leaders?

In many ways it is more of what we saw at level two, just with greater skill. But it is also a significant shift in culture. It is the complex ability of letting go—so that others can step in and step up to undertake high-level leadership roles that were once the preserve of the senior minister—while also keeping hold. Don't abdicate your role as leader. Leaders can give away and delegate their role too easily, effectively abdicating responsibility instead of managing the various growing teams so that they work together to achieve something far greater than any one person can achieve alone.

Giving other leaders responsibility is not like giving them money (once you had it, but now you've given it to them). It's more like taking the flame that is burning on your candle and sharing that same fire with another person, who is holding their own candle.[3] Now, you both carry responsibility for the task. How is this kind of leadership expressed? By leading leaders in such a way that you remain in their lives and remain in their work. For example, you now establish meetings between the leaders of various parts of the work to ensure that the whole work moves forward in a coordinated and aligned way. This means learning how to run meetings with high-level leaders, which is a skill in itself. It's all part of letting go and holding on all at the same time.

These things are difficult. But again, we won't work at doing these things and developing these skills unless we've felt the pain of not changing.

4. Learn to lead an organization

The fundamental principle at this level of leadership is that a body of people is bigger and more complex than the sum of its parts. Any organization, including a church, is not just a gathering of individuals; the organization (or we might prefer the word 'community') becomes, in effect, a living organism that takes on a life of its own. A network of relationships and a system of behaviours emerge, which gives a unique flavour and colour to everything that happens.

You see this dynamic at work in families. There is a whole branch of modern psychology called 'family systems' therapy, which encourages and helps people to work through their issues in the context of their 'family units'. The way a group of people relate to each other—the web of relationships, the habits that form—are all very important. Now multiply that into a community that includes 30, 50 or 100 families, and it's obvious that leaders need to be alert to all kinds of complex forces.

Step one in leading an organization is owning the fact that it is impossible to lead such a thing without getting organized. And part of getting organized is recognizing that the great purpose of church needs to be broken down. This brings us to back to the fourth of our five foundational points.

Foundation four: Break down the big things

The task of making mature disciples is large and complex. There are many components that need to come together for our disciple-making aims to be achieved as effectively as we hope. How do we achieve such big aims? It begins by embracing the fact that we lead a complex organization. And given that we're faced with such a large and multifaceted task, we need to break the larger outcome down into secondary outcomes that all serve the purpose of making mature disciples in ever-increasing numbers. In this, we are beginning to apply 'systems thinking' to the life of a church community. This isn't as 'businesslike' as it might first appear. Think instead of an 'organism' or a church 'family system' (large families often break things down to ensure the family is well loved).

There are three different ways we could break things down.

1. A basic system

In this type of approach, we simply categorize or list the elements we need to make a church—whether an existing church or a new church plant—work well. For example, we might determine that a church needs three systems to function well: a good Sunday gathering with clear and engaging preaching; a children's ministry; and a network of small groups. Depending on our situation, we might add other elements (such as a youth ministry). Whatever items we put on the list, we'd expect to see reasonable growth in most contexts once we get these elements in place and functioning well. This is perhaps the most common way to break down the elements of church life. But while its simplicity is appealing, it lacks the ability to help us analyze our ministry in a deep and biblical way. What's more, such a breakdown tends to focus on inputs rather than outputs.

2. The pathway

We might therefore turn to the second method—what we could call *the 'pathway' approach to ministry*. In this analysis, we would start with two big areas: we need to focus on *getting people* (mission or evangelism), and we need to focus on *growing people* (maturity or discipleship).

But if we stop here, we've only broken down our ministry into two very large categories: mission/evangelism, and maturity/discipleship. Therefore, it's useful to break each category down even further. In order to *get* people, we might identify that we have to: make initial contact with them; invite them to come and hear the gospel; share the gospel with them; and see them converted. In order to *grow* people, we have to do four more things: establish people in church; see them matured in the word (e.g. through being part of a small group); get them serving; and get them engaged in evangelism. This gives us a total of eight categories.

If we want our church or ministry to grow, we need all these pieces working well in various ways. A model like this can be applied in different ways at different times. When we first planted EV Church in the mid 1990s, the average person in our part of Australia had some kind of Christian understanding, so there was a good chance that they'd come to faith in Jesus through evangelistic preaching at church. But in our current climate, people are so far away from any knowledge of the gospel that we need to preach to them, and preach to them again, and again—then perhaps sit down and take them through a whole Gospel or through a specially tailored evangelistic course. It might take many months to see a person converted, and only then can we begin to establish them in the faith. In our context, we also realized that we need to engage a range of ministries and approaches to help a new Christian get established in the faith. If we dropped them into church and left it at that, they often bounced straight out again. If we engaged them in a range of ways—through one-to-many (a follow-up small group) or one-to-one Bible reading, for example—there was a much greater chance that they'd stick.

Regardless of the details of how you apply this model, one thing should jump out at you: *nobody can do this on their own*. No human being can get all eight steps firing; you need a team. This means that to get all eight steps firing, you need to be able to recruit, train and delegate. You need to lead people into ministry, then lead the leaders. This is closely followed by *the need for a strategic plan*, where you're not just flailing around and responding to everyone's demands on your time. Instead, you're focused on ensuring that each step is firing, with teams of people who are committed to the output and taking responsibility for moving people along the pathway. The leader's job is to make the whole system work. You're no longer at the mercy of everyone else's agenda: you're setting the agenda.

Part of the skill (and the challenge) of leadership in this model is working out which parts of the operation are most critical to making the whole enterprise work. What parts of the operation demand most of your time as leader?

Think, for example, about a Formula 1 team: what is it trying to achieve? The objective is fairly simple: get your car around the track more quickly than anyone else. The team principal needs to understand how each member of the team plays a part in achieving that outcome. As anyone can see, some parts of the team will have a greater impact on the outcome than others. The drivers or the chief technical director, for example, will have a much bigger impact on the output than the guy who brings everyone their lunch. The team principal will therefore allocate resources accordingly.

Now, let's say that the team principal decides to rank each part of the team out of five. The lunch guy gets three out of five because the food isn't always great. And the drivers are only hitting three out of five because they're always arguing with each other and are failing to drive well. Would the team principal prioritize fixing both areas with the same sense of concern? Of course not. It would be great for both areas to be fives, but one matters much more than the other.

The point is that we could analyze every aspect of our church, ranking it between one and five, and mislead ourselves. One of the challenges of leadership is to see that some parts of the whole are more important than others. Any area that scores one or two out of five will always be a problem, but how urgently do we address these areas? How important is it that we bring them up to a four or five? Where do we invest our time or allocate our resources?

How does a leader learn to navigate this challenge? There are many ways. You could spend time visiting a church that has worked through the issues. You could spend time with other leaders. You could read books, or attend workshops or training courses. It's such an important skill to develop, because our job as leaders is to make things work together so that the desired output is achieved.

Every leader will have their own favourite part of church life. For some, it's the small group work; for others, it's the evangelism course. It is easy to pour all your energy into one or other of these works depending on where your passion lies. But this can cause a leader to lose sight of the big picture. If all we do is invest our energy in one part, the whole will stop working. We'll end up with a church 'body' that has a huge mouth, one hand, and no legs. It won't be the church of Ephesians 4, where the leadership has equipped the saints "for the work of ministry, for building up the body of Christ" (Eph 4:12).

Which parts of your ministry are most important to achieving your purpose? The critical piece in the life of any healthy church is the ministry of the word, so it is absolutely vital that this is our highest priority. Yet we need to value all the pieces that fit together as part of the church's overall task of making disciples.

The pathway approach has many strengths, and can be very useful in helping us to analyze the ministry and see where our resources should be deployed. But it is not without its weaknesses. Perhaps its most significant weakness is that it doesn't represent all aspects of church life—especially the idea that we gather at church not just as a means to an end, but as an end in itself. We gather together to express our love for God and for each other. To put it cynically, or perhaps even a little cruelly, the pathway model might be the engineer's analysis of church life: a prosaic and functional model that doesn't capture the essence of what it means to be a Spirit-filled community of God's people.

And so, we turn to a third model: the pentagon.

3. The pentagon

Many (including me) prefer this model because it attempts to convey that the purpose of church is not just to move people through a pathway like items on a conveyor belt. The higher goal is that we are moved to praise God together and to enjoy him forever. These elements—that we praise God, and that we do it *together* as members of the body of Christ—are critical to the health of the church.[4]

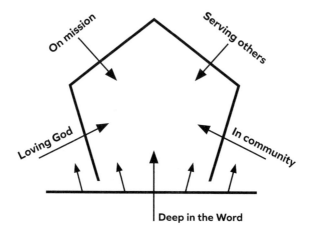

Deep in the Word

The bottom of the pentagon is 'deep in the word', showing that this is the engine for the whole model of discipleship. The word of God gives shape to every aspect of church life and permeates every other aspect of our life together. The Scriptures are the foundation for every mature disciple and for every mature church.

With this foundation in place, the four other interconnected elements of the pentagon can come together. A deep trust in the word of God will give rise to disciples who *love the Lord their God* with all their heart, soul, mind and strength, and so give themselves to lives of thanksgiving and holiness. These disciples will realize that Christ has not saved them to live as lone rangers, but that he gathers us to live in *a community of his people* in the local church—knowing and loving each other, and being known and loved by each other. Mature disciples will give themselves gladly to *serve others* in formal and informal ways. And because they share God's heart for the lost, they will be committed to *mission*, praying and working so that others are converted.

These five elements don't fit on a pathway, but they are critical to the health and life of a Christian, and to the life and health of a church.

Foundation five: Understanding the ecosystem

Personally, I believe the pentagon is the framework that best captures the various elements of how the gospel plays out in the life of God's people. But we also use the pathway as a complement. Both have their place, and both are important. But whatever tool you adopt is just that: a *tool* to help you work out how to manage and resource a ministry. No model will express the totality of what is needed in church life. You could build a hexagon, for example, that assigns a particular place to prayer—as opposed to this model, which sees prayer as part and parcel of 'loving God' and expects prayer to permeate every aspect of the ministry.

In fact, there is no great need to choose just one model. We have found that the pathway and the pentagon can work together. We move quite freely between the two models to help us analyze what's happening. We arrange ourselves around both insights, because both add something useful to the equation and help us to make sense of what's happening.

The important thing is to understand that the various parts of the Christian life, and the various parts of church life, work together as an *ecosystem*. Our models must help us create churches where ministries are not siloed off from one another. The pentagon, I believe, will help you to see a fuller, richer picture of how church life should operate. It will help you to see how each of the outputs that we are pursuing function together as interconnected parts of the whole.

ACKNOWLEDGEMENTS

It ought to be obvious, but anything that has merit in these pages will be because of the investment of others. Like everyone, I'm the product of so many influences—all of them ultimately gifts from God himself, the source of all things.

These influences go back as far as the family I grew up in. I thank God for them—a mother and father who taught me many critical lessons about life.

But more particularly, these influences relate to the very specific Christian shaping I've enjoyed: the biblical rigour of Sydney Anglican ministries; the depth and richness of Moore College; many great theologians who took time to produce books I could read and digest; men who took the time to invest in me personally—Phillip Jensen, Col Marshall, John Chapman, Brian Telfer, and so many others; a father-in-law, Michael Corbett-Jones, who helped me think harder about how humans work; and the many different teams I've worked in and with.

Ministry for me has always been a team affair. We are all so much better together. I've been incredibly blessed to have been surrounded by great teams of people. And this was particularly the case as Cathie and I launched into planting the church that is now called EV (it began its life as 'Central Coast Evangelical Church', but very quickly we realized no-one could pronounce it or even understand what it meant, so 'EV' it became). Other earlier ministries gave me the opportunity to test and develop my ministry thinking and skills. I was given a great start in being able to try things with lots of support and feedback (again, thank God for the fellowship of Anglican churches in Sydney). But the deepening and refining has happened over the past three decades with such a wonderful congregation of God's people who make up EV, and an absolutely exceptional team of leaders. This includes the many passionate volunteers who have done all they can to advance the cause of the gospel in their context and with the time available, as well as the many paid staff leaders I've had the privilege to work with. The names are too numerous to spell out and the risk is too great to miss someone so thoroughly significant. So I want to just acknowledge the blessing it has been to work together with so many fine Christian men and women. Every week I look out at the congregations of EV and see so many people who have poured themselves into the work and who have partnered in seeking to grow the work in our immediate area (and then beyond, through church planting and support of mission and national work) and I'm stirred to keep going. And then I move between various meetings where I sit with men and women who are so thoroughly captured by Christ and a desire to make him known (from senior staff meetings, to church council, to all staff, to one-to-ones, and so on). God has used all these people and all these settings to grow and shape me.

I also want to acknowledge the very direct influence of the teams of people who now make up the 'Reach Australia' network (which grew out of what we once called 'Geneva Push', which was previously only focused on promoting church planting). Over the last 10–15 years, we've tried to clarify and sharpen what it is to lead a work that makes the kind of difference God calls us to make. There has been lots of debate and discussion, all of it wonderfully helpful—and, we trust, a blessing now to others.

Even in writing this book, I have much to thank God for in the team that have been part of helping me put it together. I'm not a writer. My world is preaching, teaching, and leading in small and large settings. But God gave me a great editor by the name of Geoff Robson. If this book reads well, it's because of him! He has been infinitely patient and very insightful. God has also given me an amazingly competent PA in Anne Boyle, who has made it possible for me to carve out the time to write.

I want to acknowledge the unique contributions my children have made. When we started in paid public ministry, it was a choice Cathie and I made. But our children were conscripted. It wasn't always easy for them. But in so many ways they've contributed to my thinking and to our ministry. They are brilliant at cutting through things to the heart of what matters. Pastoral ministry is like parenting, and parenting is like pastoral ministry. The one informs the other, as the ones parented inform the parent! Now, as adults, they are gladly choosing to pursue the cause of Christ in their own settings and contexts.

Finally, in all of this is the tireless partnership of my wonderful wife, Cathie. She has given so much of herself, but has done it gladly as she herself seeks to honour her God and Saviour. She has brought many observations, critiques and insights that have been hugely helpful. She has been a special gift of God.

> We have this treasure in jars of clay to show that the surpassing power belongs to God and not to us. (2 Cor 4:7)

NOTES

Chapter 1

1   RE Quinn, *Deep Change: Discovering the leader within*, Jossey-Bass, 1996, pp 92–93.

2   D Martyn Lloyd-Jones, *Preaching and Preachers*, Zondervan, 1971, p 9.

Chapter 2

1   IH Murray, *Evangelicalism Divided: A record of crucial change in the years 1950 to 2000*, Banner of Truth Trust, 2001, pp 170–171.

2   Quoted in Murray, *Evangelicalism Divided*, p 171.

3   At the same time, beware the leader who doesn't even notice he isn't liked—that's a problem along another dimension!

4   Cited in JJ Murray, 'Are we taking error seriously?', *Christian Study Library*, 2015 (christianstudylibrary.org/article/are-we-taking-error-seriously).

5   See R Trumbull, 'Pope Paul's coming visit causes dissension among Australian Protestants', *The New York Times*, 8 October 1970 (nytimes.com/1970/10/08/archives/pope-pauls-coming-visit-causes-dissension-among-australian.html).

Chapter 3

1   I should say at this point that my interest is not in offering a simplistic critique of any and every use of the phrase "just be faithful" (or similar variations). My interest is in contemplating the deeper, underlying attitude that, in my observation, often accompanies such a statement (and in prompting thoughtful reflection from leaders who never use those words, but whose ministry practice aligns with the statement). It's possible that a Christian leader might use the word 'faithfulness' to mean something that aligns very closely with the biblical vision for ministry that I am presenting. As we all know, words can have a range of meanings, depending on context. I will say a little more about this when discussing 'inputs' and 'outputs' in chapter 7.

2   The Greek word translated "building up" (4:12; see also 4:16) could equally be translated as 'build', which would more readily indicate the two-dimensional growth intended in Paul's meaning. Add to this the fact that one of the foundational gifts given to 'build' the church is the evangelist (4:11) and it is clear God's purpose is twofold: deepen spiritually *and* add numerically.

3 See ESV footnote on Matt 18:9. Note also that Mark's record of Jesus' teaching includes the citation of Isaiah 66:24 to drive home the seriousness of hell—"where their worm does not die and the fire is not quenched" (Mark 9:48).

4 Even this request might in fact be a reference to eternal things—some expositors argue that it is a reference to the 'messianic banquet' or to the 'bread of heaven'. See ESV footnote on Matt 6:11: "Give us this day our bread for tomorrow".

5 Used with permission from his personal correspondence to friends and family during his last few months.

6 R Baxter, *The Reformed Pastor*, Banner of Truth Trust, 1974, pp 204–5.

7 The original twelve minus Judas (with Matthias not yet having been added to their number).

8 A Köstenberger and PT O'Brien, *Salvation to the Ends of the Earth: A biblical theology of mission*, New Studies in Biblical Theology, Apollos, 2001, p 108.

9 Köstenberger and O'Brien, *Salvation to the Ends of the Earth*, p 105.

10 New Testament scholar Peter Orr has argued persuasively that "the work of the Lord" does not refer to "essentially *anything* that Christians do *because* of the resurrection", but rather that it specifically refers to *"what believers do to advance the gospel among unbelievers and to establish believers in the gospel"* (emphasis original). See P Orr, 'Abounding in the Work of the Lord (1 Cor 15:58): Everything we do as Christians or specific gospel work?', *Themelios*, 38:2, pp 205–214. For a simplified version of Orr's important insights, see P Orr, 'The work of the Lord', *The Briefing*, 2 September 2014 (thebriefing.com.au/2014/09/the-work-of-the-lord).

Chapter 4

1 Notice the way that Paul starts his letters to the Corinthians and the Thessalonians by referring to recipients not as part of the church, but as *the church*.

2 See also Ps 127:1–2; Prov 19:21, 21:31; Zech 4:6; John 15:5; 2 Cor 4:3–6.

3 T Keller, *Center Church: Doing biblical, gospel-centered ministry in your city*, Zondervan, 2012, pp 13–14.

4 See, for example, DA Carson, *The Gospel According to John*, The Pillar New Testament Commentary, Eerdmans, 1991. Commenting on John 15:5–6, Carson says: "There has been considerable dispute over the nature of the 'fruit' that is envisaged: the fruit, we are told, is obedience, or new converts, or love, or Christian character. These interpretations are reductionistic. The branch's purpose is to bear much fruit (v. 5), but the next verses show that this fruit is the consequence of prayer in Jesus' name, and is to the Father's glory (vv. 7, 8, 16). This suggests that the 'fruit' in the vine imagery represents everything that is the product of effective prayer in Jesus' name, including obedience to Jesus' commands (v. 10), experience of Jesus' joy (v. 11—as earlier his peace, 14:27), love for one another (v. 12), and witness to the world (vv. 16, 27). This fruit is nothing less than the outcome of persevering dependence on the vine, driven by faith, embracing all of the believer's life and the product of his witness." It's worth adding that I believe Jesus' focus is on bearing fruit *in community*. That is, as it relates to the fruit of conversion growth, he intends believers to participate *together* in producing this fruit, rather than an individualistic reading where each believer is expected to produce conversion fruit on their own.

5 For instance, if 'just being faithful' is your goal and you achieve it, then you have 'succeeded', regardless of the outcomes.

6   Churches vary in size for a host of reasons, many of which have nothing to do with the spiritual merit or giftedness of the leader involved. Surely this is part of what Paul was combating in his engagement with the 'super-apostles' in Corinth (see 2 Corinthians 11–12).

7   For examples of this type of language being used, see: E Swanson and S Williams, *To Transform a City: Whole church, whole gospel, whole city*, Zondervan, 2010; 'Lausanne Occasional Paper: Towards the transformation of our cities/regions', *Lausanne Movement*, 2004 (lausanne.org/content/towards-transformation-citiesregions-lop-37); R Hunter, 'Should your church "transform" the city?', *The Gospel Coalition*, 30 April 2019 (thegospelcoalition.org/article/church-transform-city).

8   Edwards first preached this famous sermon, entitled 'Sinners in the Hands of an Angry God', in Enfield, Massachusetts (now Connecticut) in 1741. The full text of the sermon is available online in multiple places (e.g. monergism.com/thethreshold/sdg/edwards/edwards_angry.html).

Chapter 5

1   AH Maslow, 'A theory of human motivation', *Psychological Review*, 50, 1943, pp 370–396 (psychclassics.yorku.ca/Maslow/motivation.htm).

2   In using the phrase 'acts of charity', I'm aware that churches and Christian movements use different terminology to refer to essentially the same thing—Christians doing good works to care for the poor, the lowly and the marginalized, out of a desire to serve God and to acknowledge and share his heart for those who are least in the world's eyes. Another common label would be 'mercy ministry', but your church or movement may have its own preferred label. I'll say more about such ministries below, but please note that I'm simply seeking to be broadly descriptive, not pejorative in any way, in using such labels.

3   See J Piper, 'Christians care about all suffering and injustice', *Desiring God*, 25 August 2019 (desiringgod.org/messages/christians-care-about-all-suffering-and-injustice).

4   Think of the way that a marriage is established in the wedding ceremony, but is not consummated until some time later. In both cases (a marriage and the kingdom of God), it's natural to expect that one will follow very soon after the other. Any time delay between the two requires a very good reason.

5   See Carson, *The Gospel According to John* (especially his comments on verses such as 1:9–10, 7:7, 14:17 and 15:18–19).

6   For more on this, see V Mangalwadi, *The Book that Made Your World: How the Bible created the soul of Western civilization*, Thomas Nelson, 2011 (especially chapter 12 on university: 'Why educate your subjects?').

7   For more on this important topic, see E Thornett (ed), *Evangelism and Social Action*, Minizine, Matthias Media, 2011.

Chapter 6

1   See DA Carson, 'The beauty of biblical balance', in PG Bolt (ed), *Let the Word do the Work: Essays in Honour of Phillip D. Jensen*, Matthias Media, 2015, pp 109–116.

2   This doesn't mean we should embrace the 'seeker-sensitive' model, in which every part of the main church gathering—including the preaching—is completely reshaped around what a new person, especially an unbelieving new person, will find helpful or engaging.

Wherever it has been tried, this has meant that everything in church life has been 'dumbed down' and Christians were not properly fed and matured. The movement may have had the best of intentions (to reach more people with the gospel), but it failed to recognize that the shape and nature of the central church gathering profoundly shapes the whole tone and tenor of every aspect of church life. Bill Hybels, the founder and former senior pastor of Willow Creek Community Church—the church at the forefront of the seeker-sensitive movement—has spoken honestly and movingly about the movement's failure to properly disciple believers: "Some of the stuff that we have put millions of dollars into, thinking it would really help our people grow and develop spiritually, when the data actually came back it wasn't helping people that much. Other things that we didn't put that much money into and didn't put much staff against is stuff our people are crying out for. We made a mistake. What we should have done when people crossed the line of faith and become Christians, we should have started telling people and teaching people that they have to take responsibility to become 'self feeders.' We should have gotten people, taught people, how to read their Bible between services, how to do the spiritual practices much more aggressively on their own." See B Burney, 'First-person: A shocking confession from Willow Creek Community Church leaders', *Baptist Press*, 6 November 2007 (baptistpress.com/resource-library/news/first-person-a-shocking-confession-from-willow-creek-community-church-leaders). This wasn't easy to see in the movement's early days, when passionate evangelists saw the immediate fruit of new people in church. The only warning bells were sounded by those who had drunk deeply of the Bible's theology and wisdom. They offered the reminder that church wasn't first and foremost *for* the outsider—a point that the Bible makes very clear. But the concerns were often dismissed as the sad bleating of those who were too old to notice how much the surrounding culture had shifted.

Chapter 7

1 I'm aware that some of them might also be described as outputs. For example, church is both the outcome of all our ministries—the place where God's saved people are gathered—and a place of significant input in any number of ways. The point for now is not to neatly categorize every aspect of ministry, but simply to see that many aspects of Christian ministry are rightly described as 'inputs'.

2 See ESV footnote on John 3:8.

3 I am reminded of DA Carson's provocative comment on false antitheses: "Damn all false antitheses to hell, for they generate false gods, they perpetuate idols, they twist and distort our souls, they launch the church into violent pendulum swings whose oscillations succeed only in dividing brothers and sisters in Christ": DA Carson, *Becoming Conversant with the Emerging Church: Understanding a movement and its implications*, Zondervan, 2005, p 234.

4 For those interested in the Greek background, the phrase "in such a way" translates a single Greek word (*houtōs*). This is a 'demonstrative adverb' speaking to the manner in which something happens, and the ESV translation captures it well. I am conscious, however, that we must not claim too much for what's being said here. The precise nature and extent of the connection between the input (Paul and Barnabas' preaching) and the output (a great number of Jews and Greeks believing) is open for debate. My point is simply

to highlight the fact that Luke is drawing *some* level of connection between inputs and outputs. I am indebted to Lionel Windsor, lecturer in New Testament at Moore Theological College, for his insights on this verse in personal discussion and correspondence.

5   The phrase is literally "a wise master builder" (see ESV footnote), but given the usage of this word (*sophos*) elsewhere, it is right to see this as a reference to 'skill' as much as it is to 'wisdom'. It can be used to convey the idea of being an 'expert'.

6   'William Carey: Father of modern Protestant missions', *Christianity Today* (christianitytoday.com/history/people/missionaries/william-carey.html).

7   W Carey, 'An enquiry into the obligations of Christians to use means for the conversion of the heathens', *William Carey University*, 1792 (wmcarey.edu/carey/enquiry/enquiry.html).

8   For Carson's extended definition and discussion of 'compatibilism', see DA Carson, *How Long, O Lord: Reflections on suffering and evil*, 2nd edn, IVP, 2006, pp 179–200. Carson's discussion is particularly grounded in the issue of suffering, but the principles are applicable to other areas of life, including gospel ministry. For a slightly shorter but equally insightful discussion of the topic, see PF Jensen, *The Life of Faith: An introduction to Christian doctrine*, Matthias Media, 2022, pp 259–272. See especially Jensen's discussion of 1 and 2 Thessalonians, where he notes that responsibility for the Thessalonians' response to the gospel belongs to Paul and his fellow workers, to the Thessalonians themselves, *and* to God.

9   These are not technical definitions, but by 'hyper-Calvinism' I mean the notion that God exercises his sovereignty in such a way that we don't need to preach, pray or evangelize; he will save people with or without our involvement. 'Arminianism' refers to the opposing idea: in sending Jesus, God gives all people the opportunity to be saved, and all people can be saved; now, the decisive act must come from us, not from God, as we respond to the offer of salvation with repentance and faith. Arminianism wrongly denies that God is sovereign in salvation, while hyper-Calvinism wrongly diminishes or even dismisses the place of deliberate, active evangelism.

10 CF George and W Bird, *How to Break Growth Barriers: Revise your role, release your people, and capture overlooked opportunities for your church*, updated edn, Baker Books, 2017, p 106.

Chapter 8

1   The *Institutes of the Christian Religion* is the best-known work of the great French reformer John Calvin, in which (among many other things) he delivers a full-throated expression of the sovereignty of God.

2   Yes, we are called to die—but *sustainably*! Even as we rightly desire to sacrifice our lives to the cause of the gospel, it is right to add that we should do this in a sustainable way. This conveys the proper sense that we can best serve when we also pay attention to our own health, such that we can be about our master's work for as long as possible, rather than burning out in a great burst of unsustainable fire. One thinks of the words of Robert Murray M'Cheyne, the 19th-century Scottish pastor who died at the age of 28, shortly before his death: "God gave me a message to deliver and a horse to ride. Alas, I have killed the horse, and now I cannot deliver the message." We will return to this topic, and to the question of work hours, in chapter 13.

3   J Collins, *Good to Great: Why some companies make the leap ... and others don't*, Random House Business, 2001, p 86.

4   CH Spurgeon, *The Soul Winner: How to lead sinners to the Saviour*, Revell, 1895, pp 192–3. I am indebted to Murray Anderson for directing me to this quote.

Chapter 9

1   This is akin to the wisdom expressed in 'homogeneous unit principle' ministry, which (stated very briefly!) says that a congregation will be more readily accessible to newcomers when it contains others of the same kind; in essence, 'like attracts like'. This observation is true, but is far from the only issue to consider in shaping our ministry practice.

2   A possible critical distinction here is the question of *intent* and *motive*. A person may simply look cool without seeking to *be* cool. It would be wrong to critique the former, and wrong to brush over the latter. But discerning which is which can be tricky. Is it wrong, for example, for a young pastor to pay careful attention to his clothes, his hair, his manner and his language? Maybe. Intent and motive are crucial; but so too is the flow-on effect on those that are led. The 'Corinthian spirit' of boastful and self-aggrandizing leadership is alive and well among us. Leaders need to move people away from that spirit and not inadvertently allow it to flourish and grow.

3   P Jensen, 'We must be pragmatic—the theological necessity for pragmatism', *PhillipJensen. com* (phillipjensen.com/resources/1988-we-must-be-pragmatic-the-theological-necessity-for-pragmatism). Both series of talks are well worth listening to in full. They are available free online at phillipjensen.com.

4   Jensen, 'We must be pragmatic'.

Chapter 10

1   J Calvin, *Commentary on Corinthians—Volume 1*, Christian Classics Ethereal Library, p 294 (ccel.org/ccel/calvin/calcom39/calcom39).

2   RJ Banks, *Paul's Idea of Community: The early house churches in their cultural setting*, Baker Academic, 1994, pp 27–31.

3   This raises some questions about some of our rhetoric concerning the church-planting movement. In our desire to increase the number of churches, we can sometimes overreach and claim far more for planting than is warranted. 'Church planting' wasn't an explicit apostolic strategy so much as it was a consequence of their disciple-making strategy. They were certainly concerned to gather believers into churches: at the heart of coming to Christ was (and is) to be a 'gathered one', and gathering believers into church was no doubt a critical and proper place to embed the strategy of further disciple making. But church was the 'output', not the 'input'. It was not their strategy for taking the gospel to the world so much as it was the fruit of their (God-given) strategy for taking the gospel to the world. It is not inappropriate to make church planting a key part of our plans to see the gospel bear fruit and increase now. But this is in large measure a matter of pragmatic wisdom rather than a biblical mandate.

4   See chapter 14 for a discussion of the 'pathway' structure for understanding church life.

5   I am indebted to JB Lightfoot's book *The Christian Ministry* (Macmillan, 1901) for many of these insights.

6   The origin of the saying (about which I make no personal comment in this context!) is attributed to many people—Benjamin Disraeli, Robert Frost, George Bernard Shaw, Victor Hugo and Bertrand Russell, among many others.

7   C Marshall and T Payne, *The Trellis and the Vine: The ministry mind-shift that changes everything*, Matthias Media, 2009, p 8.

8   Marshall and Payne, *The Trellis and the Vine*, p 9.

Chapter 11

1   G Lyons, 'A candid interview with Eugene Peterson', *Church Leaders*, 2 January 2011 (churchleaders.com/pastors/pastor-articles/145302-a-candid-interview-with-eugene-peterson.html).

2   It is sometimes surprising for Christians to discover that the word 'pastor' is almost entirely absent from the most widely used English translations. For example, it appears just once in the NIV, NLT and CSB (Eph 4:11). It is not used at all in the ESV, except as a footnote to Ephesians 4:11 (which it translates with the word "shepherds"). The language of 'shepherd' is preferred in each of these translations.

3   See TS Laniak, *Shepherds after My Own Heart: Pastoral traditions and leadership in the Bible*, New Studies in Biblical Theology, IVP Academic, 2006. Note a subtle difference between translations for Isaiah 63:11: the NIV uses the singular 'shepherd' (following the LXX), but the ESV uses the plural 'shepherds' (following the Hebrew Masoretic Text). If Isaiah's original word was singular, then it refers to Moses; if plural, then the context and parallels suggest that it refers to Moses and Aaron (see Psalm 77).

4   It's worth remembering that "the good shepherd" is also "the Lamb of God, who takes away the sin of the world" (John 1:29; see also Rev 5:6–14). It's an amazing mix of imagery that is only possible in Jesus.

5   This is also a beautiful example of grace in action as Jesus restores Peter for such a task following Peter's denial of Jesus (see John 18:15–18).

6   Note the way that Paul moves from using the Greek word *presbuteros* ('elder') in Titus 1:5 to using the word *episkopos* ('overseer') in verse 7.

7   See ESV footnote.

8   Only one definite article is used for both words, which links them very closely.

9   The word 'elder' had a long history within the Jewish world (though it is not exclusive to that world), where it was used from the time of the Egyptian captivity. In the first instance, elders were most likely heads of families, although eventually limited to a particular number (Exod 24:1). By the time of Jesus, the role was well established. Elders ran the affairs of the local community and people generally acknowledged their authority. 'Overseer' was more of a Greek term. These were generally appointed by the emperor to lead captured or newly founded cities. They would regulate the affairs of the city, and particularly exercised a role of management over key organizations. For more on these terms, especially 'overseer', see DA Carson, 'Some reflections on pastoral leadership', *Themelios*, 40.2, 2015, pp 195–197. (The word 'leader' was used more broadly; the verb form of this word ('to lead') appears three times in Hebrews 13 (*hēgeomai*, vv 7, 17, 24), where the ESV translates it "leaders".) Acts 20 offers one example of how these words operated culturally: Luke reports that Paul called the Ephesian "elders" together at Miletus (v 17), but in Paul's direct speech he refers to them as "overseers" (v 28). This shift is almost certainly to do with the cultural context of the Ephesian elders. They were largely drawn from a Greek setting, and so Paul speaks to them using the most relevant term in their culture. But Luke reports on Paul's activities with the more normal Jewish language.

10 This isn't absolute, given that Timothy wasn't older than every person he led. It might be that, especially in some new church settings, there isn't an 'older man' qualified to perform the function of elder/overseer/pastor, and a younger man may need to lead. Paul told Timothy, "Let no one despise you *for your youth*, but set the believers an example in speech, in conduct, in love, in faith, in purity" (1 Tim 4:12).

11 Readers might notice that I've used the word "himself" here, and that I've assumed male leadership of churches at various points throughout this chapter. It's well beyond the scope of this book to delve into this issue in any detail. I will simply note that, as a complementarian, I believe that the Bible gives responsibility for the leadership of churches to appropriately gifted men (e.g. 1 Tim 2:11–12). I would also affirm that godly and appropriately gifted women can and should exercise all kinds of important ministries among the people of God. For more on this issue, see C Smith, *God's Good Design: What the Bible really says about men and women*, 2nd edn, Matthias Media, 2019.

12 It's beyond my purpose here to fully consider the notion of 'servant leadership', a topic which has generated its own world of thought. But leaders would do well to pause and consider Jesus' words to his disciples in Mark 10: "You know that those who are considered rulers of the Gentiles lord it over them, and their great ones exercise authority over them. But it shall not be so among you. But whoever would be great among you must be your servant, and whoever would be first among you must be slave of all. For even the Son of Man came not to be served but to serve, and to give his life as a ransom for many" (vv 42–45).

13 Given the continuity of thought across the testaments, this application of the language is telling. But noting this isn't to suggest that everything Moses and David did as leaders carries across into the New Testament. It is rather to note that there is nothing inherently inconsistent with being a shepherd of God's people *and* carrying responsibility for a large number of people. There is nothing in the New Testament that pushes against this observation. A first-century person could only form the view that a shepherd-leader led small groups if there was a significant change from Old Testament usage to something new. Shepherds often led large flocks.

14 See L Windsor, 'The work of ministry in Ephesians 4:12', in K Condie (ed), *Tend my Sheep: The word of God and pastoral ministry*, Latimer Trust, 2016. See also the summary of this chapter on the author's website (lionelwindsor.net/2016/09/20/work-ministry): "Often it is claimed that the biblical word 'ministry' (διακονία) is based on an original usage involving 'waiting at tables', and therefore that the word in the New Testament always carries connotations of 'humble service.' John N. Collins, however, has demonstrated that this claim is false. While the word is sometimes used of table-waiters, a more fundamental concept is the 'go-between.' Thus 'ministry' does not necessarily mean 'humble service'. In Ephesians 4:12, *the work of 'ministry' is more a matter of 'bringing' the saving gospel of the Lord Jesus Christ to people*" (emphasis added).

15 See Rom 16:1 and (possibly) 1 Tim 3:11.

16 See Lightfoot, *The Christian Ministry*, pp 11–16.

17 Carson, 'Some reflections', p 196.

18 Carson, 'Some reflections', p 197.

19 See chapter 8 of Marshall and Payne, *The Trellis and the Vine*: 'Why Sunday sermons are necessary but not sufficient'.

20 Carson, 'Some reflections', p 197.

21 J Calvin, *Commentary on Timothy, Titus, Philemon*, Christians Classics Ethereal Library (ccel.org/ccel/calvin/calcom43/calcom43).

22 DA Carson, 'Defining Elders', *9 Marks*, 4 January 1999 (9marks.org/article/defining-elders-2).

23 In a situation where we have already promised to operate within the bounds of a particular denomination or structure, we should continue to honour those structures and keep our promises (unless we become convicted that those structures are somehow contrary to the word of God!), while also making use of the freedoms given to us within those structures. While I hold that the Bible does not mandate a specific form of church polity, those who differ should, of course, follow their conscience and their understanding of Scripture.

Chapter 12

1 Again, I will be quick to add that we can take only *some* measure of responsibility for outcomes. I'm not suggesting we are completely responsible for outcomes. Every good outcome is, in a very direct way, the sovereign, gracious work of God. It is God who works in us "both to will and to work for his good pleasure" (Phil 2:13); "neither he who plants nor he who waters is anything, but only God who gives the growth" (1 Cor 3:7).

2 Again, notice the care to qualify: we aren't to be *simply* input-focused, but we *must* still focus on inputs. I will say more about this later in the chapter.

3 Notice at this stage that I have made no mention of *how* a leader achieves the desired outcome. Many definitions of leadership smuggle in a *way* to lead which in turn narrows the possible paths by which leadership can achieve its task.

4 J Calvin, *Commentary on the Catholic Epistles*, Christian Classics Ethereal Library (ccel.org/ccel/calvin/calcom45/calcom45).

5 This point illustrates something of the complexity. Theoretically, I could compel a person to give money—it is, after all, an outward act. But I could never compel a person to *love* giving money: true generosity of spirit is a grace gift of God. And yet I can minister in such a way that it will influence people towards having a heart filled with grace such that they give out of joy, not out of compulsion (see 2 Corinthians 8–9).

6 CH Spurgeon, *Speeches at Home and Abroad*, Passmore and Alabaster, 1878, pp 84–85.

7 PS Grimmond, 'Equipping students at Moore Theological College to develop biblically faithful, relevant application in preaching' [Doctor of Ministry thesis], Southern Baptist Theological Seminary, 2023, p 14. Excerpts from this thesis are quoted with kind permission from the author.

8 Grimmond, 'Equipping students at Moore Theological College', pp 13–15.

9 Grimmond, 'Equipping students at Moore Theological College', pp 15.

10 It is good for the soul to read John W Harris's book *One Blood: Two hundred years of Aboriginal encounter with Christianity* (Australians Together, 2018)—but it's also disturbing, as the book recounts the horrors wrought upon the Aboriginal population of Australia by early European settlement. As a nation, we have much to repent of.

11 Harris, *One Blood*, loc 1357 (emphasis mine).

12 Harris, *One Blood*, loc 1154.

13 Harris, *One Blood*, loc 3223.

14 See 2 Pet 3:18, Gal 5:22–23; Titus 2:11–13.

15 For more on this shift in focus, see chapter 2 ('Ministry mind-shifts) in Marshall and Payne, *The Trellis and the Vine*.

16 Regarding buildings, it is often noted that churches experience a high turnover of senior staff once a building program has been completed. In my view, this could well be a sign of an input-focused leader: once the building is completed, the church is thought to have reached its high mountain peak, and the energy for further engagement totally fades. By contrast, an output-focused leader will see the end of a building program as simply giving him and the ministry the tools for the job. They now have a power saw that will make the real building work—building the kingdom of God and seeking biblical outputs—that much easier. Why leave now?!

Chapter 13

1 See our discussion of 'compatibilism' in chapter 7.

2 I recommend Paul Grimmond's *When the Noise Won't Stop: A Christian guide to dealing with anxiety*, as a resource for dealing with these types of issues—especially anxiety—in much more detail (Matthias Media, 2022).

3 For a mix of theological and practical insights into the importance of sleep, see Geoff Robson's *Thank God for Bedtime: What God says about our sleep and why it matters more than you think* (Matthias Media, 2019).

4 One passage that might challenge even this view, however, is Proverbs 31, where the "excellent wife" (v 10) rises while it is still dark (v 15), and "her lamp does not go out at night" (v 18).

5 This assumes that the leader is generally healthy, that his wife and family are healthy, that he is not the primary caregiver to his children, and that he isn't bivocational.

6 J Adamson, 'In the last 12 months 35% of Australian ministers considered quitting', *Sydney Anglicans*, 4 June 2023 (sydneyanglicans.net/news/in-the-last-12-months-35-of-australian-ministers-considered-quitting/53335). No doubt COVID and its aftermath play some part in these figures, but they are startling nonetheless.

Conclusion

1 My apologies to anyone not old enough to remember the classic 80s sitcom about Cheers, the bar "where everybody knows your name and they're always glad you came" (as the theme song put it).

Appendix

1 See chapter 3.

2 See chapter 4.

3 As is often the case with these kinds of insights into ministry, a fellow leader shared this description with me some years ago—but I can't recall who! My sincere apologies to the brother or sister who shared this idea with me. Hopefully, you know who you are and can be thankful that your insight is now shared with others, even though you go uncredited. God remembers your name!

4 This diagram and other elements in this section ('the Pentagon') are drawn from material I have previously published in 'Framework: A framework for church ministry' (*Reach Australia*, 2021; reachaustralia.com.au/reach-australia-framework-ebook) and are reproduced here with permission from Reach Australia.

❧matthiasmedia

Matthias Media is an evangelical publishing ministry that seeks to persuade all Christians of the truth of God's purposes in Jesus Christ as revealed in the Bible, and equip them with high-quality resources, so that by the work of the Holy Spirit they will:

- abandon their lives to the honour and service of Christ in daily holiness and decision-making
- pray constantly in Christ's name for the fruitfulness and growth of his gospel
- speak the Bible's life-changing word whenever and however they can— in the home, in the world and in the fellowship of his people.

Our wide range of resources includes Bible studies, books, training courses, tracts and children's material. To find out more, and to access samples and free downloads, visit our website:

matthiasmedia.com

How to buy our resources

1. Direct from us over the internet:
   - in the US: matthiasmedia.com
   - in Australia: matthiasmedia.com.au

2. Direct from us by phone: please visit our website for current phone contact information.

3. Through a range of outlets in various parts of the world. Visit **matthiasmedia.com/contact** for details about recommended retailers in your part of the world.

4. Trade enquiries can be addressed to:
   - in the US and Canada: sales@matthiasmedia.com
   - in Australia and the rest of the world: sales@matthiasmedia.com.au

Register at our website for our **free** regular email update to receive information about the latest new resources, **exclusive special offers**, and free articles to help you grow in your Christian life and ministry.

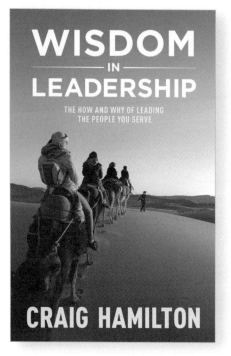

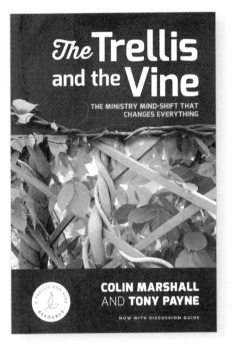

How to Walk into Church
By Tony Payne

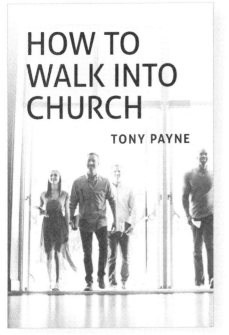

A short book for Christians on the topic of church that looks briefly at what church is, why we go and how that affects what we do while we're there.

"Loving the church can be hard work. It's easier to turn up, sit on your own, listen/pretend you're listening and go home feeling better about yourself. But that's not what what God wants. God wants us to be a family, loving one another and serving each other. Tony walks us through says we can serve with intention and in doing so glorify God. There are simple ways like thinking who we sit with or what we talk about after the service but things I often neglect out of love for my own interests. This is a short, well written and low-cost gem. If you're wanting a book on why you should bother loving the church—this is it!"

— Jonathan Carswell

For more information or to order contact:

Matthias Media
sales@matthiasmedia.com.au
matthiasmedia.com.au

Matthias Media (USA)
sales@matthiasmedia.com
matthiasmedia.com

AVAILABLE ONLINE